DISCOVER WORD 97

Keyboard Movement Keys

Press	To move...	Press	To move...
←	One character left	Ctrl + ←	One word left
→	One character right	Ctrl + →	One word right
↑	One line up	Ctrl + ↑	One paragraph up
↓	One line down	Ctrl + ↓	One paragraph down
Home	To the beginning of the line	PgUp	One screen up
End	To the end of the line	PgDn	One screen down
Ctrl + Home	To the beginning of the document	Ctrl + PgUp	Top of screen
Ctrl + End	To the end of the document	Ctrl + PgDn	Bottom of screen

The Standard Toolbar

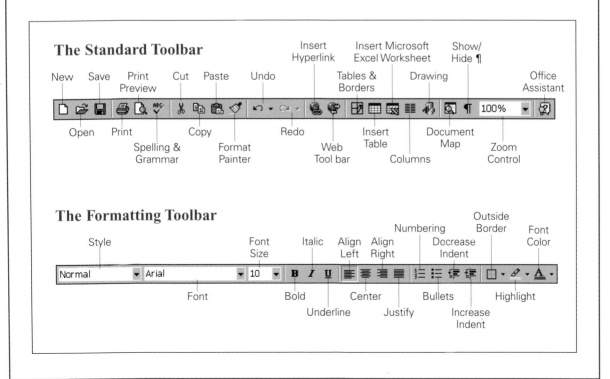

New — Save — Print Preview — Cut — Paste — Undo — Insert Hyperlink — Tables & Borders — Insert Microsoft Excel Worksheet — Drawing — Show/Hide ¶ — Office Assistant

Open — Print — Spelling & Grammar — Copy — Format Painter — Redo — Web Tool bar — Insert Table — Columns — Document Map — Zoom Control

The Formatting Toolbar

Style — Font Size — Italic — Align Left — Align Right — Numbering — Outside Border — Font Color

Normal — Arial — 10 — **B** *I* U — Align/Center/Justify — Bullets — Increase Indent — Highlight

Font — Bold — Underline — Center — Justify — Decrease Indent

Word Tasks

To:	Select:	Then:
Copy text	The text you want to copy	Click 📋 and move to where you want to paste the text. Click 📋.
Create a new document	🗋	
Delete text	The text you want to delete	Press the Delete key.
Exit Word	💾	Select File→Exit.
Move text	The text you want to move	Click ✂ and move to where you want to paste the text. Click 📋.
Open a document	📂	Open the folder containing the document, click to move up a level, use the Look in drop-down list to change to another drive. When you see the file listed, double-click it.
Preview a document	🔍	
Print a document	Select File→Print	Make any changes to print options and click OK.
Save a document	💾	Type a name, select a folder, and click the Save button.
Select text with keyboard	The start of the text	Hold down the Shift key and use the movement keys to select the text you want. Release the Shift Key.
Select text with mouse	The start of the text	Hold down the mouse button and drag it across the text you want to select. Release the mouse button.
Start Word	Start→Programs	Click the program icon to start Word.
Undo	↶ ▾	

Text Formatting

To...	Click
Make text bold	B
Make text italic	I
Make text underlined	U
Create a bulleted list	☰
Create a numbered list	☷

Alignment Options

To...	Click
Center text	☰
Left-align text	☰
Right-align text	☰
Justify text	☰

DISCOVERY CENTRAL

DISCOVER
WORD 97

DISCOVER
WORD 97

BY SHELLEY O'HARA

IDG BOOKS WORLDWIDE, INC.

AN INTERNATIONAL
DATA GROUP COMPANY

FOSTER CITY, CA • CHICAGO, IL •
INDIANAPOLIS, IN • SOUTHLAKE, TX

Discover Word 97

Published by
IDG Books Worldwide, Inc.
An International Data Group Company
919 E. Hillsdale Blvd., Suite 400
Foster City, CA 94404

http://www.idgbooks.com (IDG Books Worldwide Web site)

Library of Congress Catalog Card No.: 96-79749

ISBN: 0-7645-3049-6

Printed in the United States of America

10 9 8 7 6 5 4 3 2

1IPC/RU/QT/ZX/FC

Distributed in the United States by IDG Books Worldwide, Inc.

Distributed by Macmillan Canada for Canada; by Contemporanea de Ediciones for Venezuela; by Distribuidora Cuspide for Argentina; by CITEC for Brazil; by Ediciones ZETA S.C.R. Ltda. for Peru; by Editorial Limusa SA for Mexico; by Transworld Publishers Limited in the United Kingdom and Europe; by Academic Bookshop for Egypt; by Levant Distributors S.A.R.L. for Lebanon; by Al Jassim for Saudi Arabia; by Simron Pty. Ltd. for South Africa; by Pustak Mahal for India; by The Computer Bookshop for India; by Toppan Company Ltd. for Japan; by Addison Wesley Publishing Company for Korea; by Longman Singapore Publishers Ltd. for Singapore, Malaysia, Thailand, and Indonesia; by Unalis Corporation for Taiwan; by WS Computer Publishing Company, Inc. for the Philippines; by WoodsLane Pty. Ltd. for Australia; by WoodsLane Enterprises Ltd. for New Zealand. Authorized Sales Agent: Anthony Rudkin Associates for the Middle East and North Africa.

For general information on IDG Books Worldwide's books in the U.S., please call our Consumer Customer Service department at 800-762-2974. For reseller information, including discounts and premium sales, please call our Reseller Customer Service department at 800-434-3422.

For information on where to purchase IDG Books Worldwide's books outside the U.S., please contact our International Sales department at 415-655-3172 or fax 415-655-3295.

For information on foreign language translations, please contact our Foreign & Subsidiary Rights department at 415-655-3021 or fax 415-655-3281.

For sales inquiries and special prices for bulk quantities, please contact our Sales department at 415-655-3200 or write to the address above.

For information on using IDG Books Worldwide's books in the classroom or for ordering examination copies, please contact our Educational Sales department at 800-434-2086 or fax 817-251-8174.

For press review copies, author interviews, or other publicity information, please contact our Public Relations department at 415-655-3000 or fax 415-655-3299.

For authorization to photocopy items for corporate, personal, or educational use, please contact Copyright Clearance Center, 222 Rosewood Drive, Danvers, MA 01923, or fax 508-750-4470.

 is a trademark under exclusive license to IDG Books Worldwide, Inc., from International Data Group, Inc.

ABOUT IDG BOOKS WORLDWIDE

Welcome to the world of IDG Books Worldwide.

IDG Books Worldwide, Inc., is a subsidiary of International Data Group, the world's largest publisher of computer-related information and the leading global provider of information services on information technology. IDG was founded more than 25 years ago and now employs more than 8,500 people worldwide. IDG publishes more than 275 computer publications in over 75 countries (see listing below). More than 60 million people read one or more IDG publications each month.

Launched in 1990, IDG Books Worldwide is today the #1 publisher of best-selling computer books in the United States. We are proud to have received eight awards from the Computer Press Association in recognition of editorial excellence and three from *Computer Currents'* First Annual Readers' Choice Awards. Our best-selling *...For Dummies*® series has more than 30 million copies in print with translations in 30 languages. IDG Books Worldwide, through a joint venture with IDG's Hi-Tech Beijing, became the first U.S. publisher to publish a computer book in the People's Republic of China. In record time, IDG Books Worldwide has become the first choice for millions of readers around the world who want to learn how to better manage their businesses.

Our mission is simple: Every one of our books is designed to bring extra value and skill-building instructions to the reader. Our books are written by experts who understand and care about our readers. The knowledge base of our editorial staff comes from years of experience in publishing, education, and journalism — experience we use to produce books for the '90s. In short, we care about books, so we attract the best people. We devote special attention to details such as audience, interior design, use of icons, and illustrations. And because we use an efficient process of authoring, editing, and desktop publishing our books electronically, we can spend more time ensuring superior content and spend less time on the technicalities of making books.

You can count on our commitment to deliver high-quality books at competitive prices on topics you want to read about. At IDG Books Worldwide, we continue in the IDG tradition of delivering quality for more than 25 years. You'll find no better book on a subject than one from IDG Books Worldwide.

John J. Kilcullen

John Kilcullen
CEO
IDG Books Worldwide, Inc.

*Eighth Annual
Computer Press
Awards ≥1992*

*Ninth Annual
Computer Press
Awards ≥1993*

*Tenth Annual
Computer Press
Awards ≥1994*

*Eleventh Annual
Computer Press
Awards ≥1995*

IDG Books Worldwide, Inc., is a subsidiary of International Data Group, the world's largest publisher of computer-related information and the leading global provider of information services on information technology. International Data Group publishes over 275 computer publications in over 75 countries. Sixty million people read one or more International Data Group publications each month. International Data Group's publications include: **ARGENTINA:** Buyer's Guide, Computerworld Argentina, PC World Argentina; **AUSTRALIA:** Australian Macworld, Australian PC World, Australian Reseller News, Computerworld, IT Casebook, Network World, Publish, Webmaster; **AUSTRIA:** Computerwelt Osterreich, Networks Austria, PC Tip Austria; **BANGLADESH:** PC World Bangladesh; **BELARUS:** PC World Belarus; **BELGIUM:** Data News; **BRAZIL:** Annuário de Informática, Computerworld, Connections, Macworld, PC Player, PC World, Publish, Reseller News, Supergamepower; **BULGARIA:** Computerworld Bulgaria, Network World Bulgaria, PC & MacWorld Bulgaria; **CANADA:** CIO Canada, Client/Server World, ComputerWorld Canada, InfoWorld Canada, NetworkWorld Canada, WebWorld; **CHILE:** Computerworld Chile, PC World Chile; **COLOMBIA:** Computerworld Colombia, PC World Colombia; **COSTA RICA:** PC World Centro America; **THE CZECH AND SLOVAK REPUBLICS:** Computerworld Czechoslovakia, Macworld Czech Republic, PC World Czechoslovakia; **DENMARK:** Communications World Danmark, Computerworld Danmark, Macworld Danmark, PC World Danmark, Techworld Denmark; **DOMINICAN REPUBLIC:** PC World Republica Dominicana; **ECUADOR:** PC World Ecuador; **EGYPT:** Computerworld Middle East, PC World Middle East; **EL SALVADOR:** PC World Centro America; **FINLAND:** MikroPC, Tietoverkko, Tietoviikko; **FRANCE:** Distributique, Hebdo, Info PC, Le Monde Informatique, Macworld, Reseaux & Telecoms, WebMaster France; **GERMANY:** Computer Partner, Computerwoche, Computerwoche Extra, Computerwoche FOCUS, Global Online, Macwelt, PC Welt; **GREECE:** Amiga Computing, GamePro Greece, Multimedia World; **GUATEMALA:** PC World Centro America; **HONDURAS:** PC World Centro America; **HONG KONG:** Computerworld Hong Kong, PC World Hong Kong, Publish in Asia; **HUNGARY:** ABCD CD-ROM, Computerworld Szamitastechnika, Internetto online Magazine, PC World Hungary, PC-X Magazin Hungary; **ICELAND:** Tolvuheimur PC World Island; **INDIA:** Information Communications World, Information Systems Computerworld, PC World India, Publish in Asia; **INDONESIA:** InfoKomputer PC World, Komputek Computerworld, Publish in Asia; **IRELAND:** ComputerScope, PC Live!; **ISRAEL:** Macworld Israel, People & Computers/Computerworld; **ITALY:** Computerworld Italia, Macworld Italia, Networking Italia, PC World Italia; **JAPAN:** DTP World, Macworld Japan, Nikkei Personal Computing, OS/2 World Japan, SunWorld Japan, Windows NT World, Windows World Japan; **KENYA:** PC World East African; **KOREA:** Hi-Tech Information, Macworld Korea, PC World Korea; **MACEDONIA:** PC World Macedonia; **MALAYSIA:** Computerworld Malaysia, PC World Malaysia, Publish in Asia; **MALTA:** PC World Malta; **MEXICO:** Computerworld Mexico, PC World Mexico; **MYANMAR:** PC World Myanmar; **NETHERLANDS:** Computer! Totaal, LAN Internetworking Magazine, LAN World Buyers Guide, Macworld Netherlands, Net, WebWereld; **NEW ZEALAND:** Absolute Beginners Guide and Plain & Simple Series, Computer Buyer, Computer Industry Directory, Computerworld New Zealand, MTB, Network World, PC World New Zealand; **NICARAGUA:** PC World Centro America; **NORWAY:** Computerworld Norge, CW Rapport, Datamagasinet, Financial Rapport, Kursguide Norge, Macworld Norge, Multimediaworld Norge, PC World Ekspress Norge, PC World Nettverk, PC World Norge, PC World ProduktGuide Norge; **PAKISTAN:** Computerworld Pakistan; **PANAMA:** PC World Panama; **PEOPLE'S REPUBLIC OF CHINA:** China Computer Users, China Computerworld, China InfoWorld, China Telecom World Weekly, Computer & Communication, Electronic Design China, Electronics Today, Electronics Weekly, Game Software, PC World China, Popular Computer Week, Software Weekly, Software World, Telecom World; **PERU:** Computerworld Peru, PC World Profesional Peru, PC World SoHo Peru; **PHILIPPINES:** Click!, Computerworld Philippines, PC World Philippines, Publish in Asia; **POLAND:** Computerworld Poland, Computerworld Special Report Poland, Cyber, Macworld Poland, Networld Poland, PC World Komputer; **PORTUGAL:** Cerebro/PC World, Computerworld/Correio Informático, Dealer World Portugal, Mac*In/PC*In Portugal, Multimedia World; **PUERTO RICO:** PC World Puerto Rico; **ROMANIA:** Computerworld Romania, PC World Romania, Telecom Romania; **RUSSIA:** Computerworld Russia, Mir PK, Publish, Seti; **SINGAPORE:** Computerworld Singapore, PC World Singapore, Publish in Asia; **SLOVENIA:** Monitor; **SOUTH AFRICA:** Computing SA, Network World SA, Software World SA; **SPAIN:** Communicaciones World España, Computerworld España, Dealer World España, Macworld España, PC World España; **SRI LANKA:** Infolink PC World; **SWEDEN:** CAP&Design, Computer Sweden, Corporate Computing Sweden, Internetworld Sweden, it.branschen, Macworld Sweden, MaxiData Sweden, MikroDatorn, Natverk & Kommunikation, PC World Sweden, PCaktiv, Windows World Sweden; **SWITZERLAND:** Computerworld Schweiz, Macworld Schweiz, PCtip; **TAIWAN:** Computerworld Taiwan, Macworld Taiwan, NEW ViSiON/Publish, PC World Taiwan, Windows World Taiwan; **THAILAND:** Publish in Asia, Thai Computerworld; **TURKEY:** Computerworld Turkiye, Macworld Turkiye, Network World Turkiye, PC World Turkiye; **UKRAINE:** Computerworld Kiev, Multimedia World Ukraine, PC World Ukraine; **UNITED KINGDOM:** Acorn User UK, Amiga Action UK, Amiga Computing UK, Apple Talk UK, Computing, Macworld, Parents and Computers UK, PC Advisor, PC Home, PSX Pro, The WEB; **UNITED STATES:** Cable in the Classroom, CIO Magazine, Computerworld, DOS World, Federal Computer Week, GamePro Magazine, InfoWorld, I-Way, Macworld, Network World, PC Games, PC World, Publish, Video Event, THE WEB Magazine, and WebMaster; online webzines: JavaWorld, NetscapeWorld, and SunWorld Online; **URUGUAY:** InfoWorld Uruguay; **VENEZUELA:** Computerworld Venezuela, PC World Venezuela; and **VIETNAM:** PC World Vietnam. 2/14/97

Welcome to the Discover Series

Do you want to discover the best and most efficient ways to use your computer and learn about technology? Books in the Discover series teach you the essentials of technology with a friendly, confident approach. You'll find a Discover book on almost any subject — from the Internet to intranets, from Web design and programming to the business programs that make your life easier.

We've provided valuable, real-world examples that help you relate to topics faster. Discover books begin by introducing you to the main features of programs, so you start by doing something *immediately*. The focus is to teach you how to perform tasks that are useful and meaningful in your day-to-day work. You might create a document or graphic, explore your computer, surf the Web, or write a program. Whatever the task, you learn the most commonly used features, and focus on the best tips and techniques for doing your work. You'll get results quickly, and discover the best ways to use software and technology in your everyday life.

You may find the following elements and features in this book:

Discovery Central: This tearout card is a handy quick reference to important tasks or ideas covered in the book.

Quick Tour: The Quick Tour gets you started working with the book right away.

Real-Life Vignettes: Throughout the book you'll see one-page scenarios illustrating a real-life application of a topic covered.

Goals: Each chapter opens with a list of goals you can achieve by reading the chapter.

Side Trips: These asides include additional information about alternative or advanced ways to approach the topic covered.

Bonuses: Timesaving tips and more advanced techniques are covered in each chapter.

Discovery Center: This guide illustrates key procedures covered throughout the book.

Visual Index: You'll find real-world documents in the Visual Index, with page numbers pointing you to where you should turn to achieve the effects shown.

Throughout the book, you'll also notice some special icons and formatting:

 A Feature Focus icon highlights new features in the software's latest release, and points out significant differences between it and the previous version.

 Web Paths refer you to Web sites that provide additional information about the topic.

 Tips offer timesaving shortcuts, expert advice, quick techniques, or brief reminders.

 The X-Ref icon refers you to other chapters or sections for more information.

Pull Quotes emphasize important ideas that are covered in the chapter.

 Notes provide additional information or highlight special points of interest about a topic.

 The Caution icon alerts you to potential problems you should watch out for.

The Discover series delivers interesting, insightful, and inspiring information about technology to help you learn faster and retain more. So the next time you want to find answers to your technology questions, reach for a Discover book. We hope the entertaining, easy-to-read style puts you at ease and makes learning fun.

Credits

ACQUISITIONS EDITOR

Ellen Camm

DEVELOPMENT EDITOR

Susannah Davidson

TECHNICAL EDITOR

Paul Summitt

COPY EDITORS

Robert Campbell

Carolyn Welch

PROJECT COORDINATOR

Phyllis Beaty

GRAPHICS AND PRODUCTION SPECIALISTS

Kurt Krames

Dina F Quan

Elsie Yim

QUALITY CONTROL SPECIALIST

Mick Arellano

PROOFREADERS

Desne Border

Andrew Davis

Stacey Lynn

Candace Ward

Anne Weinberger

INDEXER

Steve Rath

BOOK DESIGN

Seventeenth Street Studios

Phyllis Beaty

Kurt Krames

About the Author

Shelley O'Hara is a freelance writer based in Indianapolis. She has written over 50 computer books, including *Discover Word 97*. In addition to writing, she does training for the Division of Continuing Studies for Indiana University Purdue University at Indianapolis. O'Hara has a BA in English from the University of South Carolina and an MA in English from the University of Maryland. She has also penned *101 Ways to Drive Your Husband Insane* and *The Marriage Trifecta*, her yet-to-be-discovered fiction work.

PREFACE

Word 97 for Windows is the latest version of the most popular and highly rated word processing program for Windows. It's perfect for creating every kind of document, from a simple memo to a complex manuscript. It's possible to open Word 97 and start creating documents immediately — without any help at all. You can just start typing. But there's a lot more to Word than just using it as a typewriter. Word includes features that can improve the look of your document, save you time, avoid embarrassing errors, and make your work shine overall. You just need to know where to look and what to do. That's where this book comes in. This book explains all the skills you need to get the most from Word 97.

Think of learning all the ins and outs of Word as a journey. On your way, you'll *discover* all kinds of things that will benefit you and your work.

Is This Book for You?

This book offers some advice and instruction for anyone using Word 97. If you are new to word processing, this book can help you learn the basics of creating a document. Each procedure is detailed in a step-by-step fashion and is illustrated with figures. You'll find yourself comfortable with the basics pretty quickly. Then you can move on to the more complicated techniques.

If you have used a previous version of Word, this book can help you convert your skills to the new version. You learn about new features and maybe even about some older features that you never tried.

If you have used another word processing program, this book can help you get up to speed with Word and show you all the cool things you can do to make your work easier.

If you have been using Word for some time but feel as if you aren't getting the most from the program, this book can help you find key features that can simplify and improve your work.

What's in This Book?

This book is divided into four parts and seventeen chapters.

Part One, "Learning the Basics," covers all the skills you need to create a document from start to finish, and starts with a Quick Tour that leads you through creating a sample document.

Part Two, "Making Your Document Attractive," focuses on the many, many formatting features included with Word. Formatting is basically changing how the text, paragraphs, lines, pages appear in a document. Think of this part as the "makeover" part.

Part Three, "Creating Special Document Types," covers some special types of documents you can create with Word, including templates, form letters, and documents that incorporate data from other programs.

Part Four, "Changing How Word Works," explains some of the ways you can set up Word so that it is personalized for you and your work situation.

Also included are the Visual Index, a troubleshooting guide, and a glossary. The Visual Index is something you will find especially helpful, because it includes several document examples. It not only illustrates some of the neat things you can do with Word, but also shows you which features were used to set up the document.

The learning process is an adventure, a journey, a path to discovery. That's the theme of this book.

Have a great journey!

Acknowledgments

It's not easy to put a new series together. You have to figure out lots of things. What should we call it? What should it include? How should it look? The person most responsible for this new *Discover* series is Ellen Camm. So much of what you see on these pages are her ideas, her concepts, her design suggestions. She worked for months and months coming up with ideas, polling other people and integrating suggestions to bring off this new series. For this and more, I thank Ellen.

Walt Bruce, Publishing Director and long-time colleague, was integral in designing the new series. I appreciate his help and insight as well.

The development editor on this book, Susannah Davidson, also played a key role. The editor is the person an author deals with day in and day out on a project, and it can be a joy or a real drag. Working with Susannah was a joy, and her perceptive suggestions have made this a better book.

I would also like to thank Paul Summitt, the technical editor, who not only reviewed the text, but also helped me get answers to questions and solutions to problems. And thanks to Robert Campbell, the copy editor.

I know there are lots of other nameless people who sat around a conference room tossing out ideas, making suggestions, and doodling designs. Even though I didn't personally work with these people, I thank them for their impact on this book.

— *Shelley O'Hara*

CONTENTS AT A GLANCE

CONTENTS

15 INCLUDING DATA FROM OTHER APPLICATIONS, 259

PART FOUR—CHANGING HOW WORD WORKS, 277

16 MANAGING YOUR WORD FILES, 279

WORD 97 QUICK TOUR

IN THIS QUICK TOUR YOU PRACTICE

HOW TO TYPE A DOCUMENT   PAGE 1

HOW TO SAVE A DOCUMENT   PAGE 3

HOW TO FORMAT A DOCUMENT   PAGE 4

HOW TO CHECK A DOCUMENT   PAGE 5

HOW TO PRINT A DOCUMENT   PAGE 6

To get an idea of the process you use to create a document, try this Quick Tour. The tour leads you step by step through a specific exercise to create a memo. You not only learn how to create a typical document, but you also get to try out some of the most common features of Word 97. Why don't you try it?

Typing a Memo

The best way to create a document is to first concentrate on the text. Then you can go back and modify the appearance of the document. Let's type the text for a simple memo.

Follow these steps:

1. Start Word for Windows by clicking the Start button on the Windows desktop. Select Programs and then Microsoft Word . You see a blank document on screen (see Figure QT-1). The insertion point is at the top of the document.

2. Type **MEMO** and press Enter twice. This step enters the heading for your document.

1

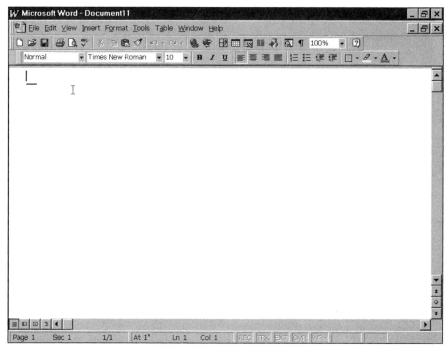

Figure QT-1 You can start typing in the blank document.

3. Type **TO:** and press Tab twice. You press Tab twice so that this entry and the other lines will stay aligned. You can also simply change where the tab stops occur. Working with tabs is covered in detail in Chapter 7.

4. Type **Sales Department** and press Enter twice. You've completed the first few lines of the document.

5. Type **FROM:** and press Tab.

6. Type **Laurie Murphy** and press Enter twice.

7. Type **DATE:** and press Tab. You can use a shortcut to insert the date here.

8. Open the ⌷ Insert ⌷ menu and select the ⌷ Date and Time ⌷ command. Click the OK button to insert the current date and then press Enter twice.

9. Type **RE:** and press Tab three times. You press Tab three times to keep the text aligned with the preceding entries. You can also change the tab stops, as covered in Chapter 7.

10. Type **Sales Seminar** and press Enter twice. You've completed the top few lines for the memo. Now you can type the text of the memo.

11. Type the following, pressing Enter after each paragraph. Go ahead and type the mistakes as they appear. You can correct them later in this quick tour.

Please plan to attend a sales seminer this Thursday at 9AM in the board room. The sales seminar will cover the following topics:

* **Mining for new contacts**
* **Manageing existing clients**
* **Following up on orders**

If you have any questions, please contact your sales manager.

You have completed the short memo shown in Figure QT-2. Now that you have typed the document, it's a good idea to save it. You should save the document periodically as you type and make changes. The next section covers how to save a document.

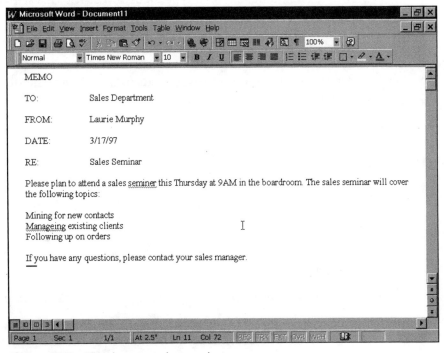

Figure QT-2   This document shows a short memo.

Saving a Document

To save your memo, follow these steps:

1. Open the File menu and select the Save command. You see the Save As dialog box (see Figure QT-3). The first time you save a document, you must assign a name to it and select a folder in which to place the file.

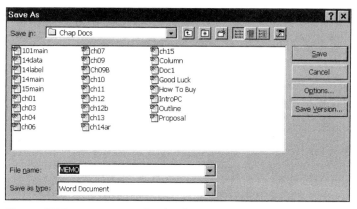

Figure QT-3 Type a name for the document.

2. In the File <u>n</u>ame text box, type **SALES MEMO**. This step assigns a name to the document.

3. Click the <u>S</u>ave button. Notice that the file name appears in the title bar.

 For more information on saving, closing, and opening documents, see Chapter 2.

Changing How the Document Looks

After you finish the contents of the document, you can go back and make changes to its appearance. You may want to change the alignment or spacing of the text. Or you may want to make some text boldface. Here you practice some common formatting changes. Part II of this book covers this topic in much more detail.

Follow these steps to make some changes to your document's appearance:

1. Select the first line of the document (MEMO). To select text, click at the start of the text and then drag the mouse across the text you want.

2. Click ▦ . This step centers the memo heading.

3. Click B . This step makes the heading bold.

4. Select the three topic lines (Mining for new contacts, Manageing existing clients, and Following up on orders). You can add a bullet to these items.

5. Click ▤ . Word applies bullets to the list items. Your document looks much more readable and appealing now (see Figure QT-4).

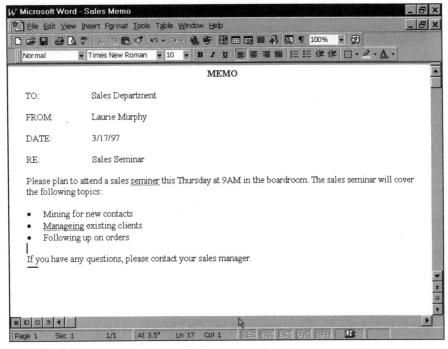

Figure QT-4 You can make some simple formatting changes to enhance the appearance of your document.

6. Click ⊞. Word saves the document with the same name and in the same file.

Checking the Document for Errors

You may notice that as you type, Word underlines some words with red, curvy lines. These are words that Word thinks are misspelled. You can make corrections to any flagged words.

Follow these steps:

1. Right-click on the word "seminer". Word displays a pop-up menu listing the correct spelling (see Figure QT-5).

2. Click the correct spelling.

3. Right-click on the word "Manageing" and select the correct spelling from the pop-up menu.

4. Save your document again using the **File** → **Save** command or the Save button.

If Word flags the FROM line in your memo, don't worry about it. This is not a mistake.

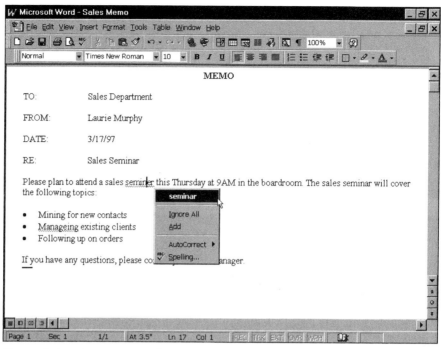

Figure QT-5 Correct any spelling errors in your document.

Previewing and Printing the Document

Now your document looks good and is error free. You are ready to print. First, preview the document to get a sense of the overall page layout. Then you can print.

Follow these steps:

1. Open the **File** menu and select the **Print Preview** command. You see a preview of your sales memo, as shown in Figure QT-6.

2. To close the preview, click the Close button. You are now ready to print.

3. Open the **File** menu and select the **Print** command. You see the Print dialog box (see Figure QT-7). Here you can select the number of copies to print, the pages to print, and more. The default options are acceptable, so you don't need to make any changes.

4. Click the OK button. Word prints your memo.

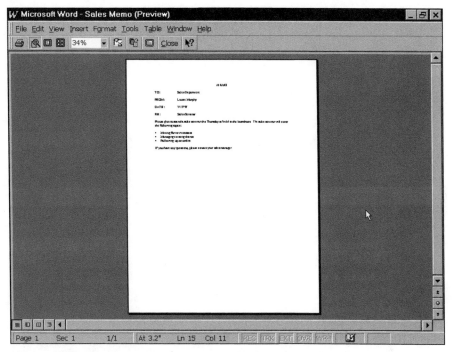

Figure QT-6 It's a good idea to preview your document before printing it.

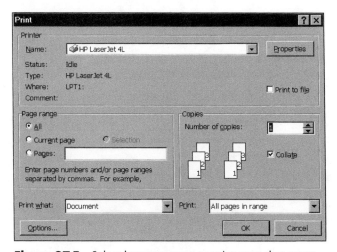

Figure QT-7 Select how you want to print your document.

This simple Quick Tour gives you a pretty good idea of how you create a document from start to end. For the most part, you will follow this same process — type, format, check, print — for all the documents you create. The Quick Tour also introduces you to some of the most commonly used features.

Now that you have whet your appetite, you can read the rest of the book for more details on typing, editing, saving, formatting, checking, and printing a document.

LEARNING THE BASICS

This part teaches you all the basics you need to know to type and edit a document. These are the skills you will use over and over and over again to create documents. If you already know some of this information, you should feel pretty confident. If you don't, you should feel relieved to know that all you need to master are the key skills in this chapter and you will be well on your way to being able to create a document.

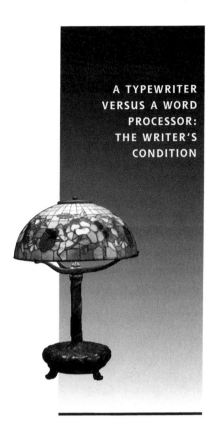

"I don't see how anyone can write without a computer these days. I really don't. I couldn't go back to retyping everything three or four times."

Eva Segar, freelance travel writer, photographer, and cryptography puzzle designer, began her writing career in 1965 with a series of hints published in *Capper's Weekly*. By interesting coincidence, one of those first hints was how to clean a typewriter.

Three children, travels from the Arctic Ocean to the Yucatan Peninsula in everything from a pop-up camper to a 30-foot fifth-wheel trailer, and 32 years later, Eva has progressed far beyond her uncle's dilapidated Remington. She has written articles for a major Midwestern newspaper about her extensive travels around North and Central America. In those travels Eva has also left her uncle's Remington behind for a Toshiba laptop.

Her computer experience varies almost as widely as her travel experience. "Don't get my husband started telling you how many computers I've had," she said as she described her first computer, a Radio Shack Model 3 with two floppy disk drives. On that trip to Mexico in the pop-up camper, she used her first laptop — also a Radio Shack — to write one of her early travel articles.

Eva appreciates her Microsoft word processing software, especially the spelling and grammar checkers. She says that often she just clicks the Suggest button and follows the rules. "I can see my mistakes before I make them," says Eva.

Word 97 allows you to change your mind. Eva feels that's important for a writer. Another important aspect of being is writer, according to Eva, is the ability to try new things. "Learn how to follow instructions," she says. "You have to want to do it!"

Currently, Eva is traveling with her husband and their dog in their RV and finishing her book *Yellow Britches*, a story of growing up in northeast Missouri in the 1920s and 1930s. "During the depression," she says, "Mom made our clothes out of feedsacks. She used soft flour sacks for baby clothes for my new sister. She made most of my clothes from yellow, tightly woven meal sacks. The meal sacks had black letters on them, most of which Mom was able to scrub out." Eva is currently looking for a publisher for her book.

Oh, and for those of you using a typewriter, Eva offers a cleaning hint. "Use the reverse switch on your vacuum cleaner and blow rather than suck the dust out of your typewriter." Word 97 doesn't require the use of your vacuum cleaner.

When you start using any program, there are some key skills you need to learn first. For example, you must learn how to start the program, get familiar with the screen, learn how to use on-screen items such as menus and toolbars, and learn how to get help. You must also figure out how to call it quits and turn off or exit the program. This chapter covers these skills.

If you have already used a previous version of Word for Windows 95, you are in luck. The new version is a lot like the previous one. (Many of the commands are similar to those in earlier versions such as Word 2.0 for Windows.) If you have used some other Windows 95 program, you will also be a few steps ahead in the game. You start, exit, look around, and get help in much the same way in any Windows 95 program. And if you haven't used a previous version of Word or any other Windows 95 program, don't fret. This chapter will have you up and running in no time.

Ladies and Gentlemen, Start Your Word Processors

The first step in using any program is to get it started. Starting is pretty simple: you just click a few commands. What can be confusing is that different systems can be set up differently. The programs you have on your system may be different than those on your neighbor Ed's. You may put your Word program icon somewhere different than the folder your coworker Camille uses. It's kind of like finding your car keys. Once you find those keys — or, in this case, the program icon — you are set.

Follow these steps to start Word:

1. Click the Start button. You see the Start menu options.

2. Click **Programs**. You see the programs and program folders you have set up on your system.

3. If necessary, click the folder that contains the Word program icon. If you have not made a change since installing Word, you can skip this step. The program item is added to the Programs folder, and you should see the Word program icon after completing step 2. If you have made a change, select the folder you used to store this program icon.

4. When you see the program icon, shown in Figure 1-1, click it to start Word.

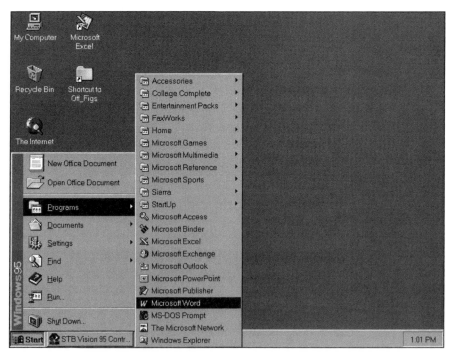

Figure 1-1   Click the Word program icon to start the program.

5. The program starts, and you see a blank document on-screen.

What's All This?

When you start Word, you see a blank document on-screen (see Figure 1-2). You can probably figure out what the big blank area of the screen is. It's like a blank piece of paper, where you will type the text of your document. You can pat yourself on the back for figuring that one out.

But as you look at the screen you may wonder, "What is all the other stuff? What are the little hieroglyphics at the top of the screen? Modern cave drawings?" The other stuff you see consists of items that help you use the program. You can use these items to select commands, move around the document, change how the document is displayed, and more. The screen also displays information about the current document, such as the page number and document name. Before you get started, you should take some time to familiarize yourself with the on-screen tools. To do so, take a look at Figure 1-2 and then use Table 1-1 to read about each item.

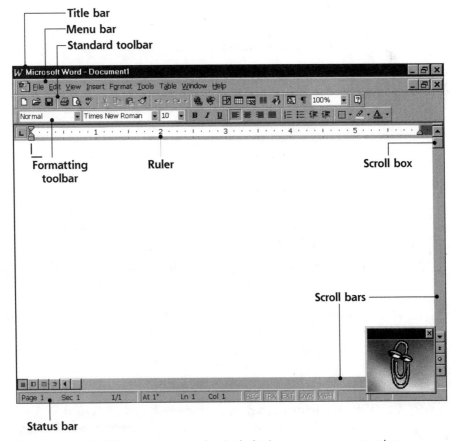

Figure 1-2 The Word program window includes items you can use to select commands, get information, move around, and more.

TABLE 1-1 Word Screen Items

Screen Item	Description
TITLE BAR	Lists the program name and document name, if you have saved the document. If you haven't saved the document, you see "Document1" in the title bar.
MENU BAR	Lists the menu names. See the section "I'll Take One of These Please" for more information.
STANDARD TOOLBAR	Includes buttons for frequently used commands. You can click the appropriate button to select a command — for instance, click the Print button to print your document. See the section "Tooling Around."
FORMATTING TOOLBAR	Includes buttons for frequently used formatting options. You can click the button to select the formatting option. For instance, click the Italic button to make selected text italic.
RULER	Includes means to format paragraphs, such as indenting text, setting tabs, and so on. For information on using the ruler, see Chapter 7.
SCROLL BARS/ SCROLL BOXES	Appear along the right side and bottom of the window. Click the scroll arrow to scroll the document window in that direction. To scroll quickly, drag the scroll box up or down to scroll in that direction. Chapter 2 covers how to move around the document.
STATUS BAR	Contains information about the current page, the current section, and the location of the insertion point.

TIP Note that the toolbar buttons have been redesigned in Word 97 (Word 8), but the screen looks much as it did in the previous Word 95 version. Most of the commands are also the same.

You may also see a little window with a paper clip icon. This is the Office Assistant, which you can use to get help. See the section "Your Helpful Assistant" later in this chapter.

FEATURE FOCUS Office Assistant is a new feature in Word 97 (Word 8). You can type questions in "regular" language, such as "How do I make something bold?" and Office Assistant will display relevant help topics.

I'll Take One of These, Please

One day you will be able to say to Word "Open this document. Make this text bold." And it will. This day will probably come sooner than you expect. For now, though, when you want Word to do something, you have to select the command you want. Word organizes its many commands into different menu categories, which appear in the menu bar. Selecting a command is easy. You can use the mouse or the keyboard.

To select a command with the mouse, follow these steps:

1. Click the name of the menu you want to open. For example, click the **File** menu. The menu drops down, and you see a list of commands (see Figure 1-3).

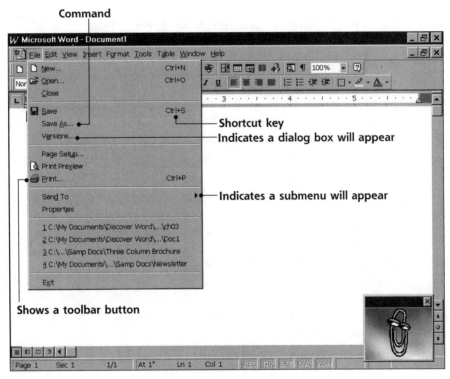

Figure 1-3 When you open a menu, you see a list of commands.

2. Click the command you want to execute. Some commands are executed right away. Other commands display a submenu or a dialog box. An arrow following a menu item indicates a submenu. If a menu item is followed by an ellipses, it means a dialog box will appear. A dialog box prompts you for additional information. See the next section for help on making dialog box selections.

3. If you see a submenu, select the command you want from this menu. If you see a dialog box, select any dialog box options you want to put into effect and then click the OK button. For more help on dialog boxes, see the next section.

To select a command with the keyboard, follow these steps:

1. Press the Alt key. This step activates the menu bar.

2. Press the key letter of the menu name. The key letter appears underlined in the menu bar. For instance, to open the ▣ File ▣ menu, press F. The menu drops down, and you see a list of commands (refer to Figure 1-3).

3. Press the key letter for the command you want. Again, the key letter is underlined.

Making Selections in a Dialog Box

To execute some commands, Word needs additional information. For example, if you intend to print a document, Word needs to know how many copies you want, the printer to use, and other options you may want to change. When there are other options for carrying out a command, Word displays a dialog box. It's kind of like ordering a meal. If you order some things — say a steak dinner — the waitress bombards you with questions. "How do you want your steak cooked? Do you want a baked potato or french fries? What kind of salad dressing?" A dialog box is like this questioning waitress. When you see one, you make your selections and then click the OK button to carry out the command.

You'll encounter dialog boxes quite a bit when you use Word, and even though the options are different, they all work the same way. Figure 1-4 shows the Options dialog box. (If you want to follow along and display this dialog box yourself, open the Tools menu and select the Options command. Click the Save tab.) Table 1-2 explains the different types of options you can find in a dialog box.

TABLE 1-2 Dialog Box Options

Item	Description
TAB	Some dialog boxes have more than one set of options, indicated with tabs near the top of the dialog box. Click the tab name to display the options for that tab.
CHECK BOX	Click the check box to check (turn on) or uncheck (turn off) the option. If a dialog box has more than one check box, you can check as many as you want.

Item	Description
OPTION BUTTON	Click the option button to turn it on (darkened) or off (blank). You can select only one option button in each group of option buttons. (Figure 1-4 does not show an option button.)
TEXT BOX	Click the text box and then type the entry. If the text box already contains an entry, drag across it to select the entry and then press Delete.
SPIN BOX	A spin box is a type of text box with spin arrows next to it. You can type an entry in the spin box. Or you can click the spin arrows to scroll through the text box values. (Figure 1-4 does not show a list box.)
LIST BOX	Displays a list of selections. Click the item you want in the list. (Figure 1-4 does not show a list box.)
DROP-DOWN LIST BOX	Displays only the first selection in a list. Click the down arrow next to the item to display other selections. Then click the item you want.
COMMAND BUTTON	Click the OK button to confirm and carry out the command. Click the Cancel button to cancel the command. Some dialog boxes also have other buttons that display other options. Click the button to display these options.

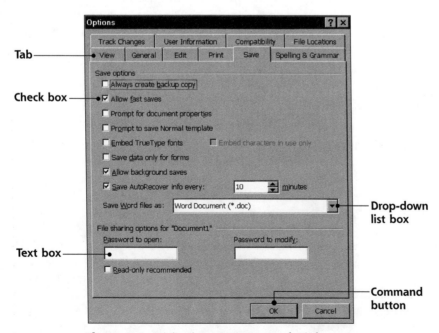

Figure 1-4 Dialog boxes prompt you for information about how to carry out the command.

TIP If you don't know what a dialog box option does, you can get help on an option. If the dialog box includes a question mark icon in the title bar, click it. The mouse pointer changes to display a question mark. Click the option on which you want help. You can also point to the item and click the right mouse button. A pop-up menu appears. Select What's This? In either case, you see a pop-up explanation of the dialog box option.

Tips on Commands

You'll select commands again and again and again in Word. So it's a good idea to learn a few tips about them:

You can use the Undo command to undo the action you just performed.

* The command you will probably value the most in Word is the Undo command. You can use this command to undo the action you just performed. For instance, if you deleted text accidentally, you can undo the command. To use this command, select Edit → Undo or click [🔙 ▾].

* Sometimes you may undo a command and then think, "Why did I undo that? Now I want to undo the undo." In that case, click the Redo button. What you just undid is undone. Think of it as going back two steps.

* If you want to execute the same command again, you can select it again or simply use the Edit → Repeat command.

* You can also use shortcut menus to select commands. To display a shortcut menu, click the right mouse button on the item you want to modify. For instance, to modify the toolbar, right-click this item. To display a shortcut menu for selected text, right-click the selected text. A shortcut menu pops up. Click the command you want.

SIDE TRIP

UNDOING A PAST ACTION

What if you don't realize you've made a mistake until after you've performed several other actions? Are you out of luck if you want to undo it? No. You can use the drop-down list next to the Undo button to display all the actions you can undo. To undo a certain one, click the down arrow to display the list. Then click the command or action you want to undo. Be careful. Some of the items listed may sound similar. Be sure to select the correct action.

✳ Another way to select commands is to use the shortcut keys. Shortcut keys appear in the menus next to the command names. The tips in this book point out some of the most common shortcut keys.

Tooling Around

Opening a menu, finding the command you want, and clicking the command takes time. As a faster way to select the most commonly used commands, Word displays two toolbars with buttons for these common commands. Rather than select a menu command, you can click the toolbar button.

TIP To find out what a button does, put the mouse pointer on the bottom edge of the button. The button name (called a ScreenTip) appears under the button.

The top toolbar is called the Standard toolbar; it includes buttons for working with files, editing text, and inserting items such as tables and worksheets. Table 1-3 shows the buttons in this toolbar. The Formatting toolbar, as you may guess from the name, includes buttons for formatting your document. Here you find buttons for applying a style, changing the font, making text bold, changing the alignment, and more. Table 1-4 shows the buttons in this toolbar.

To use a toolbar button, click it. Word carries out the selected command or feature. To use a toolbar list, click the down arrow next to the list box. Word displays a list. Click the option you want.

TABLE 1-3 The Standard Toolbar

Button	Name	Description
	NEW	Creates a new document.
	OPEN	Displays the Open dialog box.
	SAVE	Saves the document.
	PRINT	Prints the document.
	PRINT PREVIEW	Displays a preview of the document.
	SPELLING AND GRAMMAR	Checks your spelling and grammar.
	CUT	Cuts selected text.
	COPY	Copies selected text.

(continued)

TABLE 1-3 The Standard Toolbar (*continued*)

Button	Name	Description
	PASTE	Pastes cut or copied text.
	FORMAT PAINTER	Copies and pastes formatting.
	UNDO	Undoes the last command or commands.
	REDO	Redoes the last command or commands.
	INSERT HYPERLINK	Inserts a link to a file or a Web address.
	WEB TOOLBAR	Displays a toolbar with buttons for creating Web documents.
	TABLES AND BORDERS	Displays a toolbar with buttons for formatting and working with tables and paragraph borders.
	INSERT TABLE	Inserts a table.
	INSERT MICROSOFT EXCEL WORKSHEET	Inserts a Microsoft Excel worksheet.
	COLUMNS	Formats the selected section into columns.
	DRAWING	Displays the Drawing toolbar.
	DOCUMENT MAP	Displays a separate pane with an outline of your document headings. You can use this document map to navigate through your document.
	SHOW/HIDE ¶	Displays or hides paragraph marks ¶.
	ZOOM CONTROL	Zooms the document.
	OFFICE ASSISTANT	Displays the Office Assistant so that you can get help.

FEATURE FOCUS The Insert Hyperlink and Web Toolbar buttons are new features in Word 97.

TABLE 1-4 The Formatting Toolbar

Button	Name	Description
Normal ▼	STYLE	Displays a style list. Click the style you want.
▤	FONT	Displays a font list. Click the font you want.
10 ▼	FONT SIZE	Displays a size list. Click the size you want.
B	BOLD	Makes selected text bold.
I	ITALIC	Makes selected text italic.
U	UNDERLINE	Turns on underlining.
▤	ALIGN LEFT	Aligns selected paragraph(s) left.
▤	CENTER	Centers selected paragraph(s).
▤	ALIGN RIGHT	Aligns selected paragraph(s) right.
▤	JUSTIFY	Justifies selected paragraph(s).
▤	NUMBERING	Creates a numbered list.
▤	BULLETS	Creates a bulleted list.
▤	DECREASE INDENT	Decreases the indent of the selected paragraph(s).
▤	INCREASE INDENT	Increases the indent of the selected paragraph(s).
▣ ▾	OUTSIDE BORDER	Adds a border around the current paragraph. You can select a different type of border from the drop-down list.
✐ ▾	HIGHLIGHT	Highlights the selected text. The default color is yellow. You can select another color from the drop-down list.
A ▾	FONT COLOR	Changes the color of the selected text. The default color is red. You can select another color by clicking the down arrow next to the button and then clicking the color you want.

 X-REF You can turn off the toolbars if you don't use them. You can also choose to display other toolbars. For information on changing the screen display, see Chapter 17, "Customizing Word."

Your Helpful Assistant

Word is a complex program with lots of options. For the most part, you'll quickly learn the features and commands you use day after day and won't need much help remembering how to perform these common tasks. For less often used features, you may need a little reminder, though. If this book isn't at hand, you can use the Office Assistant to get help. Try the Assistant first. This feature lets you type in a question in "regular" terms and then displays relevant topics.

In addition, you can also look up help in the online help "books." For these help pages, you can look up something in the table of contents or index or search for help. Try this method when you can't find what you want using the Assistant.

Using the Office Assistant

See that winking paper clip in the little window at the lower-right corner of the Word window? That's one of the new features of Word 8; it's called the Office Assistant. You can use this animated icon to get help.

Follow these steps:

1. Click the Office Assistant. If the Office Assistant is not displayed, click the Office Assistant button in the Standard toolbar. You see a cartoon caption for the Assistant, which you can use to get help (see Figure 1-5).

Figure 1-5 Tell the Office Assistant what you want to do.

2. Type what you want to do and then click the Search button. You see all the matches (see Figure 1-6).

3. Click the topic you want. You see a help window with information about the selected topic (see Figure 1-7).

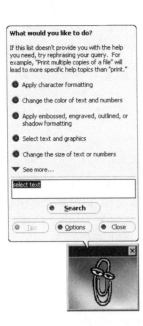

Figure 1-6 Office Assistant lists the matching things you can do.

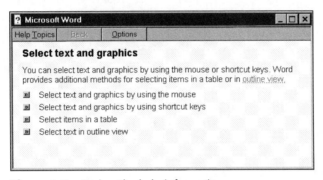

Figure 1-7 Review the help information.

Using the Help Window

When you display help, you see a help window (refer to Figure 1-7) with appropriate information. This window also includes buttons and references that you can use to navigate through the help system.

✳ To display the Help Topics dialog box, click the Help Topics button.

✳ Click the Back button to go back to the previous topic.

✳ To print the information, click the Options button and then select the Print Topic command.

✳ If you see other topics indicated with little brackets, you can display these topics by clicking the reference.

* If you see a dotted line under a word or phrase, it means that you can display a pop-up definition for the term. Point to the term and click the mouse button. A definition appears. Click back in the help window to close the definition.

* To close the window, click the Close button.

Using Help Topics or the Index

If you aren't partial to animated paper clips, you can use the more traditional help window to get help. This help system works a lot like a book. You can look up topics in the table of contents or in the index. Unlike when you are using a book, though, you can also use the help system to search for a topic.

To get help using the online help "manual," follow these steps:

1. Open the **Help** menu and select the **Contents and Index** command. You see the Help Topics dialog box.

2. To look up a topic in the table of contents, click the Contents tab. You see a table of contents of help topics. Top-level topics are indicated with book icons. Double-click the "book" you want until you see the help page you want. Help pages are indicated with question mark icons. Figure 1-8 shows both book icons and help page icons. Double-click the help page icon to display a window with specific information on the selected topic.

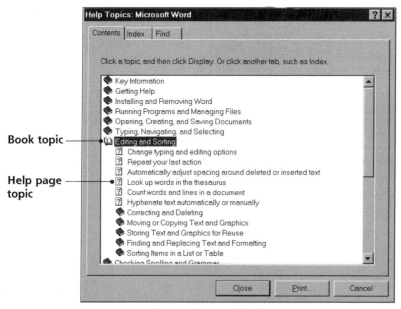

Figure 1-8 Use the Contents tab to display the topic on which you want help.

MODIFYING THE ASSISTANT

You can modify the appearance of the assistance and set options for how it works. To do so, follow these steps:

1. Click the Office Assistant.

2. Click the Options button. You see the Office Assistant dialog box, with the Options tab selected. This dialog box contains several check boxes. To turn on an option, check its check box. To turn off the option, uncheck the check box.

3. Click the Gallery tab. Using this tab select a different character for the Assistant. Use the Back and Next buttons to scroll through the characters until you find the one you want.

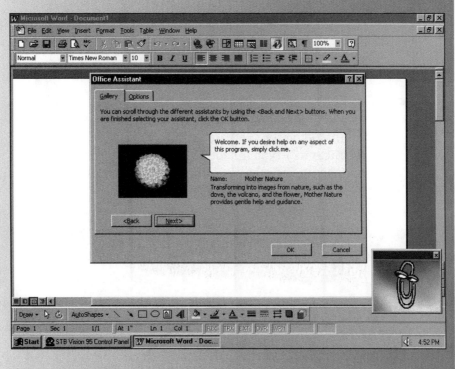

4. Click the OK button.

3. To look up a topic in the index, click the Index tab. Then type the first few letters of the topic you want. Word displays matching topics in the second half of the dialog box (see Figure 1-9). Double-click the topic you want.

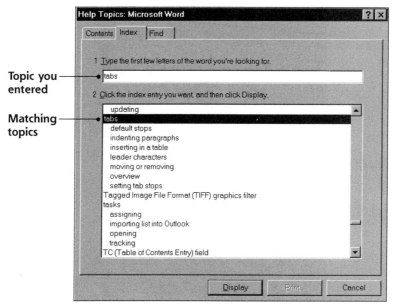

Topic you entered

Matching topics

Figure 1-9 Use the Index tab to move quickly to a topic of interest.

4. To search for help, click the Find tab. (The first time you use this command, you have to set up the word list. Follow the on-screen instructions.) Type the topic on which you want help. Word displays matches in the middle of the dialog box. Narrow the search by selecting the topics of interest as under step 2. As in step 3, double-click the topic you want (see Figure 1-10).

I'm Done

When you are finished working in Word, you can exit the program. You shouldn't just turn off your PC with Word still running because that could mess up your document and program files. Instead, be sure to save all documents that you have created. If you try to exit without saving, Word will remind you. (You will learn more about saving in the next chapter.) After all the documents are saved, you can exit Word.

Follow these steps to exit Word:

1. For now, you need not save anything. You'll learn more about saving documents in the next chapter.

2. Open the File menu and select the Exit command. You return to the Windows desktop.

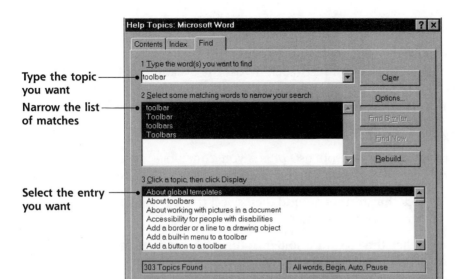

Type the topic you want

Narrow the list of matches

Select the entry you want

Figure 1-10   Use the Find tab to search for help on a particular topic.

TIP   You can also click the Close button in the application window toolbar or press Alt+F4 to exit the program.

BONUS

Shortcuts for Starting Word

Word may be a program you use all the time or at least most of the time. You may in fact start your work day by starting Word. Rather than use the Start menu, you can use some shortcuts for starting the program:

* If you want to be able to start Word from the desktop, you can create a shortcut icon. That's how I start Word.

* If you want to work on a particular document, you can open that document and start Word at the same time. I also use this method a lot when I want to edit a document I've recently worked on.

This bonus section discusses these shortcuts for starting Word.

Creating a Shortcut Icon

If you look around your "real" desk, you may see that you have everything you need close at hand. You can just reach across the desk, for instance, to pick up your pen. (Maybe you have to shuffle some papers around. Or maybe you have to crawl under the desk to find the pen. Or maybe it would take a search and rescue team to find a pen on your desk. You get the idea, though. Stuff you use often is right there on your desk.)

If Word is something you use often, you can place access to it on your Windows desktop, making it easy to find and access. To do so, follow these steps:

1. Right-click the Start menu and then select the **Open** command. You see the folders on your Start menu.

2. Double-click the Programs folder. You see the program folders and the program icons in this folder. If you have not changed the location of the Word program icon, you should see it in this window.

3. Point to the program icon and click and hold down the right mouse button. Be sure to use the right button.

4. Drag the program icon to the desktop and release the mouse button. When you release the mouse button, you see a menu (see Figure 1-11).

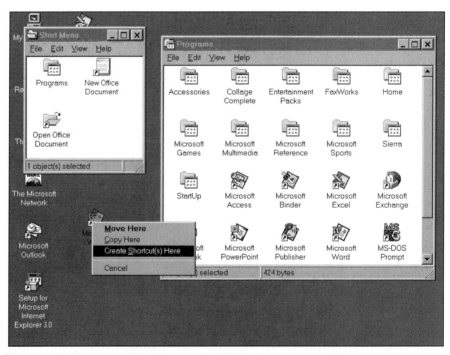

Figure 1-11   Drag a copy of the Word program icon to your desktop to create a shortcut icon.

5. Select Create Shortcut(s) Here . Windows creates the shortcut and places it on your desktop.

You can use the shortcut icon to start Word. To do so, double-click it.

Starting Word and Opening a Document

You will often start work by going back to a document that you just worked on. You could start Word and then find and open that document. Or you can use a shortcut. Windows keeps track of the last fifteen documents you worked on. You can select any of these documents from the Documents menu and both start the program and open that document.

Follow these steps:

1. Click the Start menu.

2. Select Documents . You see a list of documents you have recently worked on (see Figure 1-12).

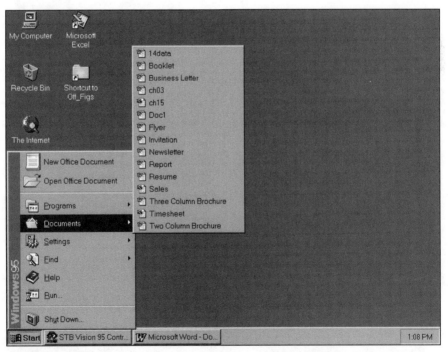

Figure 1-12   Use the Documents command to open a recently used document.

3. Click the document you want. Windows starts the associated program (Word in this case) and then opens the document. All in one fell swoop!

Summary

This chapter covered the basics of getting started using Word. Here you learned how to start the program, select menu commands, use the program, get help, and exit. Now you are ready to create a document, as covered in the next chapter.

WEB PATH ➡ **Visit this Web site for a quick introduction to the features and specifications of Word.**

`http://www.microsoft.com/msword/productinfo/brochure/wquick.htm`

CREATING A DOCUMENT

2

When you create a document, you always follow the same basic procedure. You type it, save it, and possibly open it again if you need to edit it. This chapter covers this cycle. No matter what type of document you create — a memo, a report, a manuscript page, a newsletter, a business letter, or whatever — you follow this same routine. The skills in this chapter, then, are important because you use them almost each time you use Word.

From A to Z

When you start Word, you see a blank document on-screen. Yes, a blank area just waiting for your words of wisdom. Waiting for you to commit to paper your grand scheme, your ideas for changing the world, or at least your ideas for next month's pitch-in party. To create a document, you can just start typing away.

As you type, the characters appear on-screen, and the flashing vertical bar, called the insertion point, moves to the right (see Figure 2-1). This insertion point always indicates where new text will appear when you start typing. Keep typing until you reach the end of the line. Then type some more. Notice that Word will automatically wrap text to the next line. Unlike in the old days of typewriters, you don't have to listen for a little ding and wear your arm out pressing carriage return, carriage return, carriage return.

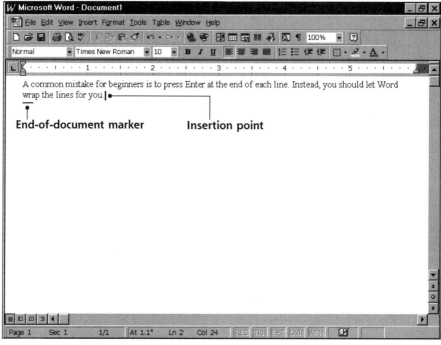

Figure 2-1 Type the text of your document.

One mistake many new users make is to press Enter at the end of each line.

In fact, one mistake many new users make is to press Enter at the end of each line. You shouldn't do this because if you have to add or delete text, your lines won't automatically readjust. You should press Enter only at the end of a paragraph or when you want to insert a blank line.

TIP   Word inserts a hidden paragraph mark when you press Enter. If you want to see where the breaks occur, click ¶ in the Standard toolbar. You see marks for paragraphs, spaces, tabs, and other hidden characters.

Inserting Tabs

If you want to insert a tab, simply press the Tab key on the keyboard. By default, Word has tabs set every ½ inch. (You can change the tab stops, as covered in Chapter 7.) Word inserts the tab and moves the insertion point over. You can then type your text.

A common mistake for beginners is to use the spacebar to tab over in a document. That's another typing no-no. Spaces don't always align entries exactly, so instead be sure to use the Tab key.

X-REF   **Tabs are great for a simple alignment setup such as memo headings. For something more complex, though, use a different feature. For instance, if you want to indent paragraphs, don't use tabs. Instead, use the paragraph indent features, covered in Chapter 7. If you want to set up a list, don't use tabs. Set up a table instead, covered in Chapter 10.**

Inserting Page Breaks

Word also automatically inserts page breaks, as necessary. When a page fills up, Word inserts a break and creates a new page. If you add or delete text, Word adjusts the page breaks. This means that you don't have to worry about text running off the page.

In some cases, you may want to force a page break. For instance, you may want to create a title page. You could just force a page break by inserting a lot of blank returns until Word inserts a page, but you shouldn't (another no-no). This method will mess you up if you add or delete text later. Instead, insert a hard page break.

The easiest way to insert a hard page break is by using the keyboard shortcut: press Ctrl+Enter. You can also use a menu command:

Follow these steps:

1. Open the ⟦ **Insert** ⟧ menu and select the ⟦ **Break** ⟧ command. You see the Break dialog box (see Figure 2-2). The ⟦ **Page break** ⟧ option is the selected option.

Figure 2-2   Insert a hard page break using this dialog box.

2. Click the OK button. Word inserts a manual page break, indicated with a dotted line with the text "Page Break" in the middle of the line. This page break will not be adjusted when you add or delete text.

To delete a hard page break, move the insertion point right after the page break and press Backspace.

Inserting the Date and Time

As a society, we are very time and date conscious. We date-stamp everything — letters, memos, manuscript revisions, newsletters. You can probably come up with a good reason to include a date in just about every type of document you create. Because including the date in a document is so common, Word provides a shortcut for inserting the date or time. No more shuffling through your desk looking for a calendar. No more taking a wild guess.

You can insert the date as just plain old text. Use this option for letters, memos, or other documents when you don't want to update the date. The date is "frozen" so that you always know the exact date you entered. You can also insert the date as a field that is automatically updated. This option works best for templates (covered in Chapter 13), form letters (covered in Chapter 14), and documents that you may work on for several days (or weeks or months or years — those great American novels take *time*). For instance, suppose that you are creating a report that will probably take you all week. You can insert the date as a field when you first create the document. Then when you finally finish and print the document, Word will update the field to the current date.

TIP   If you want, you can include the date or time in a header or footer that will print on every page. For information on setting up headers and footers, see Chapter 8.

To insert the date or time in your document, follow these steps:

1. Place the insertion point where you want to insert the date.

2. Open the **Insert** menu and select the **Date and Time** command. You see the Date and Time dialog box (see Figure 2-3).

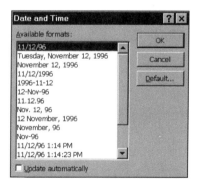

Figure 2-3   Select any of these date and time formats to insert the date and time.

3. Click the date or time format you want to use.

4. If you want to have the date automatically updated, check the Update automatically check box.

5. Click the OK button. Word inserts the date or time in the format you selected.

To delete the date, use the Edit → Undo command immediately after you insert the date. Or just select the date or time and press Delete.

DATE AND TIME WRONG?

What if the date and time are wrong? Word uses the date and time from your system clock. If this date or time is incorrect, you can update it by following these steps:

1. In the Windows taskbar, you should see the time in the lower-right corner. Right-click this area. You see a shortcut menu.

2. Select the ‹Adjust Date/Time› command. You see the Date/Time Properties dialog box with the Date & Time tab selected.

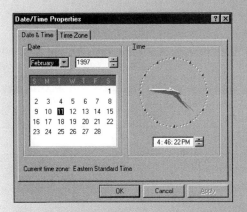

3. Select the correct date using the calendar or the drop-down list boxes.

4. Select the correct time using the clock or the spin arrows.

5. Click the OK button.

From Here to There

The insertion point is the "You Are Here" arrow. When you want to add or delete text, you start by moving the insertion point to where you want to make the change. When you want to select text, you move the insertion point to the start of the text. You can use either the mouse or the keyboard to move the insertion point.

The horizontal line in the page area indicates the end of the document. You cannot move the insertion point past this indicator. If you click beyond this line, nothing happens. Word doesn't permit the insertion point to move where nothing exists. Only after you enter text or spaces on-screen can you move the insertion point.

Using the Mouse

To move the insertion point with the mouse, move the pointer to the spot you want and click the mouse button. The insertion point jumps to that spot. Remember that the insertion point (the vertical flashing line) and the mouse pointer (the I-beam) are two separate items. You can't just point to the spot you want. You have to point and click to place the insertion point.

Using the Keyboard

If you prefer to keep your hands on the keyboard, you can use the arrow keys and other key combinations to move the insertion point. Table 2-1 lists the common movement keys. Note that if the key combination is joined with a plus sign, you must press and hold the first key, and then press the second key.

TABLE 2-1 Keyboard Movement Keys

To Move	Press
ONE CHARACTER LEFT	←
ONE CHARACTER RIGHT	→
ONE LINE UP	↑
ONE LINE DOWN	↓
TO THE BEGINNING OF THE LINE	Home
TO THE END OF LINE	End
TO THE BEGINNING OF THE DOCUMENT	Ctrl+Home
TO THE END OF THE DOCUMENT	Ctrl+End
ONE WORD LEFT	Ctrl+ ←
ONE WORD RIGHT	Ctrl+ →

To Move	Press
ONE PARAGRAPH UP	Ctrl+↑
ONE PARAGRAPH DOWN	Ctrl+↓
ONE SCREEN UP	PgUp
ONE SCREEN DOWN	PgDn
TOP OF SCREEN	Ctrl+PgUp
BOTTOM OF SCREEN	Ctrl+PgDn

Scrolling the Document

In a long document, you may simply want to scroll through the text without moving the insertion point. You can do this using certain of the key combinations in Table 2-1 as well as by using the scroll bars. See Figure 2-4 for a view of the different kinds of scrolling options.

To scroll the document using the mouse, do any of the following:

✳ To scroll left, click the left scroll arrow. To scroll right, click the right scroll arrow.

✳ To scroll up through the document, click the up scroll arrow. To scroll down through the document, click the down scroll arrow.

✳ To scroll a relative distance in the document, drag the scroll box up or down. If you have several pages in the document, you can tell which page you are on by looking at the pop-up page number that appears (see Figure 2-4). If that page includes a style heading, the heading name also appears. When you get to the page you want, release the mouse button.

✳ To scroll to a relative location without dragging, click within the scroll bar to move to that location screen by screen.

Keep in mind that when you use the scroll arrows, you are *not* moving the insertion point. The insertion point remains in the original spot. If you scroll to a different location and want to make a change, be sure to click the I-beam to place the insertion point before you make the change.

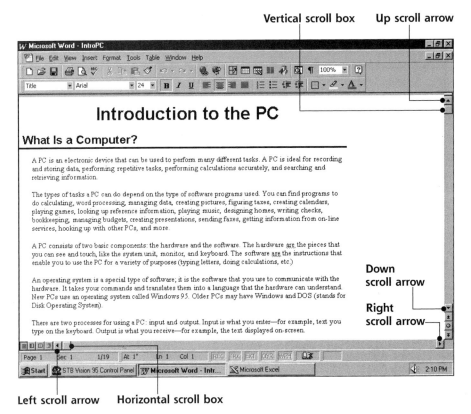

Vertical scroll box **Up scroll arrow**

Down scroll arrow

Right scroll arrow

Left scroll arrow **Horizontal scroll box**

Figure 2-4 Drag the scroll box to move in a document.

Oops!

I think the hardest part of writing is that first sentence. You don't know how many times I start a sentence and then backspace, backspace, backspace to erase what I just typed. I start another sentence that sounds good in my head but looks ridiculous in the cold glare of the PC screen. Backspace, backspace, backspace again.

The biggest thrill of using a word-processing program program is the ease with which you can make changes. As you type, you can make some simple corrections. (For more detailed information on editing a document, see the next chapter.) You can delete characters and insert new text with ease.

Correcting Mistakes

As you type, you see the characters on-screen. If you notice a mistake, you can correct it using either the Backspace key or the Delete key. Press the Backspace key to delete characters to the left of the insertion point. (Think *back, Back*space.)

Press the Delete key to delete characters to the right of the insertion point. (Think forward for the Delete key.) When you delete character(s), Word moves existing text up to fill in the gap.

Adding Text

If you are fairly young, you may have never had the privilege of using a typewriter. You won't *even* appreciate how easy it is to add and delete text. You won't remember having to retype an *entire* document just to add an idea you forgot (or your boss thought was critical).

Yes, Word makes it easy to add text, adjusting the existing text to make room. To add text, place the insertion point where you want the new text. Then type the text. New text is inserted, and existing text moves over to make room.

If you ever start typing and text disappears, you are in Typeover mode (rather than Insert mode). You can use Typeover mode to type over text, although I can't think of a good reason why you would. You usually want to stay in Insert mode, where new text is inserted in the document. You toggle between Typeover and Insert mode using the Insert key. So if text disappears, check the status bar. If you see OVR, press the Insert key to return to Insert mode.

For All Posterity or at Least Tomorrow

There is one advantage of using a typewriter over a word-processing program program. With a typewriter, you never had to worry about saving your document. You never had to worry that after you'd typed page after page, your document could go bye-bye in one short power outage.

With Word, you *must* remember to save your document. Why do you have to save? Because the words on-screen are stored in a temporary spot, the computer's memory. If something happens to the computer — someone accidentally turns it off or you have a power failure — all that information is lost. To make a permanent copy of the on-screen document, you need to save the document to a file on your hard disk.

With Word, you must always remember to save your document.

You shouldn't wait until you finish the document to save, and don't think that saving just once is enough. There's nothing more frustrating than spending several hours getting the content just perfect and then losing all that hard work because you've forgotten to save. If you wait until you are finished with the document, you run the risk of losing all your work if something happens before you finish.

You should also save periodically as you work on the document. The disk version reflects all the changes you made before you saved. As you continue to work and make changes, you need to update the disk file with the changes on-screen.

SIDE TRIP

SAVING DOCUMENTS AUTOMATICALLY

You may notice a message in the status bar that says "Autosaving document." To help you if you don't remember to save, Word is set up to save your document automatically every ten minutes. If you wish, you can turn off this feature or change the time limit.

Follow these steps:

1. Open the Tools menu and select the Options command.

2. Click the Save tab. You see the Save tab of the Options dialog box.

3. To create a backup copy each time you save, check the Always create backup copy check box. When you save the current document, Word keeps the original document but changes the extension to .BAK. Word saves the on-screen version with the extension .DOC.

   To change how often the document is saved, type a new value or use the spin arrows to enter a new value in the minutes text box next to Save AutoRecover info every check box. To turn off the automatic save feature, uncheck this check box.

4. Click the OK button.

Saving and Naming the Document

The first time you save a document, you are prompted for a name. Naming the file enables you to find and open that file again. You also select the drive and folder where the file will be stored. By default, Word uses the Personal folder to store your documents. You can place your file in another folder. In fact, it's a good idea to spend some time thinking about how you want to organize your documents. See Chapter 16 for some advice on setting up folders for your Word documents.

To save and name a document, follow these steps:

1. Open the File menu and select the Save command or click 🖫. You see the Save As dialog box (see Figure 2-5).

Select a drive

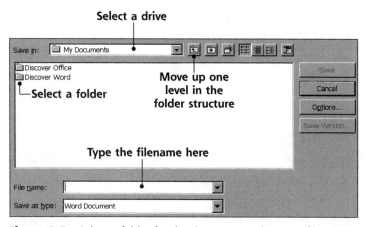

Figure 2-5 Select a folder for the document and enter a filename.

2. To select another drive, display the Save in drop-down list and select the drive you want.

3. To select another folder, double-click it in the folder list. You may have to move up a level in the folder structure using the Up One Level button to find the folder you want.

4. In the File name text box, type a name for the document. You used to be limited to 8 characters before Word 95. Now you can type up to 255 characters and include spaces in the filename. Use a descriptive name that will remind you of the contents.

5. Click the Save button. Word saves the document. The filename appears in the title bar.

Saving a Document Again

Once you save and name a file, you don't need to enter the name again. You can save the file again by simply selecting File → Save or clicking the Save button. If you like keyboard shortcuts, use Ctrl+S to save a document.

Using Save As

If you use Windows 95, you know that you can use it for file management tasks such as copying, renaming, or moving a document. You can also accomplish the same thing using the Save As command. For instance, suppose that you type your annual Christmas letter to your old roommate and save it as MARY.DOC. Now you also have to write a letter to your other roommate, Maureen, saying practically the same thing. You could retype the document. You could copy the text to a new document. Or you could use the Save As command and save a copy of the file. For example, you could save MARY.DOC as MOE.DOC. Then you could edit MOE.DOC and have two separate letters.

You can also use Save As is to change the folder where you placed the document or to change the name of a document. In both cases, remember that the original file remains in the same spot, with the same name.

Follow these steps to use the Save As command:

1. Open the **File** menu and select the **Save As** command. You see the Save As dialog box, the same dialog box you see when you save a document for the first time. The original name is listed.

2. To save the document to another drive or folder, select the drive from the Save in drop-down list or select the folder from the folder list. You can use the Up One Level button to move up through the folder structure.

3. Type a new filename.

4. Click OK.

Word saves the on-screen document with the new name. That document remains on-screen. The original file is closed and is kept intact on disk.

Closing a Document

After you save a document, it is not closed. It remains open so that you can continue working. When you are finished, you should save and then close the document. You can have several documents on-screen at once, but closing documents you no longer need will save memory. You can close a document by clicking the Close button in the document window or by using the File → Close command.

When all documents are closed, you see a blank, gray area. You can create a new document or open a document you have created before, as covered in the next two sections.

Open Says-a-Me

The whole purpose of saving a document is to make this document available again for editing, printing, or reusing. To display a document you have previously saved, you use the Open command.

Follow these steps:

1. Open the **File** menu and select the **Open** command or click 🗁. You see the Open dialog box (see Figure 2-6).

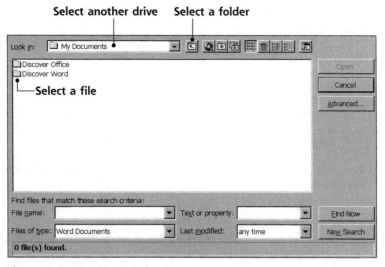

Select another drive   Select a folder

Figure 2-6   Double-click the document you want to open.

2. If you see the file listed, skip to step 3. If the file is stored on another drive, display the Look in drop-down list and select the drive you want. If the file is stored in another folder, open that folder. If you see the folder listed, double-click it. You can also use the Up One Level button to move up through the folder structure.

3. Click the file you want and then click the Open button. As a shortcut, you can double-click the filename. The document is displayed on-screen.

TIP   **To open a document you have recently worked on, open the File menu. Notice that the last four files opened are listed at the bottom of the menu. Simply click the file you want to open.**

A New Blank Sheet of Paper

When you start Word, you see a blank document on-screen. You always have this same blank sheet of paper available. When you want to get out another "sheet" of paper, you can do so using the File → New command.

Follow these steps:

1. To create a document based on the default template, click the New button and skip the rest of the steps. To use a different template, open the File menu and select the New command.

You see the New dialog box, with the Blank Document template selected (see Figure 2-7). You can base documents on different templates. For information on other templates, see Chapter 13.

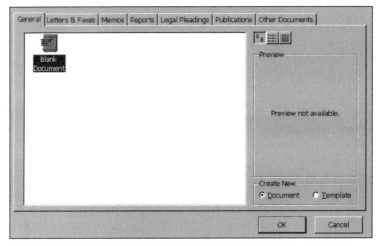

Figure 2-7 Select the template you want to use.

2. Select the template you want to use.

3. Click the OK button. Word displays a new document on-screen.

BONUS

Shortcuts for Moving Around

Moving around a short document is simple. You may be able to see the entire text of a short document in one window. To move, all you have to do is point and click. For longer documents, though, moving around isn't as easy. If you work a lot with long documents, you can use some shortcuts for moving around.

* If you have several pages, you can go quickly to a certain page in a document.

* Use the new Document Map feature to move quickly to sections.

The Document Map feature is new in Word 97.

This section describes these shortcuts for moving around.

Going to a Page

If you have tried scrolling through a document, you know it's not an exact science. The scroll box gives you some idea of where you are in the overall document. And when you drag, the page numbers do appear, but scrolling may not be the best method in a really long document. You can go directly to a page using the Go To command.

Follow these steps:

1. Open the **Edit** menu and select the **Go To** command. You see the Go To dialog box (see Figure 2-8). You can go to a page, section, line, footnote, bookmark, and other items. Most commonly you will use this feature to go to a page, and Page is the default.

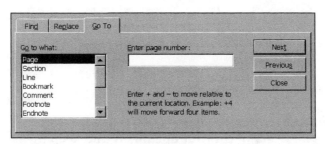

Figure 2-8   Use the Go To dialog box to go to a particular page or bookmark.

2. Type the page number. When you type a page number, the Next button changes to the Go To button.

3. Click the Go To button. You move to that page. Word also places the insertion point at the top of the page.

Navigating Using Your Document Map

If you have assigned heading styles to the headings in your document, you can use the Document Map, a new feature, to navigate through your document. (For information on using these heading styles, review Chapter 9.)

To display a document map, click . You see two separate panes. The left-most pane shows all the level-1 and level-2 headings in your document. The current section is highlighted. The rightmost pane shows the text of the document (see Figure 2-9).

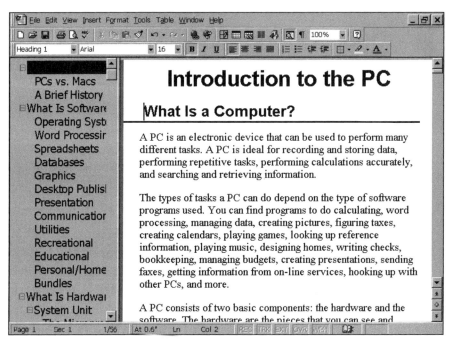

Figure 2-9   Use the new Document Map feature to navigate around your document.

To move to another section, simply click the heading in the leftmost pane. Word moves you to that section.

TIP   The Document Map is not only a good way to navigate, it's also a good way to see an overview of your document and keep the document organization in mind as you write and edit.

Summary

f you get each and every document perfect the first time you create it, then you are lucky indeed. Most of us mere mortals have to go over a document again and again — making editing changes and formatting changes — until we achieve perfection. The next chapter in this book tells you how to edit your document.

O ne of the greatest things about using a word-processing program program such as Word is how easily you can make changes. Forget a word, a phrase, or an entire paragraph? You can add text. Decide you don't like a word, a phrase, or an entire paragraph? You can delete text. When you add or delete text, Word adjusts existing text accordingly — moving text over to make room for additions or moving text up to fill in the gaps from deletions.

Adding and deleting text is not all that you can do. Suppose that you decide you like a different order — that your conclusion makes a better introduction. You can move text to another spot in the document or to a new document. You can also copy text that you want to reuse.

This chapter covers the most common editing changes you make to a document. You learn how to work with text: selecting, adding, deleting, moving, copying, finding, and replacing text.

This Is It!

The most important editing and formatting skill you can learn is how to select text. Most tasks you perform start with this basic step: Select the text you want to work with. Select text, select text, select text — you'll get tired of reading that step.

The most important editing and formatting skill you can learn is how to select text.

Once the text is selected, you can make changes to that text. You can delete it, move it, copy it, make it bold, change the font, change the color, frappé it, and so on. Selecting text is critical, then, to most editing and formatting skills.

Selecting text is similar to highlighting, and you will find it's simple to select text. You can use either the mouse or the keyboard, and you can select a character, a word, a phrase, a sentence, a paragraph, even the entire document.

Selecting Text with the Mouse

You may prefer to use the mouse to move around. If so, you'll probably be most comfortable selecting text with the mouse.

Follow these steps:

1. Move the insertion point to the start of the text you want to select.

2. Click and hold down the mouse button and drag across the text you want to select.

3. When all the text is selected, release the mouse button. The text appears in reverse video (see Figure 3-1).

 TIP Sometimes you may select text by mistake. To unselect text, simply click outside of the selected text or press an arrow key. Presto. The text is not selected.

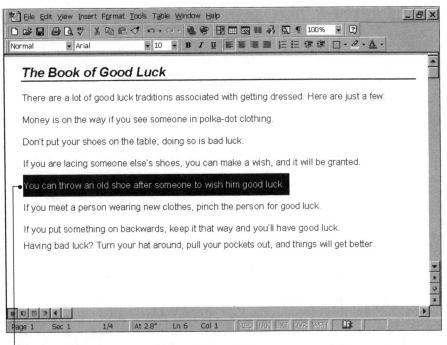

The Book of Good Luck

There are a lot of good luck traditions associated with getting dressed. Here are just a few:

Money is on the way if you see someone in polka-dot clothing.

Don't put your shoes on the table; doing so is bad luck.

If you are lacing someone else's shoes, you can make a wish, and it will be granted.

You can throw an old shoe after someone to wish him good luck.

If you meet a person wearing new clothes, pinch the person for good luck.

If you put something on backwards, keep it that way and you'll have good luck.

Having bad luck? Turn your hat around, pull your pockets out, and things will get better.

This is called the selection area. You can click here to select text.

Figure 3-1 Selected text appears highlighted on-screen.

ACCIDENTALLY MOVING INSTEAD OF SELECTING TEXT BY ACCIDENT

Many beginners make this common mistake: They select some text and release the mouse button. Then they want to select some additional text — that is, extend the selection — so they try dragging the highlight. This doesn't work. What happens is that they end up moving the text. You can select and then drag text, as covered later in this chapter.

If text mysteriously moves, this is probably what happened. Simply undo the move by clicking the Undo button. If you have this same problem a lot, you may want to turn off Drag-and-drop editing. To do so, open the Tools menu and select the Options command. Click the Edit tab. Uncheck the Drag-and-drop text-editing check box.

Selecting Text with the Keyboard

If you are a fast typist, you may prefer to keep your fingers on the keyboard. In this case, you let your fingers do the selecting.

Follow these steps to select text using the keyboard:

1. Move the insertion point to the start of the text you want to select.

2. Hold down the Shift key and use the movement keys (← , ↓ , and so on) to highlight the text you want.

3. Release the Shift key. The text is selected.

Selection Shortcuts

Because selecting text is so common, Word provides several shortcuts for selecting text. You can double-click within a word to select it. Click three times within a paragraph to select it.

Feeling pretty fancy with the mouse? You can also click with the selection bar (the blank area along the left side of the Word document) to select text. Click once next to the line you want to select the entire line. Click twice next to the paragraph you want to select the entire paragraph. Click three times to select the entire document. Click forty-five times to select every document you've ever typed. (Just kidding on that last one.)

And if you're a keyboard fan, you can press Ctrl+A to select the entire document.

Get Outta Here

Have you ever said something and then wished you could swallow your words? Told your boss that his toupee didn't look *that* bad? Asked a woman "When is your baby due?" when the baby was born two months ago? Unfortunately Word can't help you with the spoken word, but it can help you get rid of words, phrases, and sentences that just don't make sense in your document.

You can prune your text down so that it is concise, to-the-point, and devoid of any repetition. (See, I could benefit from a little editing myself: In the preceding sentence I say the same idea — concise — in three different ways.)

You can delete any amount of text by following these steps:

1. Select the text you want to delete. You can select a word, a phrase, a sentence, a paragraph, part of a paragraph, part of a document, the entire document — you get the idea.

2. Press the Delete key. Word deletes the text and fills in the gap.

TIP **Make a mistake? If you delete text by mistake, use the Edit → Undo command to undo the deletion. You can also click ⏎▾.**

No Heavy Lifting Required

In prehistoric times (that is BPC or **B**efore **PC**s), you had to create a document by writing it out in longhand on paper. When you wanted to edit it, you had to scribble out, write over, and add little notes to yourself. If you wanted to use a different order for the text, you had to use some scheme. Maybe you used numbers like 1, 2, or 3 to indicate the new order. Or maybe you literally cut and pasted the text in the order you wanted (that's what I used to do, having little bits of handwritten "wisdom" cut into strips and scattered around my room). After all this work, you then had the arduous process of committing these scribbles to the typewriter. Good luck getting it right!

Thank goodness those times are over. Now with a word-processing program program, you can easily rearrange the text. Without scissors and paste! Word does use the same metaphor of cutting and pasting. You cut the text from its original location and then paste it into its new location.

Follow these steps to move text:

1. Select the text you want to move (see Figure 3-2).

2. Open the **Edit** menu and select the **Cut** command or click ☐. The text is removed from the document and placed in a temporary holding area called the Clipboard.

3. Move to where you want to place the text. You can move to another location in a document, to another document, or even to another type of document. (For information on cutting and pasting from one program to another, see Chapter 15.)

4. Open the **Edit** menu and select the **Paste** command or click 📋 in the toolbar. The text is pasted into its new location (see Figure 3-3).

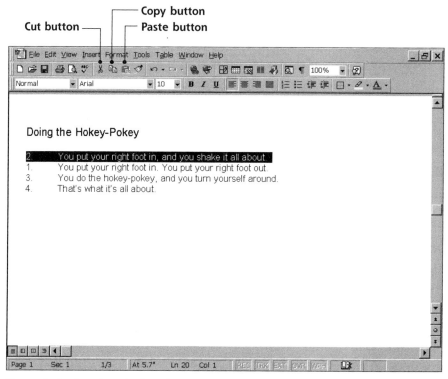

Cut button ⎯⎯ Copy button
Paste button

Figure 3-2   Start by selecting the text you want to move.

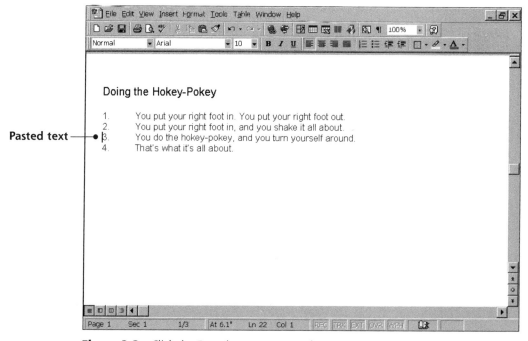

Pasted text ⎯⎯

Figure 3-3   Click the Paste button to paste the cut text.

So Nice I'll Say It Twice

Copying text is a lot like moving, except that the selected text appears in both places — the original location and the spot to which you copy it. Copying is handy when you want to use the same or similar text again. For instance, the steps for moving and copying text are similar. Thus when I was writing this book, I copied the steps for moving text and then edited the steps so that they now explain how to copy text.

Like moving, making a new copy of text involves two processes: copying the text (as opposed to cutting it) and pasting the text. When you copy the text, it is placed in the Clipboard, a temporary holding area. You can paste more than one copy because the text remains in the Clipboard until you copy or cut something else.

When you cut or copy something, you must paste the selection before you cut or copy something else. The Clipboard always holds the last selection you've cut or copied. So if you copy something and then copy something else, the Clipboard only stores the second thing you copied.

Follow these steps to copy text:

1. Select the text you want to copy (see Figure 3-4).

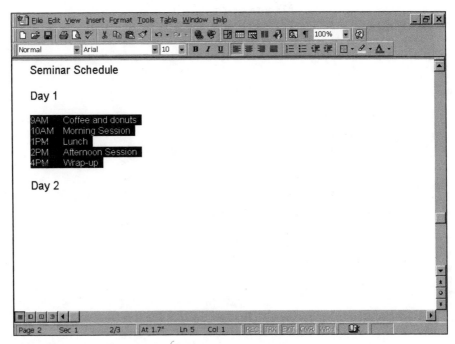

Figure 3-4 Start by selecting the text you want to copy.

2. Open the `Edit` menu and select the `Copy` command or click .

3. Place the insertion point where you want the copy of the text to appear. You can copy the text to another location in a document, to another document, or even to another type of document.

X-REF For information on copying and pasting from one program to another, see Chapter 15.

4. Open the `Edit` menu and select the `Paste` command or click . The text is copied (see Figure 3-5).

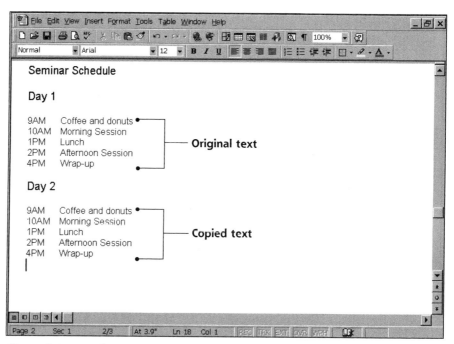

Figure 3-5 Use the Paste button to paste the copied text.

TIP You can also use these keyboard shortcuts: Press Ctrl+X for Cut, Ctrl+C for Copy, and Ctrl+V for Paste.

If you decide you don't want the copy, you can undo it. Select Edit → Undo. Or just delete the copied text.

Where Is That Word?

The Bonus section in Chapter 2 covered some shortcuts for moving around. Another way to move quickly to a particular part of your document is to use the Find command. In a long document, you may have trouble scanning and scrolling to find a section you want. Perhaps you want to check a fact and are looking for a particular word or phrase. Looking through an entire document for one word can make you blind. Instead, use the Find command to find and move to the text you want.

Understanding How the Search Works

When you search, Word starts at the location of the insertion point and searches through your text to the end of the document. When Word finds a match, it highlights it, and the dialog box remains open. You can continue to search until you find the match you want. If Word can't find a match, you see an error message telling you so.

Word, by default, finds the text you enter, no matter what the case and no matter if what you enter is part of another word. For instance, if you search for *ten*, Word will stop on *ten*, *Ten*, *tennis*, *often*. Anyplace those characters appear. You can set options that tell Word to match the case as you type it and to find whole words only. The later section "Search Tips" covers using these options.

Searching for Text

To find text, follow these steps:

1. Open the **Edit** menu and select the **Find** command. You see the Find and Replace dialog box (see Figure 3-6).

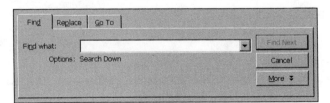

Figure 3-6   Enter the text you want to find and then click the <u>F</u>ind Next button.

2. In the Fi<u>n</u>d what text box, enter the text you want to find. You can enter a word or phrase. Try to think of something unique. If you search for something common, you'll have to wade through a lot of matches before you find the one you want.

TIP Word keeps track of what you have searched for in the document. If you see an entry in the Fi<u>n</u>d what text box, it means you have already done a search. If you don't want to use this text, drag across it and then type the text you do want to find. You can also click the down arrow next to the Fi<u>n</u>d what text box and select an entry that you have previously searched for.

Press Ctrl+F to select the **Edit** → **Find** command. Press Shift+F4 to repeat the search.

3. Click the <u>F</u>ind Next button. Word moves to the first match and highlights it (see Figure 3-7). The dialog box remains open so that you can search again.

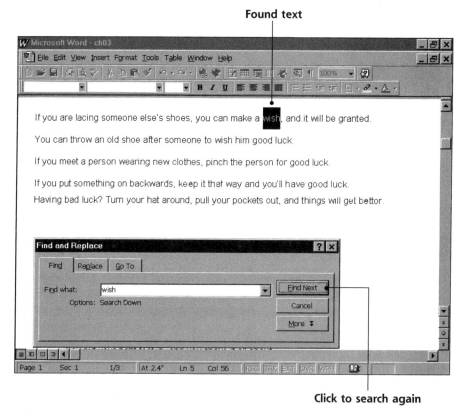

Found text

Click to search again

Figure 3-7 Click the <u>F</u>ind Next button to search for the next occurrence.

4. To search again, click the <u>F</u>ind Next button. Continue to do so until you find the match you want.

5. To close the dialog box, click the Cancel button.

Search Tips

If you don't find what you want or if you find too much of what you want, you can try some tips to fine-tune your search. In the Find and Replace dialog box, click the More button to expand the dialog box and show additional options (see Figure 3-8). This list explains which options to try in the dialog box as well as some other strategies:

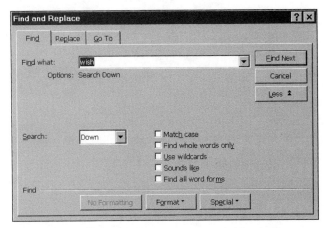

Figure 3-8 You can fine-tune your search by selecting some of these options.

* Word isn't picky about matching the case of your entry. If you enter *Foreman*, it will stop on *foreman*, *FOREMAN*, or *Foreman*. You can have Word match the case as you've entered it. To do so, check the Match case check box.

* Word also isn't picky about where your entry appears. It can be a whole word or part of a word. If you search for *bat*, Word will stop on *bat*, *Batman*, *combat*, and so on. If you want to stop only on whole words, check the Find whole word only check box.

* The same word can appear in different forms. For instance, you can have *carry*, *carries*, *carrying*, and so on. If you want Word to find all forms of the word, check the Find all word forms check box.

* By default, Word searches down through the document. You can change the search direction, by clicking the Search drop-down list and selecting Up.

* In addition to searching for text, you can also search for formatting. For instance, you can search for boldface type. To search for formatting, click the Format button and then select the appropriate formatting command. In the dialog box that appears, select the formatting you want to find. For more information on formatting options, see Part Two of this book.

* You can also search for special characters such as tabs, paragraph marks, and page breaks. To do so, click the Special button and then select the item you want to find.

* The two other options, Use wildcards and Sounds like, can also help you fine-tune a search. To me, they aren't worth the time. I've never used them. You can more easily try searching for another word or phrase. If you want more information on these options, right-click them and then select the What's This? command.

* If you can't find a match, try one of two things. First, try searching for something else. Maybe you thought you used the word *peccadillo* in your document, but you really used *petty sin*. Try another word or phrase in the section you want to find. Second, be sure that your previous entries aren't restricting your search. Word does not clear the search options with each search. So you may have options set that you don't know about. Be sure to check the expanded dialog box (click the More button) for options you may not know were set.

Changed My Mind

The Find command helps you move to a particular spot in the document. Its counterpart, Replace, helps you make replacements. For instance, suppose that you are typing up a proposal for a new product called Ralph's Canned Chili, but you decide that *Ralph's* really isn't the best name. You like *Earl* better. You could find each time you used *Ralph* and replace it manually with *Earl*. Or you can have Word make the replacements.

Replacing text is similar to finding text. You first tell Word the text you want to find and replace. Then you tell Word what text to use as the replacement.

Follow these steps:

1. Open the **Edit** menu and select the **Replace** command. You see the Find and Replace dialog box (see Figure 3-9).

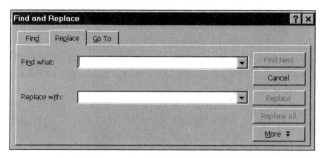

Figure 3-9 Enter the text you want to find and the text you want to use as the replacement.

TIP If you want to search and replace just part of the document, select the text first. Then select Edit → Replace.

2. In Find what text box, type the text you want to find. For instance, type *Ralph* here. If you see an entry already, it means you have searched and/or replaced something already. You can drag across the entry and type the new one to replace it.

3. In the Replace with text box, type the text you want to use as the replacement. For instance, type *Earl*.

4. Click the Find Next button to start the search. Word moves to the first match and highlights the found word or phrase. The dialog box remains open (see Figure 3-10).

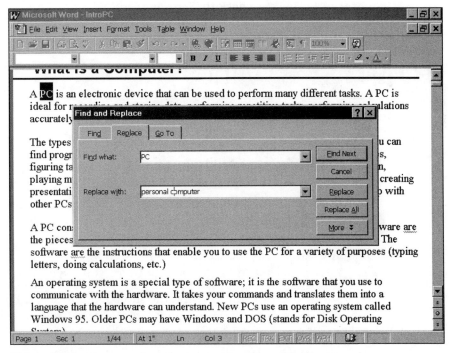

Figure 3-10   You can select whether you want the replacement made.

5. To make the replacement, click the Replace button.

To leave this text as is and move to the next match, click the Find Next button.

To make all the replacements without confirmation, click the Replace All button.

It's usually a good idea to go through a few replacements before you replace everything at once. Doing so ensures the replace is working as you intended. It's easy to make replacements that you didn't intend. For instance, if you replace all occurrences of *man* with *person*, you can end up with some weird words like *personager* (replacement for *manager*).

7. When Word is done searching the document, you see an alert message.

8. Click the OK button to close the alert box. Then click the Close button to close the dialog box.

You can also set the same options for replacing text that you do for finding text. For instance, you can search and replace formatting or special characters. You can have Word match the case or find whole words only. See the section "Search Tips."

BONUS

Saving Time Typing Text

The thing you will be doing most when you create a document is type. You type, type, type. Unfortunately, the ideas have to come from you. Word can't help you there. But Word can help you save time typing text that you often use. This is the topic of this bonus section.

Here are some ideas and examples for saving time typing text:

* Suppose that you want to send the same letter to several people. Do you have to retype the letter again and again? No. The easiest way to create a letter for several people is to do a mail merge.

For complete information on mail merge, see Chapter 14.

* If you are job hunting, you may have a letter that you send out for job ads. For each letter you send out, you may want to say about the same thing but modify it for the specific job advertised. Rather than type an entirely new letter, you can open the first letter and use the File → Save As command to save a copy of the original letter. You can then modify the copy and send it out. You can do this for any document that you want to reuse.

X-REF For the steps on using the <u>F</u>ile → Save <u>A</u>s command, see Chapter 2.

* Sometimes you may want to include the same or similar text twice in a document. For instance, in this chapter are the steps for moving and copying text is similar. I could have typed the text twice, once for moving and once for copying, but instead, I copied the steps for moving and then edited them so that they worked for copying. Copying text is covered in this chapter.

* The final tip for saving time typing text is a feature called AutoText. You may not be able to tell from the name, but this is one of Word's greatest little features. You can use this feature to avoid retyping words, phrases, even entire paragraphs that you use frequently. This next section gives complete information on this feature.

Using One of Word's AutoText Entries

Word includes some AutoText entries commonly used in memos and letters. You can select an attention line, a closing, a header or footer, mailing instructions, reference initials, a reference line, a salutation, a signature company, or a subject line. Some entry types have several different versions. For instance, for the attention line, you can select *Attention:* or *ATTN:*

To view or use one of these AutoText entries, follow these steps:

1. Open the `Insert` menu and select the `AutoText` command. You see a list of different entries you can use.

2. Click the type of entry you want to insert. You see a submenu with additional choices for this entry (see Figure 3-11).

3. Click the entry you want. Word inserts the text.

You can also simply start typing the AutoText entry. Word will then display a ScreenTip with the entry. If you want this entry, simply press Enter. For example, try typing *Sept.* Word displays a ScreenTip that says *September.* Press Enter to have Word complete the entry.

Creating Your Own AutoText Entries

Word's AutoText entries are handy for memos and letters, but you can also create AutoText entries of your own to save time with text that you type again and again. For instance, suppose that you have a complex company name like Yabadabadoo, A Division of Fred & Barney Enterprises. You can quickly tire of typing that over and over again.

Instead of typing the text, you can create an AutoText entry and have Word enter it for you. All you have to do is first create the entry. You only have to do this once. Then you can easily insert the entry.

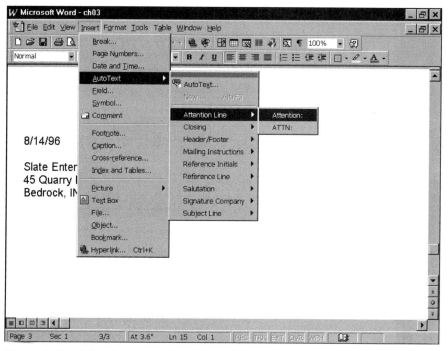

Figure 3-11 Select from one of Word's predefined AutoText entries.

CREATING AN AUTOTEXT ENTRY

Follow these steps to create an AutoText entry:

1. Select the text you want to save as an AutoText entry. You can select a word, a phrase, or an entire paragraph or more. You can either select the text from a document you have already created or type the text in a blank document.

2. Open the **Insert** menu and select the **Auto Text** command. From the submenu that appears, select the **New** command. You see the Create AutoText dialog box (see Figure 3-12).

Figure 3-12 Create an AutoText entry using this dialog box.

3. Type the name you want to assign to this entry. The best names are the shortest. You can even use just one character for the name. Use a name that is easy to remember.

4. Click the OK button.

TIP **Type a short name to save time. Most of my AutoText entries are just one character, usually the first letter of the entry — for instance, *w* for *Word for Windows*.**

INSERTING AN AUTOTEXT ENTRY

Once you have created the entry, you can insert it quickly and easily.

Follow these steps to insert an AutoText entry:

1. Open the `Insert` menu and select the `Auto Text` command. You see a list of AutoText categories.

2. Select the category you want. Your AutoText entry is probably placed in the category Normal.

3. Select the AutoText entry. Word inserts the text.

TIP **To delete an entry, select <u>I</u>nsert → <u>A</u>utoText → AutoTe<u>x</u>t. In the dialog box that appears, select the entry you want to delete from the AutoText dialog box. Click the Delete button.**

I think the keyboard shortcut is the fastest way to insert an AutoText entry. You don't have to take your hands away from the keyboard. But you do have to remember the keyboard shortcut.

To insert an AutoText entry using the keyboard, follow these steps:

1. Move to where you want to insert the entry.

2. Type the name you assigned to the entry.

3. Press F3. Word inserts the entire entry.

Summary

This chapter covered how to edit your document. You learned how to select, delete, move, copy, find, and replace text. You also learned a cool trick for saving time when typing commonly used words or phrases.

In addition to checking your document yourself, you can have Word perform some checks on your spelling and grammar. You can also use the thesaurus to look up words, as covered in the next chapter.

CHAPTER FOUR

CHECKING YOUR DOCUMENT

You can spend all the time in the world getting your document to sound good and look good, but if your document includes a glaring mistake such as a spelling error or grammatical mistake, it ain't going to be good. To help you avoid embarrassing mistakes, Word includes spell-check and grammar-check programs. In fact, Word can flag spelling mistakes and grammar problems as you type. You can choose to make corrections as you type, or you can wait until the document is complete and then check the spelling and grammar. In addition to these two features, Word also includes an online thesaurus that you can use to find just the right word. And you can also count the words in your document.

PROOFREAD YOUR DOCUMENT!

Remember that the spelling program does not replace a careful proofreading of your work. Word does not know the difference between *there, their,* or *they're.* Word doesn't know when you mean *weather* and when you mean *whether.* The program just knows when a word is misspelled. You can have perfect spelling and still look like an ignoramus. Proofread your document!

The same is true for grammatical mistakes. Just because you got an A+ according to the grammar checker doesn't mean your document doesn't include errors. You still must proofread. You'd be surprised at how many problems Word doesn't flag.

No More Squiggles

As you type, you may notice that Word puts a squiggly red line under some words and that some sentences are flagged with a squiggly green line (see Figure 4-1). These squiggly lines are Word's red flags alerting to you to possible misspellings (red) or grammar mistakes (green). You can ignore these flags and continue working, or you can make corrections as you create the document, as covered in this section.

If you don't see these squiggly lines, this feature may have been turned off. Select Tools → Options and click the Spelling & Grammar tab. Be sure the Check spelling as you type and Check grammar as you type check boxes are checked.

Correcting Spelling Errors

You can think of Word's automatic spell check as a nagging English teacher standing by with her red pen. Everyone had one memorable English teacher. Usually she had those half-glasses on a chain around her neck. Wore her hair in a bun. Enunciated each and every word. Mine's name was Mrs. Pickard. Make one little mistake and boom! she's there with that pen. (Luckily for you, she doesn't have her ruler with her too, or you could get a swat on the hand!)

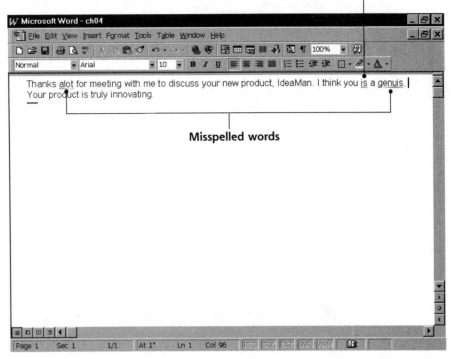

Figure 4-1 Word flags spelling and grammar mistakes in the document.

When Word's Mrs. Pickard flags a mistake, you can ignore it and check your spelling when you are done (covered later). Or you can make a correction. You can do any of the following:

* If you made a typo or know the right spelling, you can press Backspace to delete the misspelled word. Then retype the word.

* If only a few characters are wrong, you don't have to retype the entire word. You can also edit the word to correct the misspelling.

* If you don't know the right spelling, you can have Word display some choices. To do so, right-click the misspelled word. You see a pop-up menu (see Figure 4-2). If you see the correct spelling, click it. Word makes the replacement. You can also choose to ignore the misspelling, add the misspelled word to the dictionary, or start the spelling program by selecting the appropriate command. (These commands are covered in the section on checking the entire document.)

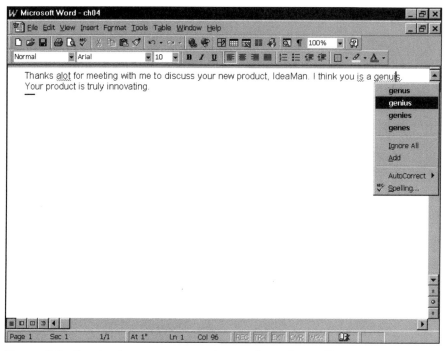

Figure 4-2 Use the shortcut menu to select an alternative spelling.

You can continue typing words and correcting mistakes until you complete the document. If this method interrupts your writing concentration, you can just ignore the lines and check the spelling later, as covered in the next section in this chapter.

Correcting Grammar Errors

In addition to flagging spelling errors, Word 97 also alerts you to grammatical errors — or at least what it thinks are grammatical errors. I have never been fond of the grammar feature of this or any word-processing program — probably because I was an English teacher. English 101. College Composition. (No. I don't have half-glasses, a bun, or a ruler. At least not handy.) The mistakes I see flagged aren't always mistakes. Plus, I've seen the grammar checker skip over some really obvious grammatical mistakes. If you want to use the grammar checker, just remember that it's not foolproof.

Word underlines what it considers questionable phrases and sentences. You can spot these grammatical errors by the squiggly green underline. You can choose to ignore the errors and check your grammar later, or you can make corrections as you go.

You can retype the word, the phrase, or the sentence to fix the problem. Or you can edit it. You can also display grammatical suggestions by right-clicking the green underlined word(s). You see a pop-up menu that lists suggestions (see Figure 4-3). If one of the suggestions is correct, click it to replace your original text with the new suggested revision. You can also choose to ignore the sentence (select Ignore Sentence) or start the grammar checker (Grammar).

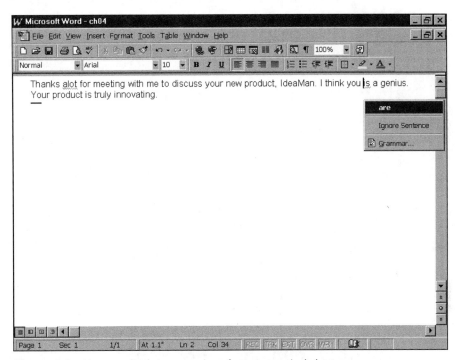

Figure 4-3 You can display suggestions for grammatical changes.

You can make all the corrections as you type. Or you can wait until you complete the document and then check the grammar, as covered later in this section.

Automatic Spelling Corrections

In addition to flagging some words or phrases, Word will automatically correct some mistakes. For example, try typing *teh*. You can't. Word automatically replaces this common typo with the correct word *the*. Word recognizes some common misspellings and typographical mistakes and makes the replacements automatically. You can also add words to the list Word "knows". For instance, I commonly mistype *chapter* as *chatper*. Rather than correct this mistake in each document, I added an AutoCorrect entry so that Word makes the replacement for me.

In the next section you learn how to add an AutoCorrect entry during a spell check. The Bonus section also tells you how to customize this feature.

Check Please

When you are trying to concentrate on your writing, you may not want to be bothered with spelling or grammar mistakes. You may want to keep your train of thought going and worry about corrections later. If so, you can run the spell check program to check the words in your document. By default, Word also checks the grammar in your document.

How the Spell Check Works

The spell-check program works by comparing words in the document to words in its dictionary. When the speller cannot find a word, it flags it as misspelled and displays a dialog box. Keep in mind that just because a word is flagged doesn't necessarily mean it is misspelled. It just means Word cannot find the word in its dictionary. Proper names and some terminology, for instance, may be flagged although they are spelled correctly.

When Word flags a word and displays the dialog box, you have the option of replacing the word with a suggested spelling, correcting the word yourself, skipping the word, creating an AutoCorrect entry, or adding the word to a custom dictionary. After you select an option, Word moves to the next flagged word.

Word will also flag double words such as *the the*. You can choose to delete the second occurrence or skip it.

How the Grammar Check Works

The grammar check knows and checks for adherence to certain grammatical rules such as subject-verb agreement. When the grammar check finds a word, a phrase, or a sentence that breaks one of these rules, it flags the error and makes suggestions on how to correct the problem.

When Word flags a grammatical error, it displays the Spelling and Grammar dialog box with suggested corrections. You can choose to change to one of the suggestions, manually edit the sentence, or ignore the sentence. You can also use the Office Assistant to display help on the grammatical problem.

Checking Your Document

To start a spell and grammar check, open the Tools menu and select the Spelling and Grammar command or click .

 TIP To check just part of the document, select the part you want to check, then press F7 to select the Spelling and Grammar command.

SPELLING ERRORS

For spelling errors, Word highlights the word and displays the Spelling and Grammar dialog box (see Figure 4-4). The Not in Dictionary: list displays the misspelled word, and the Suggestions list displays any alternative spellings. You can do any of the following:

* To skip this occurrence but stop on the next one, click the Ignore button. To skip all occurrences of this word, click the Ignore All button. Use this option for names or terms that are spelled correctly but that Word just doesn't include in its dictionary.

* To replace the word with one of the suggested spellings, click the spelling in the Suggestions list. Click the Change button to change this occurrence. Click the Change All button to replace all occurrences of the word.

* If none of the replacements is correct, you can correct the error manually. The insertion point is in the Not in Dictionary list box. Move the insertion point and edit the text or delete and retype the correct spelling. Then click the Change button.

* Click the Add button to add the word to the dictionary. This word will then no longer be flagged as misspelled. Do this for words, such as common names or terms, that you don't want to have to check continually. For instance, I've added my first and last name to the dictionary so that they are no longer flagged.

* If Word flags a repeated word, click the Ignore button to ignore and keep the repeated word. Or click the Delete button to delete one of the words.

* If you want to add the error and its correction to the AutoCorrect list, click the AutoCorrect button. When you make this same mistake, Word will automatically replace the misspelled word with the correct spelling.

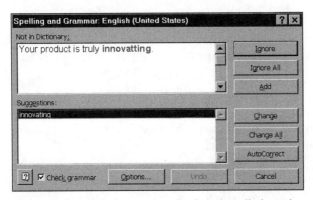

Figure 4-4 Select how to handle the misspelled word.

GRAMMAR ERRORS

For grammar errors, Word highlights the word, phrase, or sentence and also displays the Spelling and Grammar dialog box. This dialog box lists the problem as well as suggestions (see Figure 4-5). You can do any of the following things:

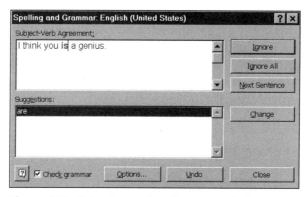

Figure 4-5 Select how to handle grammatical errors.

✳ If you don't quite understand why the sentence was flagged, click the Office Assistant button. You see a pop-up explanation of the problem as well as some examples (see Figure 4-6). To turn off this feature, click the Office Assistant button again.

FEATURE FOCUS The Office Assistant is a new feature in Word 97.

✳ To use one of the suggested changes, click the one you want in the Suggestions list. Then click the Change button.

✳ To make a correction manually, edit the existing sentence or type a new sentence in the text box. Then click the Change button. Word moves on to the next questionable sentence.

✳ To ignore the flagged sentence and move to the next one, click the Ignore button. To ignore this same error throughout the document, click the Ignore All button.

✳ To skip to the next sentence and leave this sentence flagged, click the Next Sentence button.

✳ To undo a change you made, click the Undo button.

Continue making corrections until you've gone through the entire document. When you see the message that the spelling and grammar check is complete, click the OK button.

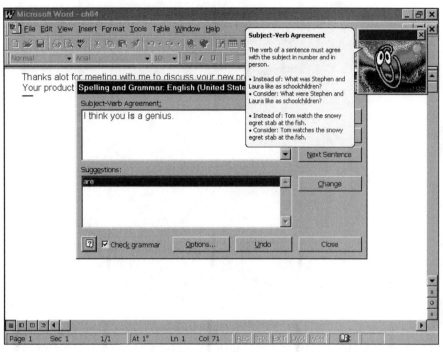

Figure 4-6 You can display help on any of the flagged grammatical problems.

As You Like It

As with most of Word's features, you have a great deal of control over how the feature works. For instance, you may prefer to check just the spelling and not the grammar. Or you may want to customize the rules used for the grammar check. You can do this and more, as covered in this section.

Check Spelling? Grammar? Or Both?

I personally don't use the grammar checker, so it is annoying to have to check the grammar when all I want to do is check the spelling. Luckily for me (and you too if you don't use this feature), I can change what is checked.

To make a change, follow these steps:

1. Open the Tools menu and select the Options command. You see the Options dialog box.

2. Click the Spelling & Grammar tab. You see the options for these features (see Figure 4-7).

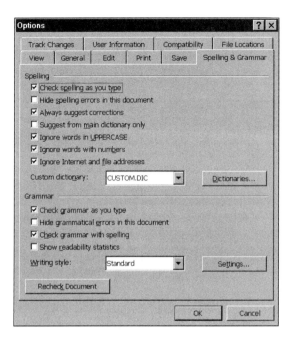

Figure 4-7 Set spelling and grammar options in this dialog box.

3. If you don't want grammar checked, uncheck the Check grammar with spelling check box.

4. Click the OK button.

What Spelling Errors Are Flagged?

The Spelling & Grammar tab (refer to Figure 4-7) also includes options that control how the spell check is performed. (To display this dialog box, select Tools → Options and then click the Spelling & Grammar tab. You can also click the Options button in the dialog box that appears during a spell check.) Word, for instance, always displays suggested alternative spellings. If you don't want these displayed, you can turn off this option. Table 4-1 describes the other spelling tab options. Make your selections and click the OK button.

TABLE 4.1 Spelling Options

Option	Description
CHECK SPELLING AS YOU TYPE	Word flags misspellings in your document. If you don't want the spell check performed as you type, uncheck this option.
HIDE SPELLING ERRORS IN THIS DOCUMENT	Spelling errors are flagged with a squiggly red underline. If you want to hide these errors, check this check box. The error is still flagged, but you just don't see the underline.
ALWAYS SUGGEST CORRECTIONS	When Word performs a spell check, it automatically lists suggested alternative spellings. This can slow down the spell check. To turn off this feature, uncheck the box.
SUGGEST FROM MAIN DICTIONARY ONLY	Word lists suggested spellings from the main dictionary only. If you want to list suggestions from the custom dictionary as well, uncheck this box.
IGNORE WORDS IN UPPERCASE	Word ignores words in uppercase. To check these words, check this check box.
IGNORE WORDS WITH NUMBERS	By default, Word ignores words with numbers — for instance, part numbers that contain text and numbers. To check this type of entry, check this check box.
IGNORE INTERNET AND FILE ADDRESSES	Word ignores Internet and file addresses, such as http://www.molson.com. To check this type of text, check this check box.
CUSTOM DICTIONARY	Word sets up one dictionary, CUSTOM.DIC, which contains the words you add during a spell check. If you want, you can create and use more than one dictionary. Use this drop-down list to select the dictionary to use. For most users, one dictionary is enough. If you are in some specialized field, you may want to set up more than one dictionary. Use the Dictionaries button to display a dialog box to do so. Use the Help button to get more information on this topic.

What Grammar Errors Are Flagged?

Word uses business writing rules when it does its grammar check. You may want to use a more formal writing style or a less formal writing style. You can also select whether a spell check is performed and whether readability statistics are displayed. Display the Spelling & Grammar tab in the Options dialog box (open the Tools menu, select the Options command, and click the Spelling & Grammar tab). Make your selections, as covered in Table 4-2, and then click the OK button.

TABLE 4-2 Grammar Options

Option	Description
CHECK GRAMMAR AS YOU TYPE	Word flags possible grammatical errors in your document. If you don't want the grammar check performed as you type, uncheck this option.
HIDE GRAMMATICAL ERRORS IN THIS	Grammatical errors are flagged with a squiggly green underline. If you want to hide these errors, check this check box.
CHECK GRAMMAR WITH SPELLING	If you want to check just spelling and not grammar, uncheck this check box.
SHOW READABILITY STATISTICS	If you want readability statistics displayed after a spelling and grammar check, check this check box.
WRITING STYLE	To select another writing style, display this drop-down list and select the writing style you prefer. You can select Standard (default), Casual, Formal, Technical, or Custom.

The Perfect Word

Finding the right word can make the difference between a mediocre writer and true talent. As you write, you may want to tinker carefully with your word selection. There's nothing more frustrating than having a word right on the tip of your tongue. It means *fabulous*, but it's not *that* word. What is it?

Rather than go insane (crazy, mad, bonkers), you can have Word display a list of synonyms. If you find the word you want in this list, you can replace the word you looked up with the new, *improved* word. If you find a word that's close, you can look up that word, until you find the word you want.

With Word, not only can you look up words and see several meanings and synonyms for each of those meanings, but for some words, you can view antonyms or related words.

To look up a word in the thesaurus, follow these steps:

1. Click before or within the word you want to look up.

2. Open the **Tools** menu and select the **Language** command.

3. From the submenu, select the **Thesaurus** command. Word displays a list of synonyms for the selected word. If the selected word has additional meanings, the meanings are listed on the left half of the dialog box. If antonyms or related words are available, the Meanings list displays *Antonyms and Related Words* as a final item (see Figure 4-8).

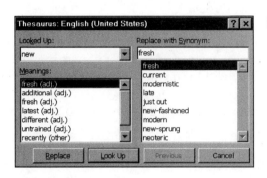

Figure 4-8 Use the online thesaurus to look up synonyms and antonyms.

4. Do any of the following:

   * To look up synonyms for another meaning, click the meaning you want in the Meanings list. Word displays synonyms for the selected meaning. For instance, Figure 4-9 shows looking up the meaning *latest*.

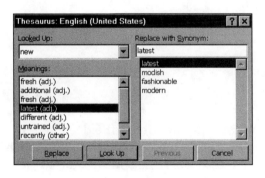

Figure 4-9 If a word has several meanings, you can look up synonyms for the meaning you want.

   * To look up synonyms for another listed synonym, click the word you want in the Replace with Synonym list. Then click the Look Up button. Word displays synonyms for the selected word.

   * If you look up other words and want to go back to a word you previously looked up, click the down arrow next to the Looked Up drop-down list. Then click the word you want. Word returns to that list of synonyms.

* To use one of the listed synonyms, click the word you want to use and then click the Replace button.
* To close the dialog box without making a replacement, click the Cancel button.

If Word cannot find the word you are looking up, the dialog box displays Not Found and the selected word. An alphabetical list appears in the dialog box. If you see the word you want in this list, click it and then click the Look Up button.

One Word, Two Word . . .

Many times a writer needs to know the number of words in a document. For instance, magazine and newspaper writers may be given a certain word count to stay within. If you want to review these and other statistics on your document, you can do so. Open the Tools menu and select the Word Count command. Word displays the Word Count dialog box, shown in Figure 4-10, listing the number of pages, words, characters, paragraphs, and lines.

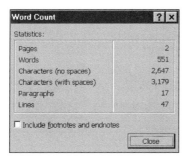

Figure 4-10 You can count the number of words in your document.

> If you want to find out the number of words or characters in your document, use the Word Count feature.

You can get additional information about the document by displaying the Properties dialog box. Open the File menu and select the Properties command. You see the Properties dialog box. Click the Statistics tab to view document statistics as well as to create, modify, access, and print dates for the document (see Figure 4-11). Click the Cancel button to close the dialog box.

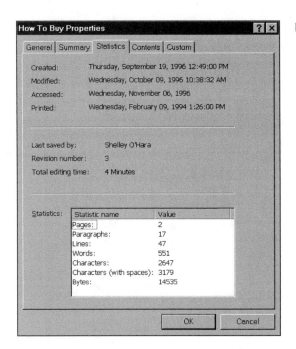

Figure 4-11 You can review other document information in the Properties dialog box.

BONUS

Customizing AutoCorrect

As you can tell from this chapter, Word tries to help you create a document that is free from error. You can't even type incorrectly if you want to! The feature that makes spelling changes automatically is AutoCorrect. You can review the AutoCorrect entries that are already set up, add entries manually, and control what other AutoCorrect options apply.

To customize AutoCorrect, follow these steps:

1. Select `Tools` → `AutoCorrect`. You see the AutoCorrect dialog box (see Figure 4-12).

2. AutoCorrect makes a lot of replacements, such as capitalizing the first letters of sentences. To turn off any of these automatic replacements, uncheck the appropriate check box:

   ✳ Correct TWo INitial Capitals — If you type two capital letters at the beginning of a word, Word changes them to an initial cap. Uncheck this box if you don't want this change made.

* Capitalize first letter of <u>s</u>entences — If you want Word to automatically capitalize the first letter of each sentence, keep this box checked.

* Capitalize <u>n</u>ames of days — If you type any of the days of the week, Word capitalizes them automatically. To turn off this feature, uncheck this check box.

* Correct accidental usage of CAPS <u>L</u>OCK key — It's easy to press Caps Lock and type in all caps when you didn't intend to. Word will correct this error automatically. If you don't want this correction made, uncheck this check box.

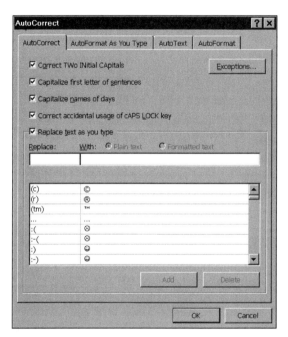

Figure 4-12 Review and make changes to how AutoCorrect works in this dialog box.

3. The easiest way to add words to AutoCorrect is to add them during a spell check. You can also manually add words. To add new words to the AutoCorrect list, type the misspelling in the <u>R</u>eplace text box. Type the correct spelling in the <u>W</u>ith text box. Then click the <u>A</u>dd button.

4. To delete a word, click it in the AutoCorrect list. Then click the <u>D</u>elete button.

5. When you are finished making changes, click the OK button.

Summary

This chapter covers the different ways you can check your document for errors. You can check your grammar and your spelling, as well as look up words in the thesaurus. After making sure your document is perfect, you can then print it. The next chapter covers how to preview and print your document.

VIEWING AND PRINTING YOUR DOCUMENT

IN THIS CHAPTER YOU LEARN THESE KEY SKILLS

M ost documents are created for someone else to look at. You type reports for your boss. You type memos for your staff. You type letters to your clients. You type reminder notes to yourself. Most documents are intended to be printed and distributed.

This chapter covers how to preview your document and then print it. In addition to learning how to print a document, you also learn how to print an envelope and send a document via fax.

Note: Before you print your text, you may want to tinker with the appearance of the document — make text bold, center the page, change the margins, indent lines, and so on. Part II of this book covers formatting.

A Doc with a View

A s with any masterpiece, you may want to take a step back and take a peek at how your document looks. Is it long enough? How does it look on the page? Does it look professional? Taking a look at a document before you print is especially important when you make formatting changes, covered in the next part of this book. You can make sure the document looks acceptable before you print it.

Word enables you to look at your document in several different views. The most commonly used one is Print Preview. But you can also zoom a document and change to a different layout view, as covered in this section.

Previewing a Document

Your screen shows only a part of the document, and you can't really get a sense of how the document will look on the page. When you want to see how the document will look when printed, preview it. You can see whether the document is balanced, whether the margins are right, whether the headers and footers look OK. (These formatting features are covered in Part 2.) If the preview looks good, you can print right from the preview window.

To preview a document, open the File menu and select the Print Preview command or click ⬚. You see a full-page preview (see Figure 5-1). Notice that the toolbar includes buttons for working with this preview. Table 5-1 shows each button and explains what you can do in preview mode.

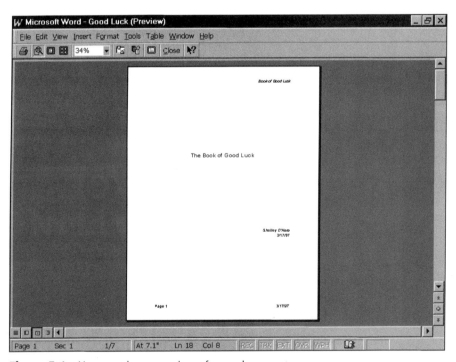

Figure 5-1 You can view a preview of your document.

TABLE 5-1 Preview Buttons

Button	Name	Click to . . .
	PRINT	Print the document.
	MAGNIFIER	Enlarge the view. Click the button. Then move the pointer (which looks like a magnifying glass) to the document. Click the area you want to see. Click again to zoom back out. Figure 5-2 shows a magnified view of a page.
	ONE PAGE	View a single page.
	MULTIPLE PAGES	View multiple pages. Click the button and then select from the drop-down palette the number of pages you want to view. Use this view to see how the pages will look side by side. Figure 5-3 shows a side-by-side view of two pages.
100%	ZOOM CONTROL	Display other zoom percentages. You can zoom in or out on the document or select other page views (Whole Page, Two Pages, Page Width).
	VIEW RULER	Display an on-screen ruler. You can use the ruler to change the page margins, as covered in Chapter 8.
	SHRINK TO FIT	Shrink the document to fit in one window.
	TOGGLE FULL-SCREEN VIEW	Hide the menu bar and toolbars.
Close	CLOSE	Return to the regular document view.
	CONTEXT-SENSITIVE HELP	Get help. Click the button. The pointer changes to a pointer with a question mark. Click the command, toolbar button, or area of the screen for which you want help.

5

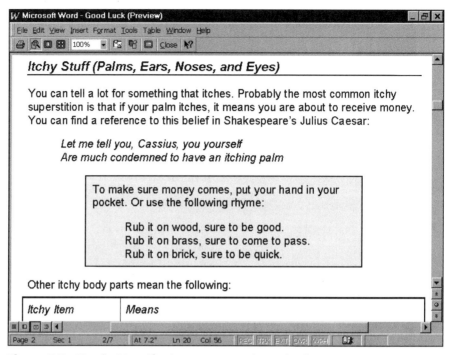

Figure 5-2 Use the Magnifier button to zoom in on the document.

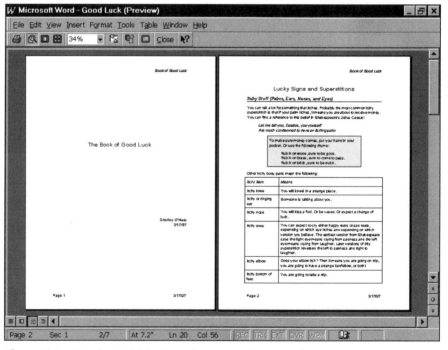

Figure 5-3 Use the Multiple Pages button to view several pages at once.

Displaying a Page-by-Page View of the Document

When you create a new document, you see the text in the default Normal view. This view works best most of the time because you can easily see the text and most formatting changes. When you are making more complex formatting changes, such as using multiple columns or adding a picture, you can change to Page Layout view. (For some formatting tasks, you must be in this view.) Page Layout view shows you the margin areas of the page as well as any headers or footers you have added. You get a sense of where the text falls on the page. You also see the effects of columns and page breaks as they will appear when you print the document. For instance, rather than a continuous document with dotted lines for a page break, you see the document page by page.

To try this view, open the View menu and select the Page Layout command. You see the document in Page Layout view (see Figure 5-4).

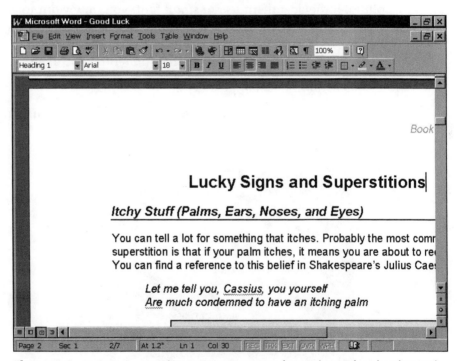

Figure 5-4   In Page Layout view, you can see page formatting such as headers and footers.

The Page Layout command is not a toggle. To turn off Page Layout view, you must select another view. To return to Normal view, select the Normal command from the View menu.

TIP If you work with outlines or create Web pages using Word, you can also change to and work with views appropriate for these types of documents. (For more information on these features, consult online help.) You can also use the view buttons in the lower-left corner of the screen to switch views. Click the view button you want. If you aren't sure which button does what, put your pointer on the button to display the ScreenTip name.

Zooming a Document

You may also want to zoom in or out on a document. If the document is wide, you may want to shrink the view so that you can see an entire line without scrolling. If the document uses a small font, you may want to enlarge it so that you can easily read the text. The default view of a document is 100%. Keep in mind that the larger the zoom percentage you select, the larger your document will be. The smaller the percentage, the smaller the document.

To zoom a document, follow these steps:

1. Open the **View** menu and select the **Zoom** command. You see the Zoom dialog box (see Figure 5-5).

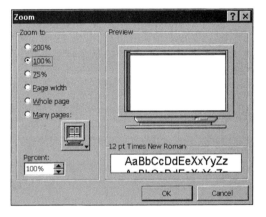

Figure 5-5 Select the zoom percentage you want.

2. Do one of the following:

   ✳ In the Zoom to area, click the amount to zoom. You can select 200%, 100%, or 75%.

   ✳ To select a different percentage, type it in the Percent text box or use the spin arrows to set the zoom percentage.

   ✳ To reduce the document so that it fits within the left and right margins, click the Page width option. Figure 5-6 shows a document viewed with this option.

* To reduce the document so that the entire page fits within the document window, click the <u>W</u>hole page option.

* To display multiple pages, click the <u>M</u>any pages option and then click the number of pages you want to view.

3. Click the OK button.

TIP You can also use the Zoom Control button in the toolbar to select a zoom percentage. Click the down arrow next to the button and then select the zoom level you want.

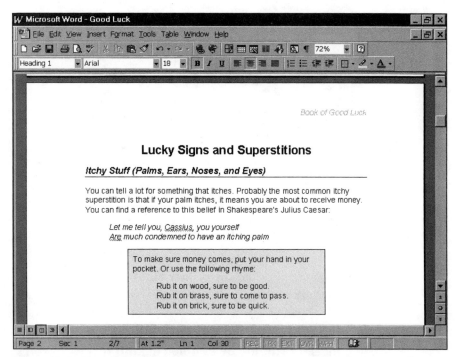

Figure 5-6 You can shrink the document view so that you don't have to scroll to see an entire line.

Putting It on Paper

When you finally complete a document, you may think it's perfect. No changes needed. But then after you print it, you usually see *something* that isn't quite right. There's something different about actually holding that document in your hand and taking a look at it.

You will most likely print a copy of your document to proof it and then again when the document is finally complete. Printing is the payoff for all your hard work.

To print a document, follow these steps:

1. Open the **File** menu and select the **Print** command or click 🖨. You see the Print dialog box, listing the current printer (see Figure 5-7).

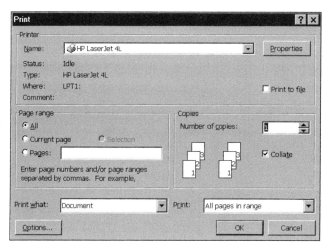

Figure 5-7 Use this dialog box to select printing options.

2. To print one copy of the document on the default printer, click the OK button.

Or make changes to the printer options (covered next) and then click the OK button.

TIP   **When Word is printing, you see a little printer icon in the taskbar. You can cancel a print job by double-clicking this icon. You see a list of all the current print jobs. Right-click the job you want to cancel and then select the Cancel Printing command. You have to be quick because Word sends the document to the printer pretty fast.**

Most of the time you will print one copy of all pages of the document on the current printer. In that case, you don't need to make any changes to the Print dialog box. Just click OK and the document is printed. In some special cases, you may want to make a change. For instance, you may not want to print the entire document. Or you may have several printers installed and what to switch among them. Here are some of the changes you can make:

* If you have more than one printer installed, you can switch to a different printer. To do so, display the Name drop-down list and select

the printer you want to use. (This printer must be set up through Windows 95). To display printer information, click the Properties button.

✳ If you want to print just the current page or a range of pages, select what you want to print in the Print range area. Select Current page to print the current page. You can also select the text you want to print and use the Selection option to print just that text. To print a page range, enter the page numbers in the Pages text box.

✳ As an alternative to entering the page range, you can also choose to print all odd pages or all even pages. To do so, display the Print drop-down list and select which pages to print.

✳ To print more than one copy, enter the number to print in the Number of copies text box. You can also select whether the pages are collated or not by checking (or unchecking) the Collate check box.

✳ You can print other information about a document such as comments, styles, and properties. To do so, display the Print what drop-down list and select what you want to print.

✳ To display additional print settings, click the Options button. (You can also display this tab by selecting the Tools → Options command and clicking the Print tab). Check the options you want to turn on. Uncheck options you want to turn off. For instance, if you want to print comments with the document, check the Comments check box in the Comments area (see Figure 5-8). If you aren't sure what each option does, right-click it, select What's This?, and then read the pop-up explanation.

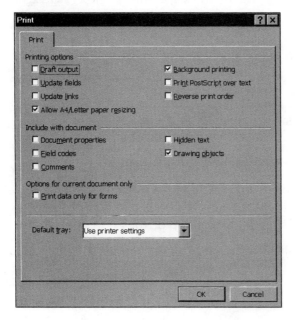

Figure 5-8 Set printer options using this dialog box.

Address Please . . .

A few years ago, it was truly a pain to print an envelope using a word-processing program and a printer. You had to set up the margins for the envelope and hope the address somehow got on the envelope. You had to have special trays or feeders for envelopes. Most people simply kept a typewriter and did the envelopes manually. Not so anymore. New printers have simplified handling envelopes, and word-processing programs, such as Word, have simplified setting up the envelope layout.

Don't type envelopes manually. Instead, use Word to print your envelopes quickly and painlessly.

If the document includes an address, you don't even have to type it. Word can find and use the address from a letter. If the document doesn't include an address, you can type it manually.

Follow these steps to print an envelope:

1. If the document contains the address you want to use, make sure it is displayed on screen. If the document doesn't include the address, it does not have to be displayed.

2. Open the `Tools` menu and select the `Envelopes and Labels` command.

3. If necessary, click the Envelopes tab. You see the Envelopes and Labels dialog box (see Figure 5-9). If your document contains an address, Word displays it in the Delivery address area. The Return address shows your name and address if you have used this feature and entered your address.

4. If necessary, make any corrections to the Delivery address. If the document does not include an address, you can type it here.

5. In the Return address area, type your return address if needed. If the address is already entered, make any needed changes.

6. After you type your return address once and print an envelope, Word will ask whether you want to use this address as the default. If you choose Yes, you won't have to type the address again.

7. If your envelopes have your return address preprinted, you can either delete all the text in the Return address text box or check the Omit check box.

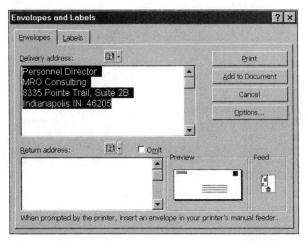

Figure 5-9 Enter the recipient and return address for the envelope.

8. Insert the envelope in the manual feed for your printer. If you aren't sure how to feed the envelope, check out the Feed picture on your printer and in the dialog box.

9. Click the Print button. Word prints the envelope.

BONUS

Faxing a Document

I f you have a fax modem, you can use Word to fax a document. You can use either the software provided with your fax modem or Word's fax features.

Using Word's Fax Software to Fax a Document

You can use Word's Fax Wizard to create and send a fax. This wizard leads you step by step through the process of setting up a fax.

Follow these steps:

1. Open the File menu and select the Send To command. From the submenu that appears, select the Fax Recipient command. You see the

first step of the Fax Wizard (see Figure 5-10). The left side of the dialog box lists the steps you go through to set up and send a fax.

Figure 5-10   Use the Fax Wizard to send a fax.

2. Click the Next button. You are prompted to select the document you want to fax (see Figure 5-11). You can choose to send the current document with or without a cover sheet. Or you can send just a cover sheet with a note.

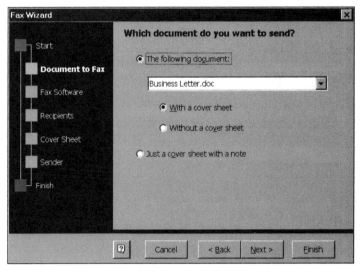

Figure 5-11   Select which document you want to fax.

3. Select what you want to fax and then click the Next button. You are prompted to select the fax program to use. You can use Microsoft Fax or your own fax program. Or you can simply print the document and then fax it on a "regular" fax machine.

4. Select which fax program to use and click the Next button. You are prompted to enter the recipient(s) for the fax.

5. In the Name text box, enter the name of the person. In the Fax Number text box, enter the fax number. You can send the fax to more than one person by completing a box for each one.

6. Click the Next button. You are prompted to select a style for the cover sheet, as shown in Figure 5-12.

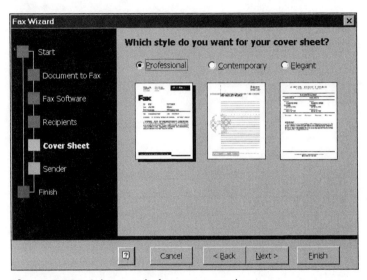

Figure 5-12 Select a style for your cover sheet.

TIP **If you have previously entered names and numbers, you can display the drop-down list and select from it. You can also select names from an address book if you have one.**

7. Select a style — Professional, Contemporary, or Elegant — and then click the Next button. If you are sending a cover sheet, you are prompted to enter your fax information, including your name, company, mailing address, phone, and fax number. If you are not sending a cover sheet, skip to step 9.

8. Enter your name, company, mailing address, phone, and fax number. Then click the Next button. You see the final screen.

9. Click the Finish button.

Summary

Most documents you create will be printed. In this chapter you learned how to view and print (and fax) a document (and an envelope). The next part of the book discusses formatting changes you can make. Formatting means changing the appearance of your document. The most common formatting change is to change the look of text, the topic of the next chapter.

Sometimes getting the look of the document just right is as important as the content. You have a great deal of control over how the text, paragraphs, and pages appear in a document. For example, you can change the appearance of your document to help make it more readable, add emphasis to certain points or ideas, and help convey the message you intend. This part covers most of the formatting features. The first three chapters cover the tools you are likely to use over and over again. The remaining chapters get into more specialized formatting features that you might want to try as you expand your Word skills.

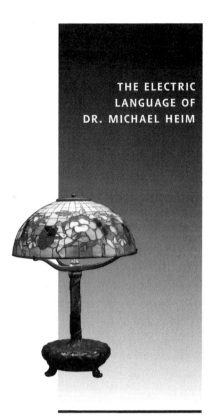

In *Electric Language* (first published in 1987, with a new edition due in 1997), Dr. Michael Heim, an academic philosopher, suggested that the computer tools we use affect the way we think. "When I wrote *Electric Language* I thought that the impact I was describing would be visible in the larger culture in fifty years. The changes that I have seen in the last ten years, however, have occurred much more rapidly than I thought."

Heim believes that we approach things in a much more tentative way today than we did in the past. He says that this is apparent in the way we speak and think. "We often put our assertions forward as questions, that is, as possibly revisable." As we think and write using a word processor, our words are fluid, tentative, and easily changed.

Word is a good instance of our culture's increasingly visual approach to communication. Heim believes that our visualization skills will improve as we use word-processing tools that enable us to create more visual output. For example, we can use an increasing number of fonts, we can import graphics into documents easily, and we can control frames on the screen. Eventually, what was once the exclusive domain of the typographer and the printer will be available to every person. "It will take time," says Heim, "before we will develop the taste and the ability to discern, the visual literacy to be able to make distinctions that we'll see more clearly. This visualizing ability will come on par with our text competence. It will become increasingly important to shape our thinking visually."

One of Word 97's features is its capacity to turn a document into a Web page. Heim is troubled as he envisions the results of the blurring of the distinctions between the user's computer and the Internet. With the user's computer connected to the Internet, the distinction between the private information in the user's files and the vast Internet world of image and text files continues to blur more and more. "In a way it is the microcosm of the world we're creating with information and the difficulties of maintaining a sense of private self. Many people see this synergy of a new culture built upon the end of the private individual. A new kind of collectivity. A virtual community."

Some of Heim's research today deals with the relationship between the alphabet and the Virtual Reality Modeling Language (VRML). Through his research, he seeks to bring new power to text through 3-D visualization and modeling. "It is a new challenge. I don't think that the alphabet is going to get up and dance away, as is sometimes suggested. Text provides us with the democratic tool of criticism. It enables us to critique images and to explain those images."

CHAPTER SIX

FORMATTING TEXT

IN THIS CHAPTER YOU LEARN THESE KEY SKILLS:

The most common formatting change you are likely to make to a document is to change the look of the text. You may think that changing the text is simply frivolous, but the look does modify the meaning. Take a look at the following sentences:

* The book wasn't that bad.
* The book wasn't *that* bad.

If you read these sentences aloud, I'm guessing, the second one will sound different. The use of italics helps clarify what to emphasize in the sentence. Now take a look at the following sentences:

* *You are invited*
* *You are invited*

What would you wear to the first party? What would you wear to the second one? As you can see, text changes can help convey the nuances of a particular message. This chapter covers the text formatting changes you can make, including making text bold, italic, or underlined; changing the font and font size; highlighting text; and changing the text color.

6

Pay Attention

The three most common types of text changes are bold, italic, and underline. Bold and italic can be used to add emphasis to your written words. Underlining adds emphasis too, but is pretty much a carryover from the days of typewriter. You may use underlining for bibliographies or other types of references. The fastest way to make text bold, italic, or underlined is to use the toolbar.

Follow these steps:

1. Select the text you want to change.

2. Click **B** to make text bold.

3. Click *I* to make text italic.

4. Click <u>U</u> to make text underlined.

The fastest way to make text bold, italic, or underlined is to use the toolbar.

Word makes the change. Figure 6-1 shows an example of each of these text attributes. You can also make these changes using the Font dialog box, covered later in this chapter.

LET YOUR FINGERS DO THE BOLDING

I learned to use Word before it had all the fancy toolbar buttons. Also, I'm a fast typist, so I like to keep my fingers right on the keyboard. If you too prefer the keyboard, you may want to learn the following keyboard shortcuts for bold, italic, and underline:

To make text . . .	Press . . .
Bold	Ctrl+B
Italic	Ctrl+I
Underlined	Ctrl+U

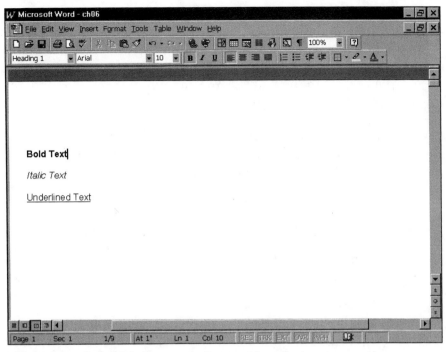

Figure 6-1   Use bold, italic, or underline to add emphasis to your words.

TIP   To undo the change, click the Undo button. Or select the text again and click the formatting button a second time. Doing so turns off the style.

Fun with Fonts

Another way to change how your text looks is to change the font. A font is a set of characters and numbers in a certain style. Each font looks different from another font. Some fonts — for instance, Times New Roman — look professional and are suited for business documents. Some fonts — for instance, Bedrock Light — are decorative or even goofy. Some fonts — such as Symbol and Wingdings — are actually sets of symbols. You can use these fonts to insert special characters into your document.

Your choice of a font helps convey the tone of the document. For instance, imagine a report in this font (Carver ICG):

✳ **Sales Report**

Imagine a love letter in this font (Courier):

✳ Dear Sean,

Part of selecting a font is choosing one appropriate for the document. You can use any of the fonts available on your system. Some fonts (called TrueType) are included with Windows 95 and with Word 97. TrueType fonts have a TT next to their name in the font list. Your printer also includes fonts, indicated with a printer icon in the font list. You can also purchase font packages to add other font choices to your system.

The easiest way to change the font is to use the toolbar. This is a quick method for making a change and is the first method covered in this section. You can also use the Font dialog box to make changes. When is this method appropriate? When you want to see how the text will look before you apply the change or when you have several changes to make at once.

Changing the Font with the Toolbar

The formatting toolbar lists the currently selected font in the Font list box. You can use this list box to display and select another font.

Follow these steps:

1. Select the text you want to change.

2. Click the down arrow next to the Font list box. You see a list of available fonts (see Figure 6-2). Word lists the most recently used fonts at the top of the list, separated from the main body of the list by a double line. Printer fonts are indicated with a printer icon; TrueType fonts are indicated with TT. Depending on your printer and font files, you may see different fonts listed.

Figure 6-2   Click the font you want.

3. Scroll through the list until you see the font you want. Then click that font. Word applies the font and closes the list.

Figure 6-3 shows some different font selections so that you can get an idea of the variety of available fonts. Remember that your system may have different font selections.

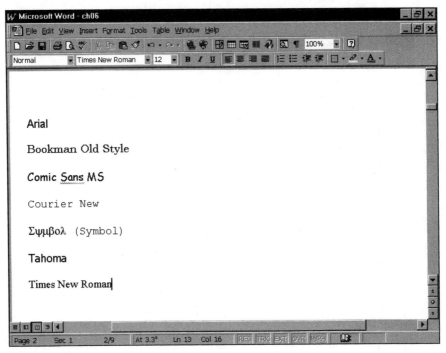

Figure 6-3 You can select from a variety of font styles.

Changing the Font Using the Font Dialog Box

Sure, the toolbar is quick, but not so quick if you have to select five or six fonts until you find one you want. If you aren't sure which font you want to use, you may want to use the Font dialog box. The dialog box displays a sample of the selected font so that you can see the change and then make up your mind. This dialog box also is more convenient when you want to make several changes at once; you can use the dialog box to select the font, the font size, the font style, the underline style, and special effects.

To change the font using the dialog box, follow these steps:

1. Select the text you want to change.

2. Open the Format menu and select the Font command.

3. If necessary, click the Font tab to display the font options, shown in Figure 6-4.

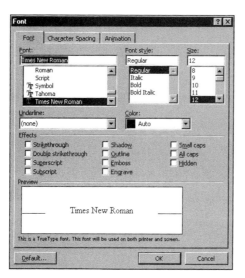

Figure 6-4 Select the font, the style, and the size you want from this dialog box.

4. In the Font list, click the font you want. Notice that you see a sample of the text in this font in the Preview area.

5. In the Font style list, click the style you want.

6. In the Size list, click the font size you want. (Changing the font size is covered next.)

7. To change the font color, select the color you want from the Color drop-down list.

8. To underline text, display the Underline drop-down list and select the style of underline you want. (See the Bonus section for more information on special underline effects.)

9. Click the OK button. Word makes the change.

CHANGING THE DEFAULT FONT

The default font used in all new documents is Times New Roman 10-point type. If you don't like this font, you don't have to change each new document you create. Instead, you can change the default font. Word will then use the new font for all new documents. For instance, I like to use Arial 12-point type because I think it is more readable. You may prefer a different font and font size.

To change the default font, follow these steps:

1. Open the ☐ Format ☐ menu and select the ☐ Font ☐ command. If necessary, click the Font tab.

SIDE TRIP

2. In the Font list, click the font you want to use as the default.

3. In the Font style area, click the default style you want.

4. In the Size list, click the default font size you want.

5. Click the Default button. You are warned that this change will affect all documents based on the Normal template. (For more information on templates, see Chapter 13.)

6. Click the Yes button.

Little Big Text

The size of the text is also important. Think of legal contracts. What size font do you think of? Think of advertisement headlines. What size font would you select? Think of a document title. What size font would work best? Think of a footnote. What font size do you envision?

As you can see, you can select an appropriate size for any portion of your document for clarity. The size of a font is measured in points, and there are seventy-two points to an inch. The larger the point size, the larger the type.

The fastest method to make a change is using the toolbar, as covered here. You can also use the Font dialog box, covered in the preceding section.

Follow these steps to change the font with the toolbar:

1. Select the text you want to change.

2. Click the down arrow next to the Font Size list box. You see a list of font sizes (see Figure 6-5).

3. Click the size you want. Word changes the font size of the selected text and closes the list. Figure 6-6 shows some different font sizes to give you an idea of the range of sizes.

TIP To increase the selected text to the next font size, press Ctrl+>. To decrease the font to the next available size, press Ctrl+<.

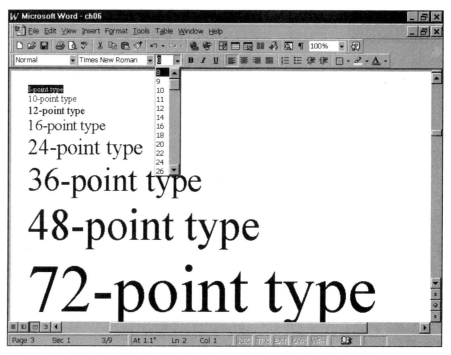

Figure 6-5　The Font Size list displays the available point sizes for the font.

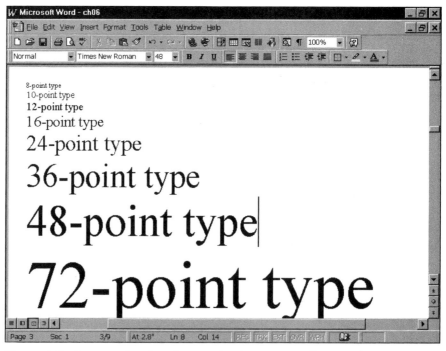

Figure 6-6　You can select font sizes ranging from very small to very large .

All the Colors of the Rainbow

olor printers are becoming more and more popular. You may even have one. In that case, you can add some splash to your documents by changing the color of text. If you don't have a color printer, but the document will be displayed on-screen, you can also make color changes. These changes do appear on-screen but will print as shades of gray on your black-and-white printer.

Follow these steps to change the text color:

1. Select the text you want to change.

2. Click the down arrow next to . You see a palette of color selections (see Figure 6-7).

FEATURE FOCUS The Font color toolbar button is a new feature in Word 97.

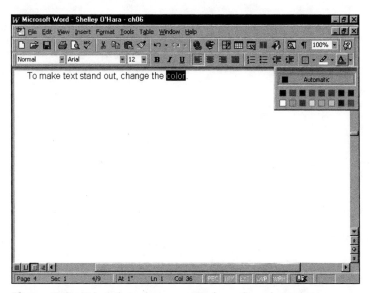

Figure 6-7 Select the color you want from the color palette.

3. Click the color you want. Word makes the selected text that color. Notice also that the toolbar button displays that color. You can apply this same color to other text by selecting the text and clicking the button.

You can also use the Font dialog box to change the color, as described in the section "Changing the Font Using the Font Dialog Box" earlier in this chapter.

Pay Some More Attention

When you read something important in a book, a magazine, a report, or any document, you may take a yellow highlighter pen and drag across it. You can then use these highlighted sections to review or find the key points in the document. Those pens remind you of college, don't they? My roommate when shopping for used books would find one with what she considered the "best" highlighting. Then she'd simply read what the other student highlighted (and hope and pray the previous owner was a decent student).

You can help your reader identify important ideas by highlighting text in your document. The default highlight color is yellow, but you can also select a different color.

Follow these steps to highlight text:

1. Select the text you want to highlight.

2. To use the yellow highlight, click ![highlight button]. Word applies the highlight. Figure 6-8 shows some highlighted text, although you'll have to take my word that it is yellow since this is a black-and-white book.

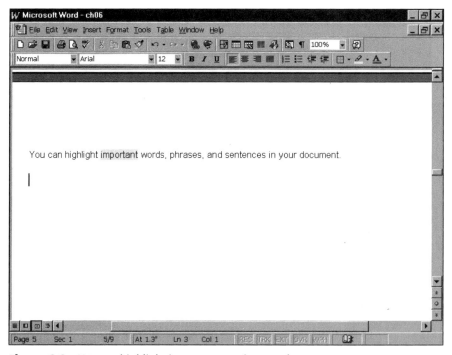

Figure 6-8 You can highlight important text in your document.

3. To use a different color, click the down arrow next to ✐▾. Then click the color you want. Word applies the highlighting.

To remove the highlighting, select the text, click the down arrow next to ✐▾, and select None.

BONUS

Special Text Effects

You've already learned the most common formatting changes, but as you get more and more skilled with Word, you may want to get fancy. This section covers some special effects you can create:

✳ You can apply other font effects such as shadow, outline, small caps, and strikethrough.

✳ You can create different effects by experimenting with the different underline styles.

✳ You can combine changes such as a pattern (covered in the next chapter) and a text color to create special effects such as white text on a black background.

✳ You can select from some text animations, such as Black Ants Marching or Las Vegas Lights.

Text Special Effects

You can select other special text effects, such as strikethrough, from the Font dialog box. Figure 6-9 shows an example of each of the different effects. To make the change, select the text and then select the Format → Font command. Check the appropriate text box for Strikethrough, Double strikethough, Superscript, Subscript, Shadow, Outline, Emboss, Engrave, Small caps, All caps, or Hidden.

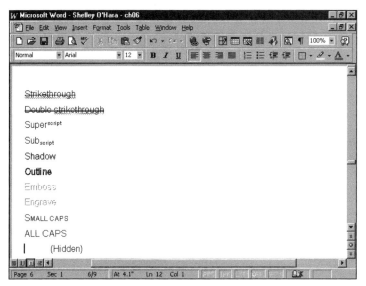

Figure 6-9   Select special effects such as these using the Font
dialog box.

**FEATURE
FOCUS**   Shadow, Outline, Emboss, and Engrave are all new features in Word 97.

Underline Special Effects

If you use the toolbar button for underlining, you get a single underline beneath
all words and spaces. If you want to use a different underline style, you can do
so from the Font dialog box. Select the text you want to underline. Then open
the Format menu and select the Font command. Click the Font tab and then display the Underline drop-down list. Select the type of underline you want: Single
(the default), Words only, Double, Dotted, Thick, Dash, Dot dash, Dot dot dash,
or Wave. Figure 6-10 shows examples of each of these underline styles.

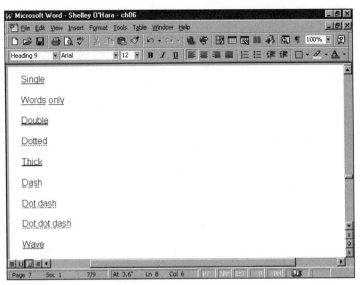

Figure 6-10   You can select a different underline style.

Reversed Text: White on Black

Another text special effect you might want to use is reversed text: the text is white and the background is black. You can create this special effect, shown in Figure 6-11, by combining the black shading and white text color.

Follow these steps:

1. Select the text you want to change.

2. Open the ⬛ **Format** menu and select the ⬛ **Font** command.

3. If necessary, click the Fo<u>n</u>t tab.

4. Click the down arrow next to the <u>C</u>olor list box and click White. Because it is white, you can't see the text, but it is still in the document.

5. Click the OK button to close the dialog box. The text should still be selected.

6. Open the ⬛ **Format** menu and select the ⬛ **Borders and Shading** command.

7. Click the <u>S</u>hading tab. You see the options for paragraph shading (covered in the next chapter).

8. Display the St<u>y</u>le drop-down list and select Solid. Leave the color as Auto.

9. Click the OK button to close the dialog box.

   The paragraph is now shaded in black, and the white text appears.

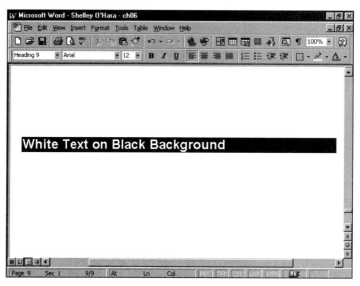

Figure 6-11 You can create reversed text.

Text Animations

FEATURE FOCUS Text animations are an entirely new feature in Word 97.

You can also include text animations in your document. Yes, you can put your text in the bright lights. In a movie marquee!

To make this type of change, follow these steps:

1. Select the text you want to animate.

2. Open the **Format** menu and select the **Font** command.

3. Click the Animation tab. You see the Animation dialog box.

4. Select the animation you want to use. For instance, Figure 6-12 shows the Marching Black Ants animation. You see a preview of the selected animation.

5. Click the OK button. The selected text is animated, using the animation you selected.

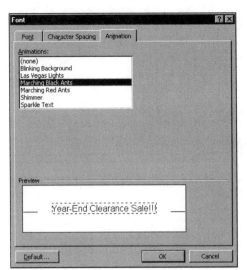

Figure 6-12   You can animate text.

Summary

In this chapter you learned how to make changes to the look of your text. You can make text bold, italic, or underlined. You can change the font or font size, use a different color for the text, or highlight text. You can even create such special effects as animated text.

Text goes together to make paragraphs. The next chapter focuses on formatting changes you can make to your paragraphs of text.

FORMATTING PARAGRAPHS

E ach time you press Enter, you create a new paragraph. You have a lot of control over how the paragraphs appear on the page. For example, you can indent the first line of each paragraph. You can center a line. You can create bulleted and numbered lists. All of the paragraph formatting options are covered in this chapter.

Formatting not only makes your document look better, but it can also help your reader. Take a look at the documents in Figures 7-1 and 7-2. The text is the same, but the second document has been formatted. Which document looks better? Which document conveys the message better? Most likely you answered, "the one in Figure 7-2." The heading clearly identifies what the document is about. Main points are easy to spot. The paragraphs are easy to read and follow. As you can see, formatting can really improve the readability and usefulness of a document, as well as enhance its appearance.

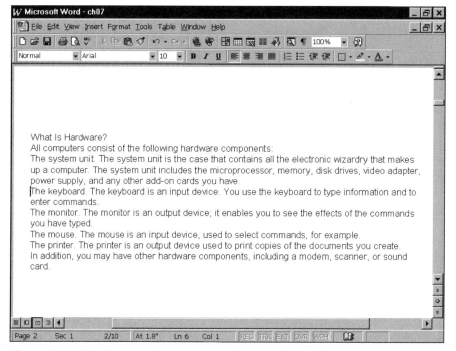

Figure 7-1 This document has no paragraph or text formatting.

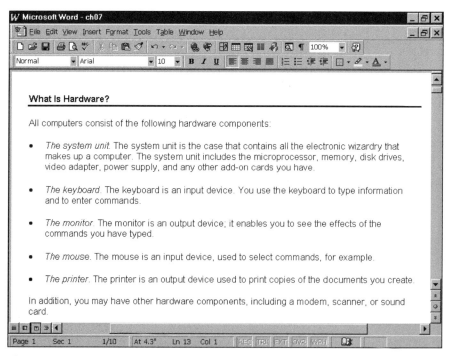

Figure 7-2 Here, the same document has been formatted.

Those Finicky Paragraph Marks

As you review this chapter, keep in mind that a paragraph is any text followed by a hard return. (A hard return is inserted every time you press Enter. Soft returns are inserted by Word and are adjusted when you add or delete text.) A single line, for instance, can be a paragraph. You can apply the formatting options covered in this chapter to a single paragraph or to several paragraphs. Each paragraph, for example, can have different tab settings.

Also, each time you press Enter, the paragraph options for that paragraph are carried down to the next paragraph. And if you delete the paragraph marker, the paragraph takes on the formatting of the following paragraph. If you type a line, center it, and press Enter, the next line is centered as well. If you have a double-spaced paragraph followed by a single-spaced paragraph and delete the paragraph mark at the end of the first paragraph, the new combined paragraph will then be single-spaced. This is confusing for beginners who wonder how a paragraph got formatted without anyone making a change. You can think of the paragraph marker as the storehouse for all formatting options for that paragraph.

If something bizarre happens, try undoing the change using <u>E</u>dit → <u>U</u>ndo. If you have trouble visualizing where the paragraph marks appear, you can display them by clicking the Show/Hide ¶ button.

Words to the Left, Words to the Right

When you type in Word, all text is left-aligned, and the right margin is ragged, or uneven. For most text, this alignment works great. For other paragraphs, you may want to make a change. For instance, you can center the document title. Or you can right-align text like a newspaper banner. You can justify the text in the paragraphs to keep both the left and right margins even.

You can select four types of alignment, and the best way to make a change is to use the Formatting toolbar.

Follow these steps:

1. To change the alignment of one paragraph, click within that paragraph. To change the alignment of several paragraphs, select the ones you want to change.

2. Click ▤ to left-align text. Click ▤ to center text. Click ▤ to right-align text. Click ▤ to justify text.

Figure 7-3 shows an example of each type of alignment.

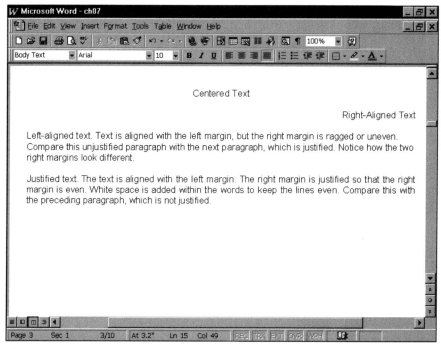

Figure 7-3 You can select from four types of paragraph alignments: left, centered, right, or justified.

TIP To undo the change, click the Undo button or select the Edit → Undo command. If you realize later that you want to use a different alignment, select the paragraph(s) and then click another alignment button.

You can also use these keyboard shortcuts to change the alignment:

Center	Ctrl+E
Left	Ctrl+L
Right	Ctrl+R
Justify	Ctrl+J

And you can use the Paragraph dialog box to change the alignment. This method involves several more steps and offers no advantages over the toolbar method, though. If you are curious, however, here's how to use this method. Display the dialog box by selecting the Format → Paragraph command and clicking the Indents and Spacing tab. Display the Alignment list box and select the alignment you want. Click the OK button to close the dialog box.

Movin' on Over

Alignment changes are most appropriate for headings or other special paragraphs in your document. But what about the main body of the document? What types of changes are appropriate? Glad you asked.

Think about one long, unending page of text. Like an article on existentialism or some other l-o-n-g article you had to read in school. Were you excited about reading it? Nope. Nobody likes a long, never-ending treatise. Just looking at this type of document makes you yawn.

To make your document easy and inviting to read, you can use some of the features in this chapter, including indents. You may, for instance, indent the first line of each paragraph. This visual clue helps your reader see how the document is divided into paragraphs. You may also indent paragraphs, such as quotations, that you want to set apart from the main document text. As another option, you may want to use a special kind of indent, called a hanging indent, for numbered lists.

You can indent text in the amount you want, and you can use either the Formatting toolbar or the Paragraph dialog box to make a change, as covered in this section.

Indenting Text with the Toolbar

If you want a left indent — useful for setting off a paragraph from the main body text — you can use the toolbar to set the indent. Click ⊞. The paragraph is indented $1/2$-inch from the left margin. You can click the button again to increase the indent. Each time you click the button, the paragraph is indented another $1/2$-inch.

If you indent too much or if you want to undo the indent, click ⊞ to decrease or undo the indents.

Indenting Text with the Paragraph Dialog Box

The Increase Indent and Decrease Indent buttons are useful if you want to indent text from the left. If you want to indent from the left and the right or if you want to create a special kind of indent, you need to use a different method. You must use the Paragraph dialog box.

Follow these steps to indent text using the Paragraph dialog box:

1. Move the insertion point to the beginning of the paragraph you want to indent. To indent several paragraphs, select those paragraphs.

2. Open the **Format** menu and select the **Paragraph** command.

3. If necessary, click the Indents and Spacing tab. You see the Indents and Spacing tab of the Paragraph dialog box (see Figure 7-4).

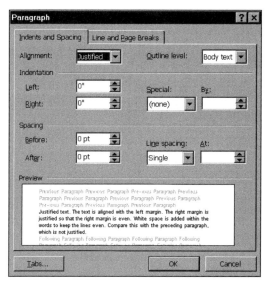

Figure 7-4 Use this dialog box to select paragraph formatting options such as indents.

4. Do any of the following:

   ✳ To indent text from the left, type in the Left spin box the amount you want to indent the text, or use the spin arrows to select a value.

   ✳ To indent text from the right, type the amount in the Right spin box, or use the spin arrows.

   ✳ To create a first-line or hanging indent, display the Special dropdown list and select the type of indent you want. In the By spin box, enter the amount you want to indent.

5. Click the OK button.

Word indents the paragraph(s). Figure 7-5 shows examples of different types of indents.

TIP Press Ctrl+M to indent the paragraph left. Press Ctrl+Shift+M to unindent or decrease the indent. Press Ctrl+T to create a hanging indent. Press Ctrl+Shift+T to undo a hanging indent.

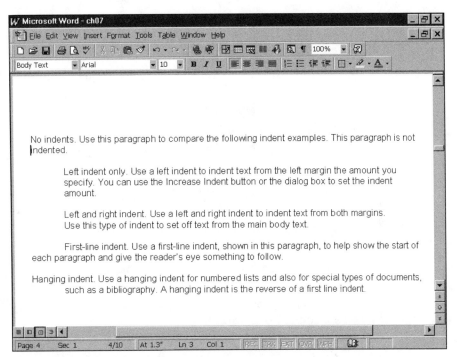

No indents. Use this paragraph to compare the following indent examples. This paragraph is not indented.

Left indent only. Use a left indent to indent text from the left margin the amount you specify. You can use the Increase Indent button or the dialog box to set the indent amount.

Left and right indent. Use a left and right indent to indent text from both margins. Use this type of indent to set off text from the main body text.

First-line indent. Use a first-line indent, shown in this paragraph, to help show the start of each paragraph and give the reader's eye something to follow.

Hanging indent. Use a hanging indent for numbered lists and also for special types of documents, such as a bibliography. A hanging indent is the reverse of a first line indent.

Figure 7-5   You can use different types of indents to format your paragraphs.

Expand-o-Text

Many of the formatting options in this chapter call to mind long, boring documents. Think again of that article on existentialism or something else yawn-inducing. (Sorry to all you existentialists out there.) Was there any room between the lines? Any break at all for you, the reader? Most likely it was single-spaced, crammed full of text, all swimming around on the page like one big long sentence. At least they could have double-spaced the document to make it a *little* easier to read.

By default, Word single-spaces the text in your document. This spacing works well for short documents such as letters and memos, but in longer documents such as manuscripts, you may want to use a different spacing increment. You can choose single, 1.5, double spacing. Or you can enter an exact amount, a minimum amount, or an amount to multiply by (for instance, to add 20 percent).

To change line spacing, follow these steps:

1. Select the paragraph(s) that you want to change.

2. Open the **Format** menu and select the **Paragraph** command.

3. If necessary, click the Indents and Spacing tab. You see the Indents and Spacing tab of the Paragraph dialog box (refer to Figure 7-4).

4. Display the Line spacing drop-down list box.

5. Select one of the following:

✳ To single-space the document, select Single. Word adjusts the line to accommodate the largest font and adds a small amount of space. The amount depends on the font size in the selected paragraph.

✳ To add $1^1/_2$ lines, select 1.5 Lines.

✳ To double-space the document, select Double.

✳ To specify the minimum amount of spacing, select At Least and then enter the spacing interval you want in the At box.

✳ To specify an exact amount of spacing, select Exactly and enter the spacing value you want. If characters are chopped off, you need to enter a larger value.

✳ To specify an amount by which to multiply, select Multiple and enter the value you want. For instance, the value 1 is single spacing; 1.2 would increase the spacing 20 percent. The value 2 would double-space the paragraph.

6. Click the OK button.

Figure 7-6 shows some examples of different spacing intervals.

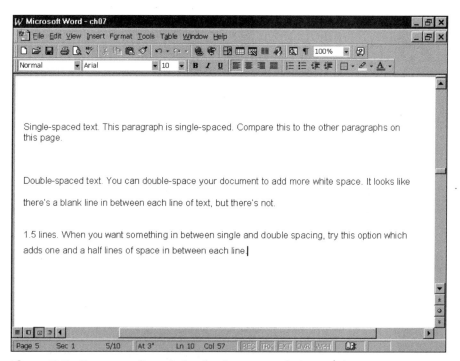

Figure 7-6 You can set line spacing for the paragraphs in your document.

TIP Press Ctrl+1 for single spacing, Ctrl+5 for 1.5 spacing, or Ctrl+2 for double spacing.

Tab-o-Matic

In your documents, you may want to include a list of columnar data. For instance, you may create a price list. One column for the product, one for the price. Or you may create a list of names and phone numbers. One column for the name, one for the phone number. The best way to set up this type of data is to create a table, as covered in Chapter 10. Tables are much easier to work with than tabbed lists, and Word includes several features for changing the look of the table. Tables have pretty much replaced plain old tabs. Still, you may find that you want to set tabs for some types of lists — for instance, when you want to align a column of numbers, use dot leaders, or just create a simple tabbed list.

You can use the ruler or the Tab dialog box to set tabs, and you can select from four different tab types (left, right, center, and decimal), as covered in this section.

Setting Tabs with the Ruler

The ruler is the on-screen formatting tool that is most useful, I think, for setting tabs. If you use the dialog box (covered next), you have to enter a precise measurement for the tabs, which you figure out simply by guessing. "How about the 4-inch mark?" you may ask. "Sounds good," that voice in your head may answer. After you take a stab at the right location and close the dialog box, you see that four inches was *way* off. So you try another measurement. This process continues until you guess right or give up.

Instead, you can set tabs by just clicking where you want them on the ruler. Follow these steps to use the ruler:

1. Display the ruler by opening the <u>View</u> menu and selecting the Ruler command. You see the ruler on-screen.

2. Select the paragraph(s) for which you want to set tabs.

 Remember that each paragraph can have individual tab settings. If you don't select all the paragraphs, your changes will apply to only the current paragraph (the one with the insertion point). Be sure to select all the paragraphs you want to format.

3. Click the Tab Alignment button until the tab type you want is selected (see Table 7-1).

TABLE 7-1 The Tab Alignment Buttons

Button	Tab Type	Function
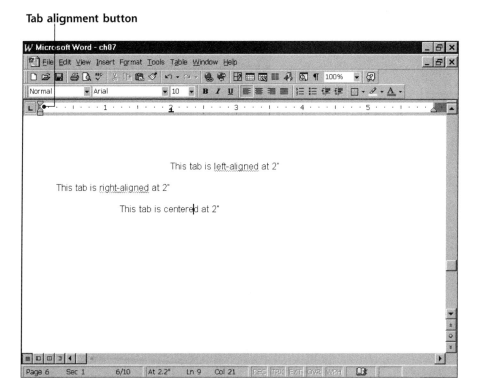 LEFT TAB	LEFT TAB	Text starts on the marker and moves right.
RIGHT TAB	RIGHT TAB	Text starts on the marker and moves left.
CENTER TAB	CENTER TAB	Text is centered on the marker.
DECIMAL TAB	DECIMAL TAB	Text is aligned on the decimal point.

Figure 7-7 shows examples of left, right, and center tabs all aligned at the same tab mark (2"). For an example of a decimal tab, see the next section.

Tab alignment button

This tab is left-aligned at 2"

This tab is right-aligned at 2"

This tab is centered at 2"

Figure 7-7 You can select different tab types and set them visually using the ruler.

4. Click the ruler at the spot you want to place the tab. The tab marker appears on the ruler, and the text is formatted with the new tab settings.

5. Follow steps 3 and 4 for each tab you want to set.

TIP To delete a tab from the ruler, click it and drag it off the ruler. To change the tab position, click it on the ruler and drag it to a new location.

Setting Tabs with the Tab Dialog Box

The ruler is easy to use because it is visual, but if you can't remember which tab button to use or if you want to set a tab at a precise measurement, you can set tabs using the Tabs dialog box.

To set tabs with the Tabs dialog box, follow these steps:

1. Select the paragraph(s) for which you want to set tabs.

2. Open the **Format** menu and select the **Tabs** command. You see the Tabs dialog box (see Figure 7-8).

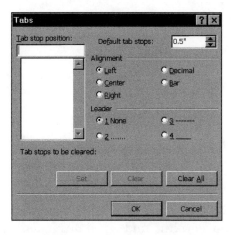

Figure 7-8 Use this dialog box to set tabs for the selected paragraphs.

3. In the Tab stop position text box, type the position for the tab. This position is measured in inches and is measured from the left margin.

4. In the Alignment area, click the type of alignment you want: Left, Center, Right, Decimal, or Bar.

5. If you want to use a dot leader for the tab, click the leader style you want in the Leader area. You can select a dotted line, a dashed line, or a solid line.

6. Click the Set button.

7. Follow steps 2 through 6 for each tab stop you want to create.

8. Click the OK button.

Figure 7-9 shows some special types of tabs you can create using the different tab types.

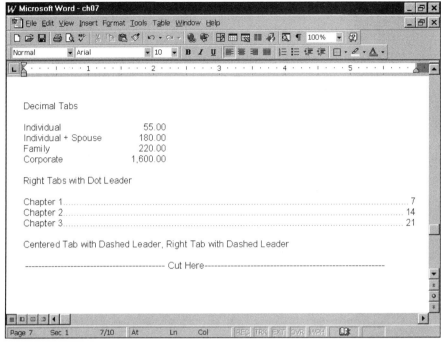

Figure 7-9 You can create special effects using different tab types.

Cross the Border

Remember when you wanted to try something fancy with a typewriter? Maybe you went back over a line and typed an underscore to create an underline. Or maybe you created borders by typing dashes or asterisks. These style flourishes are way out of date.

Now not only can you add a border, but you can also add a gray-shaded pattern to a paragraph. For example, you may want to add borders to your document headings to make them easy to scan. Or you may want to add sidebars and both shade and border these paragraphs. With the combination of borders and shading, you can create some unique effects. You can add borders to the top, the sides, or the bottom of a single paragraph or a group of paragraphs. You can specify the thickness and the style of the border.

For a quick border, use the toolbar. For more control over the line style and the placement of the border, use the dialog box. To add paragraph shading, you must use the dialog box. This section covers each method.

Adding a Border Using the Toolbar

You can select different border placements using the Border button in the formatting toolbar. You can select to place a line above the paragraph, on all sides, on the bottom, choose between two paragraphs, and so on.

Follow these steps to add a border using the toolbar:

1. Select the paragraph(s) to which you want to add a border.

2. Click the down arrow next to ▦▾. You see a palette of border selections (see Figure 7-10).

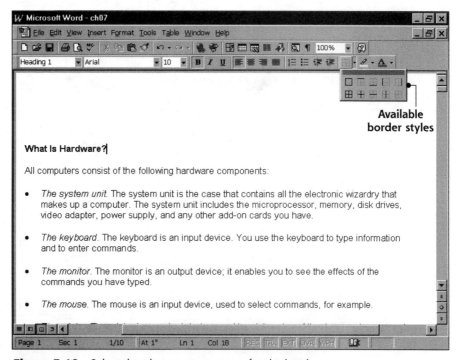

Figure 7-10   Select the placement you want for the border.

3. Click the border placement you want. Word adds the border and/or shading to the selected paragraph(s).

Adding a Border Using the Borders and Shading Dialog Box

If you want more control over the style of line, you can use a different method to add the border: the Borders and Shading dialog box. You can select from special border effects such as box, shadow, and 3-D, plus you can select different line styles.

To add a border, follow these steps:

1. Select the paragraphs you want to border.

2. Open the Format menu and select the Borders and Shading command.

3. If necessary, click the Borders tab. You see the Borders tab options (see Figure 7-11).

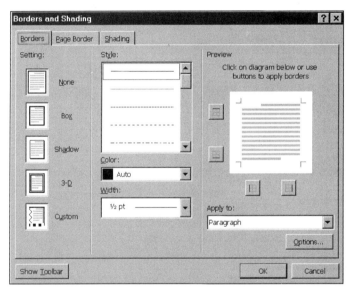

Figure 7-11   Use this dialog box to select a border style and placement.

4. In the Setting area, select the type of border you want to add: None, Box, Shadow, 3-D, or Custom.

5. In the Style list, select the line style you want.

6. To change the border color, display the Color drop-down list and then click the color you want.

7. To change the thickness of the line, display the Width drop-down list and select the width you want. (The width is measured in points.) You see a preview of your selections in the Preview area.

8. If you selected Custom, click in the preview area on the side you want to place the border. For example, click the top of the diagram to add the border to the top. Word adds the selected border to that side. Do this for each border you want to add.

9. Click the OK button to apply the border.

Figure 7-12 shows some different types of borders created using both the toolbar and the Borders and Shading dialog box.

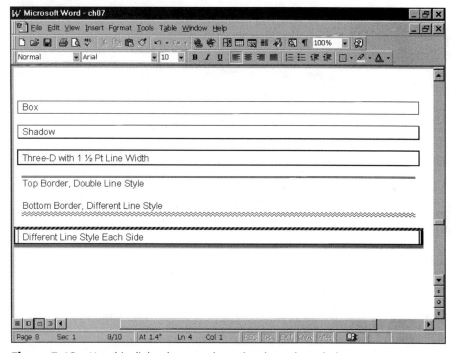

Figure 7-12 Use this dialog box to select a border style and placement.

Adding Shading

Another way to add some flash to your paragraphs is to apply shading. You may want to combine adding a border with shading (although you don't have to add a border to use shading). If you have a color printer, you can select a color for the shading, and that color will be printed. If you don't have a color printer, you can select a gray pattern.

Follow these steps to shade a paragraph:

1. Select the paragraphs you want to border.

2. Open the ❑Format menu and select the ❑Borders and Shading command.

3. If necessary, click the Shading tab. You see the Shading tab options (see Figure 7-13).

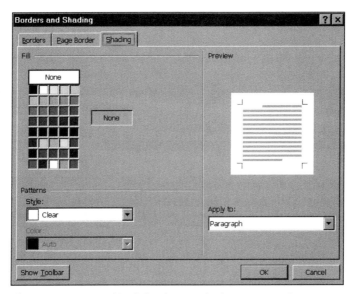

Figure 7-13 Use this dialog box to shade a paragraph.

4. Do one of the following:

* To select a gray fill pattern, click it in the Fill area. Or display the Style drop-down list and select the pattern you want.

* To use a color, click the color in the Fill area.

* To use a color and a fill, click the color you want in the Fill area. Then display the Style drop-down list and select a pattern.

   Understanding how the fills and colors work together can take some time. Just experiment in the dialog box and check the Preview, which shows you how your selection will appear.

5. Click the OK button.

Word adds the shading to the selected paragraph(s). Figure 7-14 shows some examples of shading.

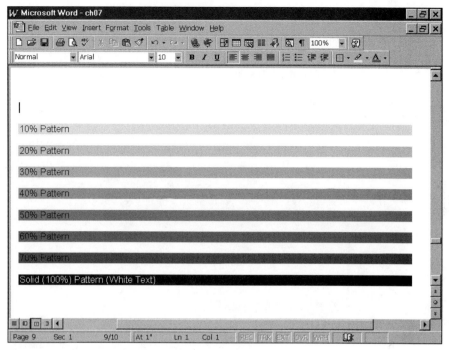

Figure 7-14 Add shading to your paragraph.

Important Points

Do you ever feel as if you are overwhelmed with information? In the information age, you are constantly bombarded with messages: office mail, e-mail, home mail. How can you tell what's important and what's not?

When you are distributing your document, you won't want your reader to struggle to find the main message. Instead, you can highlight key points to make the document easy to scan and assimilate. A well-organized document is more likely to get noticed than one that is a mishmash of ideas.

One way to set off a list of points or topics in a document is to create a bulleted list. Each item in the list is preceded by a bullet, and the text is indented. You can also create a numbered list. Numbered lists work well for directions or other points you want to present in sequence. Word automatically numbers all the items in a list, and the text is indented.

Creating a Bulleted List

The fastest way to create a bulleted list is to use the Bullets button on the formatting toolbar. When you use this method, you get a round bullet and a ½-inch indent. Perfect for most cases.

Simply follow these steps:

1. Select the text that you want to add bullets. Word will add a bullet to each paragraph within the selection, not each line. Word will not add bullets to any blank lines within the selection.

2. Click ▦. Word creates a bulleted list, as shown in Figure 7-15.

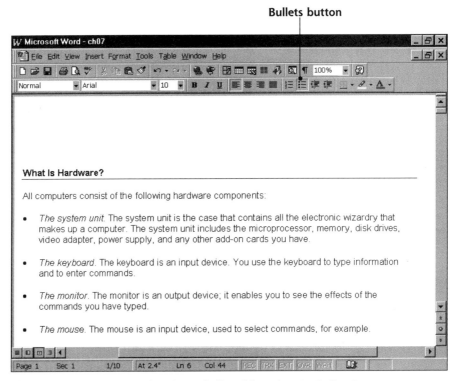

Bullets button

Figure 7-15   You can easily create a bulleted list using the Bullets button.

Creating a Numbered List

For items that appear in a specific order, such as a series of steps, you can create a numbered list. Word will add the numbers automatically and also handle indenting the paragraphs so that the text is aligned properly. All you have to do is click the button. Another great thing about a numbered list is that, if you add or delete an item within the list, Word renumbers the other items.

Follow these steps to create a numbered list:

1. Select the text you want to number. Word will number each paragraph. Blank lines within the selection will not be numbered.

2. Click . Word creates a numbered list, as shown in Figure 7-16.

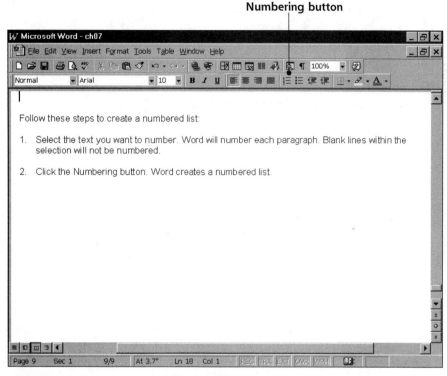

Figure 7-16   You can create a numbered list using the Numbering button.

Removing the Bullets or Numbers

To remove bullets from a list, select the list and click the Bullets button again. To remove numbers from a list, select the list and click the Numbering button again. You can also use the Edit → Undo command or the Undo button.

BONUS

Using a Different Bullet or Number Style

If you want to get creative, you can select a different type of bullet, such as a check mark, and you can select a different numbering style. You also can select the amount to indent the text. To make these changes, use the Bullets and Numbering command, as covered in this section.

Changing the Bullet Style

You can really jazz up the bulleted list by selecting a different bullet. You can select from one of several bullet characters including check boxes, diamonds, check marks, and so on.

To use a different bullet, follow these steps:

1. Select the list you want to change.

2. Open the ⌗Format⌗ menu and select the ⌗Bullets and Numbering⌗ command.

3. If necessary, click the Bulleted tab. You see the Bulleted tab options.

4. To use one of the bullets that appear in this default list, click the character you want. Skip to step 7.

    To use a different bullet character (one not shown), click the Customize button and follow steps 5 and 6 to select the character you want.

5. In the Customize Bulleted List dialog box, shown in Figure 7-17, click the symbol you want to replace. Word has room to display only six bullet styles. Word will replace this bullet style with the new one, but the original style is still available from the Bulleted tab.

6. Click the Bullet button. In the Symbol dialog box that appears, click the symbol you want to use. Click the OK button. The new bullet is selected.

 X-REF **For more information on inserting symbols, see Chapter 11.**

7. To change the placement of the bullet, enter an indent amount in the Indent at text box or use the spin arrows to select a value.

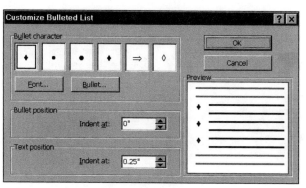

Figure 7-17 Customize the bullet character, the bullet position, and the text position using this dialog box.

8. To change the indent of the text, enter an indent amount in the <u>I</u>ndent at text box or use the spin arrows to select a value.

9. Click the OK button.

Changing the Numbering Style

Just as you can change the bullet character, you can also change the numbering style. You can select from one of the six predefined styles, or you can create your own.

To change the numbering style, follow these steps:

1. Select the text you want to number.

2. Select <u>Format</u> → Bullets and <u>N</u>umbering .

3. Click the <u>N</u>umbered tab. You see the Numbered tab options.

4. To use one of the selected numbering styles, click the style you want. Skip to step 7.

   To customize the numbering style, click the Cus<u>t</u>omize button and follow steps 5 and 6 to select the style you want to use.

5. In the Customize Numbered List dialog box, shown in Figure 7-18, display the <u>N</u>umber style drop-down list and select a style.

6. To start with a different number than 1, type it in the <u>S</u>tart at spin box. Or use the spin arrows to select a value.

7. To select a number position, display the drop-down list and select the position you want. To change the alignment spot, enter the alignment measurement (in inches) in the <u>A</u>ligned at text box.

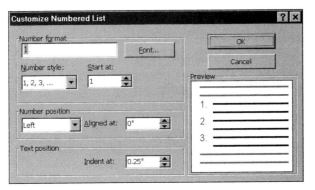

Figure 7-18 Customize the numbering style using this dialog box.

8. To change the indent of the text, enter an indent amount in the Indent at text box or use the spin arrows to select a value.

9. Click the OK button. The paragraphs are numbered with the style you selected.

Summary

Text goes together to make paragraphs, and paragraphs go together to make pages. This chapter has covered the paragraph formatting changes you can make. Turn to the next chapter for techniques and advice on formatting the pages in your document.

IN THIS CHAPTER YOU LEARN THESE KEY SKILLS:

I n the first stage of creating a document, you most likely concentrate on the content. Then you may think about how the text looks and how the paragraphs flow on the page. Finally, you may take another step back (figuratively speaking, that is) and think about how the document will be positioned on the page. Does the text look balanced? If you have a short document, all the text may be crammed at the top, and the page will look out of balance. Maybe you need to change the margins. Are the pages organized? If the document has several pages, you may want to add headers or footers to identify the document. Is there anything else that can be added to the page? You may also want to dress up a document by adding a page border. In this chapter you learn about the different ways you can format the page of a document.

TIP   Remember that you can check the overall look of the page by using the File → Print Preview command.

Give Me Some Room

Margins control how close Word prints to the edge of the page. If you have a big top margin, for instance, Word leaves white space at the top of the document. If you have a small top margin, Word prints closer to the top of the page.

The default margins are 1-inch top and bottom margins and 1.25-inch left and right margins. These settings — like most of Word's defaults — work fine for a lot of documents. If need be, you can change the margins to add more or less space along any edge of the (top, bottom, left, or right). For instance, if you print on letterhead, you may need to make the top margin larger and move the text down. As another example, you may want a bigger top margin for a short document so that the text is not crammed at the top of the page.

You can change margins using one of two methods. To figure out which is best for you, think about how you hang a picture on the wall. Do you eyeball it and then just hammer in a nail or two? If so, skip to the section "The Visual Method: Changing Margins in Print Preview." Or do you get out the level and tape measure to precisely select the wall position and then hammer in the nail. If so, read the next section.

The Precise Method: Using the Page Setup Dialog Box

If you know the amount (or approximate amount) you want for each margin, you can use the Page Setup dialog box to make a change.

Follow these steps:

1. Open the **File** menu and select the **Page Setup** command. You see the Page Setup dialog box.

2. If necessary, click the Margins tab. You see the Margin settings for the page (see Figure 8-1).

3. Press Tab to move to and highlight the margin you want to change.

4. Type the new margin setting. Or use the spin arrows to enter a new value. Notice that the Preview shows how these new margins affect the page.

If you know the amount of space you want for each margin, use the Page Setup dialog box to make a change.

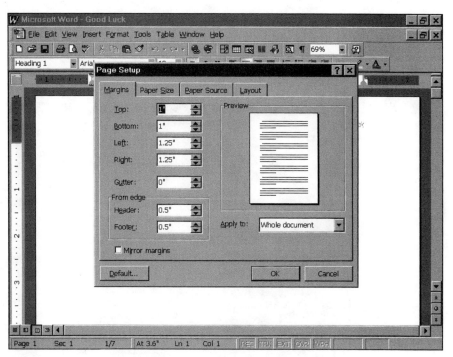

Figure 8-1   Use the Margins tab to set the page margins.

5. Follow steps 3 and 4 for each margin you want to change.

6. Click the OK button. In Normal view, the text will be adjusted for the new margins, but you won't see the overall effect on the pages. You can switch to Page Layout view or preview the document to see the change.

TIP   For information on changing header and footer margins, see the section "Changing the Header and Footer Margins."

The Visual Method: Changing Margins in Print Preview

If you aren't the precise sort, you can use Print Preview to change the margins. This method gives you an overall picture of the document and shows you how the change will affect the document.

Follow these steps:

1. Open the **File** menu and select the **Print Preview** command. You see a preview of the document. (For more information on previewing a document, see Chapter 5.)

2. If the ruler is not displayed, click the View Ruler button. You see the ruler on-screen (see Figure 8-2).

Top margin guide   Right margin guide

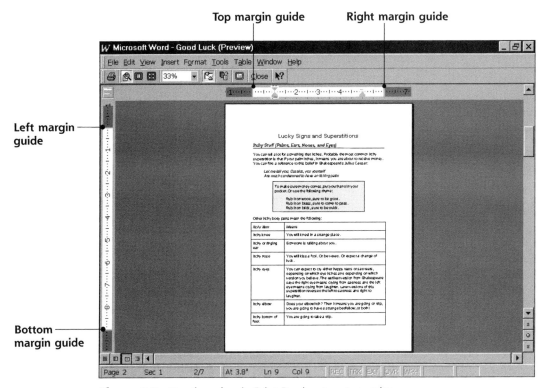

Left margin guide

Bottom margin guide

Figure 8-2   Use the rulers in Print Preview to set margins.

3. Put the mouse pointer on the margin you want to change — where the gray and white areas of the ruler come together. When the pointer is in the right spot, it looks like a two-headed arrow and the ScreenTip says the margin name.

4. Drag the margin guide to a new location.

5. Click the Close button to return to Normal view.

Front and Center

When you don't have a lot of text on the page, the page may look funny. You can try tinkering with the margins to get the text aligned on the page. Or you can simply center the page. For instance, centering a page works great for title pages.

To center a page, follow these steps:

1. Open the **File** menu and select the **Page Setup** command. You see the Page Setup dialog box.

2. Click the **Layout** tab. You see the Layout tab options (see Figure 8-3).

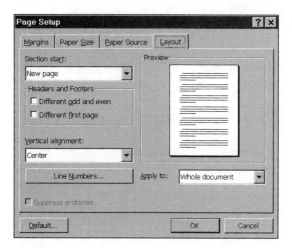

Figure 8-3 Center a page using this dialog box.

3. Display the Vertical alignment drop-down list and select Center.

4. Click the OK button. Word centers the page. In Normal view, you won't see this change. Preview the document to see the page.

Printing Down or Across the Page: Changing the Orientation

Think of a portrait. What dimensions do you think of? Usually the portrait is longer than wide, right? Now think of a landscape picture. What are the dimensions? Wider than long? These two terms carry over to Word's page orientation. You can print left to right across the short side 8½" and down the long edge 11". This orientation is called portrait. Or you can print left to right across the long side 11" and down the short side 8½". This orientation is called landscape. If your document is wider than it is long — for instance, you have a table with many columns — print in landscape.

Most documents are printed on 8½" x 11" paper. You can also select other paper sizes. For instance, you may have a printer with a bin for legal paper. You can then select and print on this paper size.

To change the orientation or the paper size, follow these steps:

1. Open the **File** menu and select the **Page Setup** command. You see the Page Setup dialog box.

2. Click the Paper Size tab to display these options, shown in Figure 8-4.

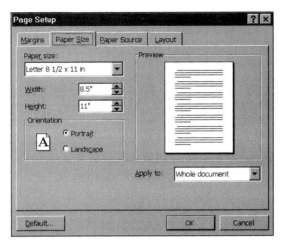

Figure 8-4 Select a paper size and orientation from this dialog box.

3. To change the paper size, display the Paper size drop-down list and select the size you want. Or enter the width and height in the spin boxes.

4. In the Orientation box, click Portrait or Landscape.

5. Click the OK button.

Numbering Pages

I magine a twenty-page document without page numbers. How would you keep the pages in order? Even if the pages were stapled or bound, how would you refer to a particular page? Count out each page until you get to the one you want? In a long document page numbers are a necessity.

Word makes it easy to insert page numbers. And when you use Word to number the pages, you don't have to worry about renumbering when you add or delete a page. The page numbers are updated automatically.

If all you want to do is insert a page number, you can do so using the Insert → Page Numbers command. This command automatically creates a footer or header, depending on where you select to place the page numbers. If you want to include additional information in the header or footer, such as the date or document name, go to the next section. You can set up the headers and footers with page numbers and any other text you want to include.

Adding Page Numbers

When you insert page numbers, you can select whether they appear at the top or bottom of the page. You can also choose to align the page number right, center, left, inside, or outside.

Follow these steps:

1. Open the **Insert** menu and select the **Page Numbers** command. You see the Page Numbers dialog box (see Figure 8-5).

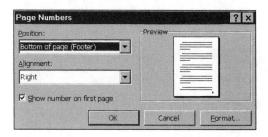

Figure 8-5 Select a position and an alignment for the page numbers.

2. Display the Position drop-down list box and select Top of page (Header) or Bottom of page (Footer).

   If you select Top of page (Header), Word creates a header and inserts the page number at the top of each page in the document. If you select Bottom of page (Footer), Word creates a footer and inserts the page number at the bottom of each page.

3. Display the Alignment drop-down list and select the alignment of the page number:

   * Left — Numbers print aligned with the left margin.
   * Center — Numbers are centered on the page.
   * Right — Numbers print aligned with the right margin.
   * Inside — Numbers print on the inside of facing pages (right-aligned on left pages and left-aligned on right pages).
   * Outside — Numbers print on the outside of facing pages (left-aligned on left pages and right-aligned on right pages).
   * If you aren't sure what an option does, select it and then check the preview. The preview shows the placement of the page number.

4. To skip a page number on the first page, uncheck the Show number on first page check box. For instance, you may not want to include a page number on a title page.

5. Click the OK button. Word creates a header or footer and inserts the page number. In Normal view, you don't see the page numbers. Switch to Page Layout view or preview the document.

Using Letters or Roman Numerals to Number the Pages

If plain old Arabic numbers aren't fancy enough for you, you can select another number style. You can even include additional numbering information, such as the chapter number. You do all this from the Page Number Format dialog box.

Follow these steps:

1. In the Page Numbers dialog box, click the Format button. (If the Page Numbers dialog box is not displayed, select Insert → Page Numbers to display it.) You see the Page Number Format dialog box (see Figure 8-6).

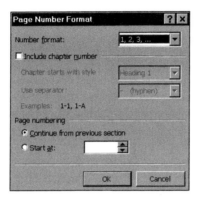

Figure 8-6 Select a number format from this dialog box.

2. To change the numbering style, display the Number format drop-down list and click the style you want. You can choose Arabic numbers, lowercase letters, uppercase letters, lowercase Roman numerals, or uppercase Roman numerals.

3. To include the chapter number and the page number, check the Include chapter number check box. Then display the Chapter starts with style drop-down list and select the style assigned to the chapter head. Display the Use separator drop-down list and select which character you want to use to separate the chapter and page number (hyphen, period, em dash, and so on).

   To use this feature, you must assign a style to the chapter head so that Word knows the chapter number. See Chapter 9 for more information on styles.

4. Click the OK button twice. Word uses the selected numbering style to number the pages.

Starting with a Different Page Number

If you have a document that is really long and is broken into several files, you may need to start numbering with a different number than 1. For instance, suppose that you are writing an epic novel, *The Overpasses of Madison Country*, with one file for each of the chapters. When you print out this tome, you want continuous page numbering.

You need to set the starting number for each chapter by following these steps:

1. In the Page Numbers dialog box, click the Format button. (If the Page Numbers dialog box is not displayed, select `Insert` → `Page Numbers` to display it.) You see the Page Number Format dialog box (refer to Figure 8-6).

 TIP If you have broken up the document into sections and want to number each section separately, click the Continue from previous section option button to turn off this option. Chapter 12 covers sections in more detail.

2. Click the Start at option button and then enter the number to use in the spin box.

3. Click the OK button twice.

Heads or Tails?

When you start creating documents that are longer than one page, you will most likely want to include some type of reference number on the page. Page numbers are practically a must. In addition, you may want to include other text that helps the reader identify the document. For example, you can include the document title, or a date, or your last name. You can include the section name to help the reader navigate through a long document. Rather than type this information on each page, create a header and a footer. Word will insert the text on each page automatically.

Just as your head is at the top of your body (or should be), a header is printed at the top of each page of the document. And where are your feet? At the bottom. Likewise, a footer is printed at the bottom of each page. (Those of you standing on your head while reading this should ignore this paragraph.)

Which one — a header or a footer — is preferable? Whichever one your little heart likes best. You can even include both a header and a footer. This section covers how to set up headers and footers.

Creating a Header

To create a header, follow these steps:

1. Open the ⧉Ⅴⅰⅇⱳ⧉ menu and choose the ⧉**Header and Footer**⧉ command. (I know that ⧉Ⅴⅰⅇⱳ⧉ seems a weird place for this command.)

   At the top of the page, you see a dotted header area. You also see the Header and Footer toolbar on-screen (see Figure 8-7).

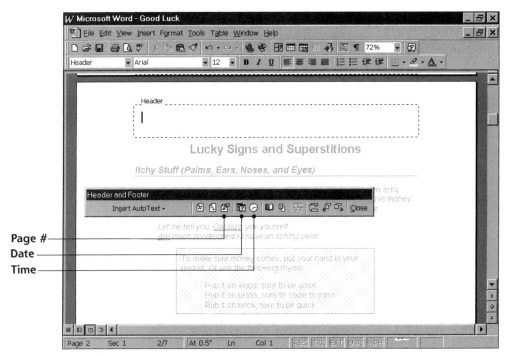

Page #
Date
Time

Figure 8-7 Type your header here.

2. Type the text for the header. You can use the toolbar to insert special text such as the page number or the date. See the section "Using the Header and Footer Toolbar."

   By default, the header includes three predefined tabs: left-aligned, center, and right-aligned. You can include text in each of these three "areas" by pressing Tab and then typing the text you want to include.

3. Make any formatting changes to the text. You can make text italic, change the font, use a different font size, add a border — just about everything you learned in Chapters 6 and 7.

4. Click the Close button. Word adds the header to the document, which you won't see in Normal view. To see the header, switch to Page Layout view or Print Preview.

Creating a Footer

You create a footer in just about the same way you do a header. You just need to use a toolbar button to move to the footer area.

Follow these steps:

1. Open the View menu and choose the Header and Footer command. You see the header area and the toolbar.

2. Click the Switch Between Header and Footer button.

You see a dotted footer area at the bottom of the page; the insertion point is within this area. The Header and Footer toolbar also appears on-screen (see Figure 8-8).

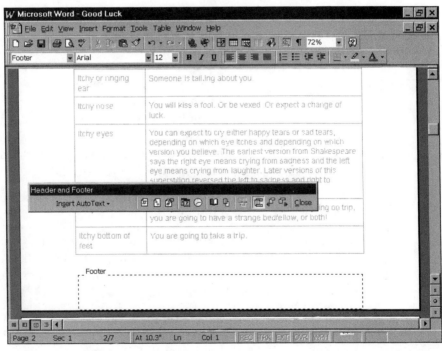

Figure 8-8 Type your footer here.

3. Type the text for the footer. You can use the toolbar to insert special text such as the page number or date. See the section "Using the Header and Footer Toolbar."

By default, the footer also includes three predefined tabs: left-aligned, center, and right-aligned. You can include text in each of these three "areas" by pressing Tab and then typing the text you want to include.

4. Make any formatting changes to the text. You can make text italic, change the font, use a different font size, add a border — just about everything you learned in Chapters 6 and 7.

5. Click the Close button. Word adds the footer to the document. To see the footer, preview the document or change to Page Layout view.

Using the Header and Footer Toolbar

You can use the buttons on the Header and Footer toolbar to insert special information in the header or footer. For instance, you can insert the page number or the date by simply clicking the appropriate button. You can also use the buttons to move among different headers and footers in the document. Table 8-1 identifies each button and includes a description.

TABLE 8-1   The Header and Footer Toolbar

Button	Name	Description
Insert AutoText ▾	INSERT AUTOTEXT	Word sets up some AutoText entries that are commonly used in headers and footers. Some examples include "Author," "Created by," "Last printed," "Page X of Y," and so on. To use one of these predefined headers or footers, display the list and select the one you want.
🔢	INSERT PAGE NUMBER	Inserts a page number that will be updated automatically.
🔢	INSERT NUMBER OF PAGES	Inserts the number of pages. You can combine the Insert Page Number button and this button to create a header or footer that says something like "Page 5 of 10."
🔢	FORMAT PAGE NUMBER	Allows you to select a format for the page numbers. See the section on page numbers for information on using this dialog box.
📅	INSERT DATE	Inserts a date field that will be updated automatically.
🕐	INSERT TIME	Inserts a time field that will be updated automatically.

Button	Name	Description
	PAGE SETUP	Displays the Page Setup dialog box so that you can make changes to the margins, paper size, and other options.
	SHOW/HIDE DOCUMENT TEXT	Hides (or shows) the document text.
	SAME AS PREVIOUS	In a document with different headers and footers, click this button to use the same header or footer as the previous section.
	SWITCH BETWEEN HEADER AND FOOTER	Moves you from the header area to the footer area.
	SHOW PREVIOUS	In a document with different headers and footers, click this button to display the previous header or footer.
	SHOW NEXT	Click to display the next header or footer. (Used with documents with different headers/footers for different pages.)

Deleting a Header or a Footer

If you want to get rid of a header or footer, all you need to do is delete the text.

Follow these steps:

1. Open the `View` menu and select the `Header and Footer` command.
2. If you are deleting a header, skip this step. To delete a footer, click the Switch Between Header and Footer button.
3. Drag across the text and press Delete.
4. Click the Close button.

Changing the Header and Footer Margins

Word prints the headers and footers $1/2$-inch from the top and bottom of the page.

If you want to use different margins, follow these steps:

1. Open the `File` menu and select the `Page Setup` command. You see the Page Setup dialog box.
2. Click the Margins tab.

3. In the Header spin box, enter the amount of margin you want for the top of the page. The header will be printed this distance from the edge. (The top margin controls where text is started on the page.)

4. In the Footer spin box, enter the amount of margin you want for the bottom of the page.

5. Click the OK button.

Fancy Stuff

FEATURE FOCUS Adding the following fancy borders is a new feature in Word 97.

Want to add something fancy to your document? Perhaps you are creating an invitation or just want to liven up an otherwise dull memo. One way to add something interesting to the page is to add a border. The steps you follow are similar to those for adding a border to a paragraph.

Follow these steps:

1. Open the Format menu and select the Borders and Shading command.

2. If necessary, click the Page Border tab. You see the Page Border tab options (see Figure 8-9).

3. In the Setting area, select the type of border you want to add: None, Box, Shadow, 3-D, or Custom.

4. In the Style list, select the line style you want.

5. To change the border color, display the Color drop-down list and then click the color you want.

6. To change the thickness of the line, display the Width drop-down list and select the width you want. (The width is measured in points.) You see a preview of your selections in the Preview area. Skip to step 9 if you want the same border on all sides.

7. When you have the line style, color, and width you want, click in the Preview area on the side where you want to place the border. For example, click the top of the diagram to add the border to the top. Word adds the selected border to that side. Do this for each border you want to add.

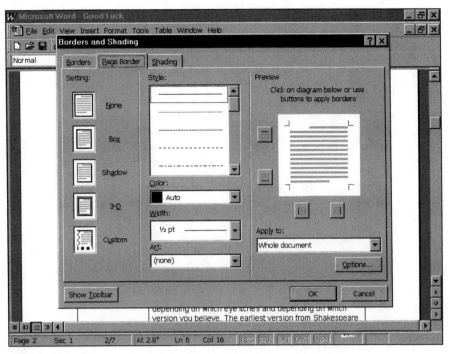

Figure 8-9   Select a page border for your document.

TIP   If you have multiple sections (covered in Chapter 12), you can control where the page border is placed. Display the Apply to drop-down list and select to add the border to all pages (Whole document), the pages in the current section (This section), the first page in this section (This section — First page only), or all pages in this section except the first one (This section — All except first page).

8. Click the OK button to apply the border to all pages in the document.

Make It Colorful

FEATURE FOCUS   Colored backgrounds are a new feature in Word 97.

M any documents are sent via e-mail and read on-screen. If your document will be displayed on-screen rather than printed, you may want to add a colored background. Colored backgrounds also work for documents created for the World Wide Web. (This topic is beyond the scope of this book.)

Follow these steps to add a background:

1. Open the Format menu and select the Background command. You see a submenu of color and fill patterns (see Figure 8-10).

2. Select the color or pattern you want. Word applies this background color or fill to all pages in the document.

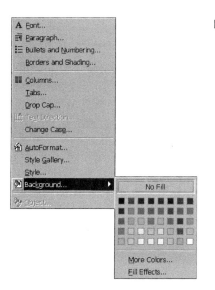

Figure 8-10 Select the color or fill you want to use for the background.

BONUS

Using Different Headers or Footers for Different Pages

I f you use Word to create long documents such as manuals, manuscripts, or really, really involved reports, you may want to vary the headers and footers on each page. For example, take a look at this book. The footer on the right side is different from the one on the left. You get *two* footers instead of just one.

You can do the same in your documents. You can elect to use different headers or footers for the first page of a document, for odd and even pages, or for different sections (if you have broken the document up into sections). Here you will learn how to create different headers and footers for different parts of the document.

X-REF **For information on dividing a document into different sections, see Chapter 12.**

Creating a Different First-Page Header or Footer

Most documents include a title page or some other page that identifies the content. On this opening page, you may not want to include a header or footer. Or you may want to include different information in the header or footer.

You can do either by following these steps:

1. Open the `File` menu and select the `Page Setup` command.

2. Click the Layout tab. You see the Layout tab options (refer to Figure 8-3).

3. Check the Different first page check box.

4. Click the OK button.

5. Go to the first page of the document and select the `View` → `Header and Footer` command. The header area should say First Page Header (see Figure 8-11).

6. Create the header. You can add a footer by clicking the Switch between Header and Footer button and typing the footer.

   If you don't want to include a header or footer on the first page, simply leave it blank.

7. Click the Show Next button. You move to the header or footer for the remaining pages in the document.

8. Create the header or footer for these pages.

9. Click the Close button.

Creating Different Headers and Footers for Odd and Even Pages

As another option, you can create different headers or footers for odd and even pages. For instance, you may want to include the chapter name in the left page header and the section name in the right page header.

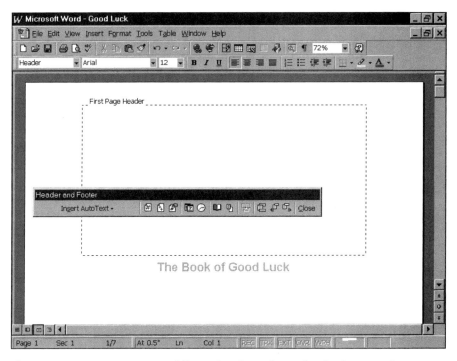

Figure 8-11 You can create a different header or footer for the first page in your document.

Follow these steps to use different headers and footers on odd and even pages:

1. Open the **File** menu and select the **Page Setup** command.

2. Click the Layout tab. You see the Layout tab options (refer to Figure 8-3).

3. In the Headers and Footers area, check the Different odd and even check box.

4. Click the OK button.

5. Go to an odd page of the document and select the **View** → **Header and Footer** command. The header area should say Odd Page Header.

6. Create the header. You can add a footer by clicking the Switch Between Header and Footer button and typing the footer.

7. Click the Show Next button. You move to the header or footer for the even pages in the document.

8. Create the header or footer for these pages.

9. Click the Close button.

Summary

You can spend a lot of time formatting a document. You may wind up tinkering with the formatting on a simple memo for *hours*. (That's one of the downfalls of having so many formatting options. It's *fun* to make your memo look great.) The next chapter covers some formatting shortcuts you can use to save time.

IN THIS CHAPTER YOU LEARN THESE KEY SKILLS

When you format a document, you may find yourself selecting the same commands over and over. For example, you may give your section headings a new font, change them to boldface, and decorate them with a border. If your document had ten section heads, you'd select thirty commands (three commands, ten times). Ugh!

Are you thinking there's got to be a better way? There is. You can use some of the formatting shortcuts in this chapter. For one or two changes, you may simply want to copy the formatting. For several text selections, you will want to investigate Word's Style command. This chapter covers both methods.

I Like It This Way

As you tinker with your text selection (a word, a sentence, a paragraph, a line, whatever), you may try an option, view the results, make some additional changes, and so on, until — ta da! — the text looks just the way you want. Now what do you do when you want to use that same set of formatting options on another line or paragraph. Start over?

If you want to use these same formatting options just one or two other places in the document, you can copy the formatting. If you plan on using them more than once or twice, create a style, as covered in the next section. Styles offer several advantages over simply copying the formatting.

To copy formatting, follow these steps:

1. Select the text (word, sentence, paragraph) that is formatted as you want it.

2. Click ![icon]. Notice that the mouse pointer looks like an insertion point with a paintbrush (see Figure 9-1).

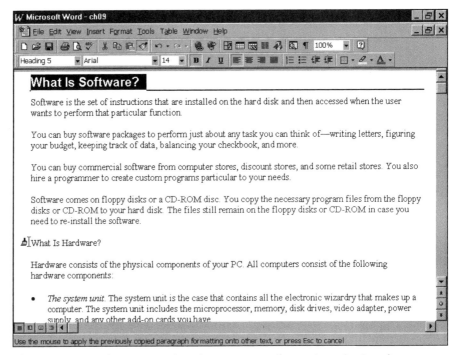

Figure 9-1   Use the Format Painter button to copy formatting selections from one piece of text to another.

3. Select the text to which you want to copy the formatting. Word applies the formatting. In Figure 9-2 the formatting for the section heading "What Is Software?" is copied to the section heading "What Is Hardware?"

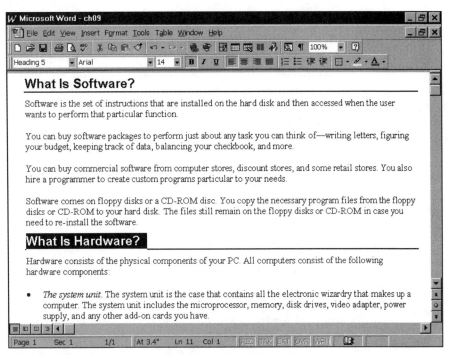

Figure 9-2 The formatting for the first heading is copied to the second heading.

For the Truly Fashionable

I f you want to use the same set of formatting options more than once or twice, you're better off creating a style. A style is a collection of character (font, size, style, color, and so on) and paragraph (alignment, indents, borders, and so on) formatting. You can apply the style to other text, and Word applies all the associated formatting options.

If you want to use the same set of formatting options more than once or twice, you should create a style.

Styles offer a lot of benefits:

* Styles save time. Rather than select the same set of commands to make the formatting changes over and over, you can create a style and then apply that style with one command.

* If you use styles, you are assured your document is formatted consistently. You don't have to worry about which font size or border to use for the headings. You simply select the heading style, and Word applies all the formatting options for you.

* If you decide to modify a style, Word automatically updates all the paragraphs tagged with that style. For example, suppose that you decide the Woodstock font is a little much for the headings in your business report. If you formatted the document manually, you'd have to go through and modify each heading. If you used a style for the headings, you modify the style once, and Word updates all paragraphs formatted with that style.

You can create styles for any type of document element you include — headings, subheadings, notes, captions, headers, footers, sidebars, and so on — and you aren't limited to the style types mentioned in the chapter. If you find yourself using the same formatting options over and over in a document, create a style.

Styles without Trying

Word's AutoFormat feature automatically makes some style changes for you as you type. For instance, if you type an asterisk, press Tab, and type some text, Word will automatically create a bulleted list. If you manually format a heading in a document, Word will create a style based on the formatting you applied. You may wonder how these changes happened. It's magic! It's AutoFormat.

To get an idea of what types of changes are made, you can check out the AutoFormat As You Type tab in the AutoCorrect dialog box. You can also turn off features you don't want to use (and turn on additional features).

To review the AutoFormat changes, follow these steps:

1. Open the **Format** menu and select the **AutoFormat** command. You see the AutoFormat dialog box.

2. Click the Options button. You see the AutoFormat tab of the AutoCorrect dialog box.

3. Click the AutoFormat As You Type tab. You see the options shown in Figure 9-3.

4. If you want to turn off an option, uncheck its check box. To turn on an option, check its check box.

 TIP Not sure what an option does? Right-click the option and select the What's This? command. Review the pop-up explanation.

5. When you are finished reviewing the options and making changes, click the OK button.

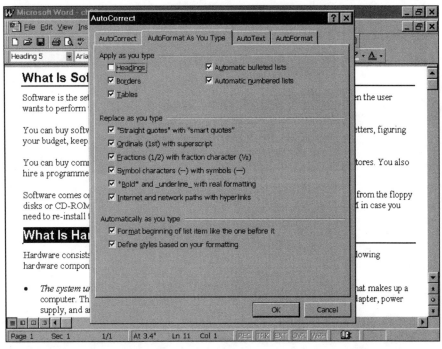

Figure 9-3 Use this dialog box to review the formatting changes Word makes automatically.

Trying Out Sample Styles

Word provides some predefined styles that you can use without going to the trouble of creating your own. Trying these styles is a good way to see how styles work. You can practice applying styles and also see what types of formatting options a style can include.

The styles that are available depend on the *template* you are using. You select the template when you choose the File → New command. For the most part, you will use the Normal template. (Templates are covered in more detail in Chapter 13.)

You can display the available styles by clicking the down arrow next to the Style drop-down list. Not only do you see the names of the styles, but you also get an idea of what each style looks like (see Figure 9-4).

To use one of these styles, select the text you want to format, display the Style drop-down list, and then select the style you want. You can find out more about applying styles in the section "Applying Styles."

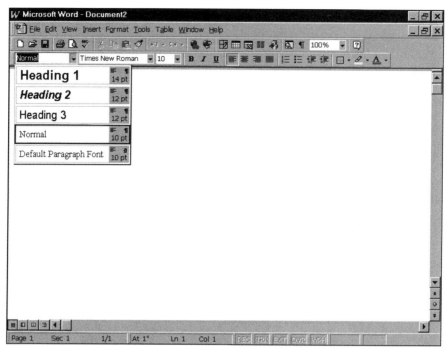

Figure 9-4   Check out the styles included in the template by displaying the Style drop-down list.

Trying Styles from Other Templates

You can also view and try the styles from other templates without actually starting with that template. (Again, templates are covered in Chapter 13.) Each template has its own set of styles, and each style can vary from template to template. For instance, the Heading 1 style in one template may look different from the Heading 1 style in another template.

You can switch to another set of styles from another template by using the Style Gallery.

Follow these steps:

1. Select Format → Style Gallery. You see the Style Gallery dialog box (see Figure 9-5).

2. Click the template you want to try in the Template list. The preview will show you how the document will look using the styles in the selected template. You can also try other previews.

3. To see an example of this template, click the Example option button. To see samples of the various styles, click the Style samples button. Figure 9-6 shows the style samples from the Professional Fax template.

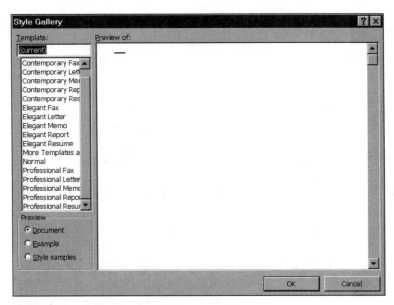

Figure 9-5 Select the template you want to see.

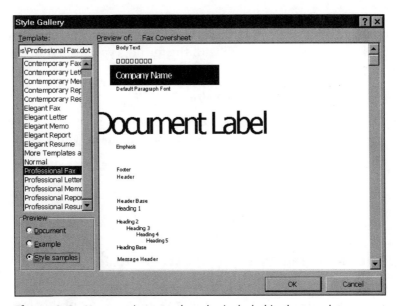

Figure 9-6 You can view sample styles included in the template.

4. To copy these styles — make them available in your document — click the OK button. To close the dialog box without copying the styles, click the Cancel button.

If you click the OK button, Word copies the new styles from this template to the on-screen document and template. You can then use any of these styles to format your text.

When you use the Style Gallery command to add styles to the document, you do not change the template that is attached. The styles are simply added to the document. If you want to use a different template, see Chapter 13.

Express Yourself

I f the predefined styles work OK for you, great! You don't need to worry about creating other styles. You may not be the picky type. On the other hand . . .

If you don't like the predefined styles or if you want to add additional styles, you can do so. You can use one of two methods to create a new style. You can create one by example or from scratch. Both methods are described in this section.

Creating a New Style by Example

You aren't limited to the predefined styles. You can also create your own styles, with the formatting options that you want to use. The easiest way to create a style is to format a paragraph with the formats you want and base the new style on this paragraph.

Follow these steps to create a new style:

1. Format the text and/or paragraph with the options you want. You can use any formatting features on the toolbar or within the **Format** menu.

2. Click in the Style list box and highlight the current name.

3. Type a new name and press Enter. Word creates the style based on the selected paragraph.

Creating a New Style from Scratch

The benefit of creating a style by example is that you can see the results of the commands. You can check that the style is as you want it before you create the style. You can also create a new style from scratch by entering a name and then selecting the formatting features you want. You can get an idea of how your selections affect the text by looking at the Paragraph preview and Character preview areas in the dialog box. You can also set other style options (covered in the Side Trip) when you use this method.

Follow these steps to create a style from scratch:

1. Open the `Format` menu and select the `Style` command. You see the Style dialog box (see Figure 9-7). This dialog box lists all styles currently in use in the document. You also see buttons for modifying an existing style and for creating a new style.

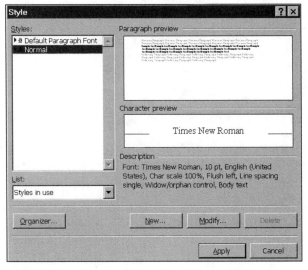

Figure 9-7 Click the New button to start building a new style.

2. Click the New button. You see the New Style dialog box, shown in Figure 9-8. Here you can enter a name for the style and use the Format button to build the style.

3. In the Name text box, type a name for the style. Use a name that will remind you of the purpose of the style.

4. Click the Format button and select the appropriate format command: Font, Paragraph, Tabs, Border, Language, Frame, and Numbering. You see the appropriate dialog box. For example, if you select the Font command, you see the Font dialog box.

5. Make the appropriate choices from the dialog boxes that appear. You can get information on these commands in Chapters 6 and 7.

6. Follow steps 4 and 5 for each formatting option you want to add to the style. For example, you can use the Font command to select a font, size, and style. Then you can also add a border using the Border command. To add space below the paragraph, use the Paragraph command.

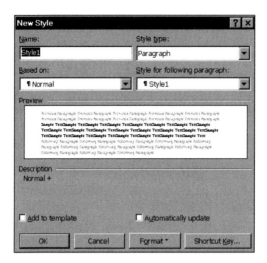

Figure 9-8 Name the style and then select the formatting options you want to include.

7. When you have selected all the formats you want, click the OK button. You see the Style dialog box again, with a preview of the style. You can also read the Description to see a list of the formatting options in effect.

8. To apply the new style to the selected paragraph, click the Apply button. To close the dialog box without applying the style, click the Close button.

Makeover City

Y ou only have to create a style once. Then you can apply it to any text in the document. The styles will also be available in other documents you create that are based on the same template.

The fastest way to apply a style is to use the Style drop-down list. You can also use the menu command. This method works best when you want to see both the Character and Paragraph previews as well as a detailed description of the style.

Selecting a Style with the Style Drop-Down List

To apply a style from the toolbar, follow these steps:

1. Select the paragraph(s) or text you want to format. If you are formatting a single paragraph, you can just place the insertion point within the paragraph. To format several paragraphs, select them. If you are applying a character style, select the text you want to format.

2. Click the down arrow next to the Style list. Word displays a list of available styles (see Figure 9-9).

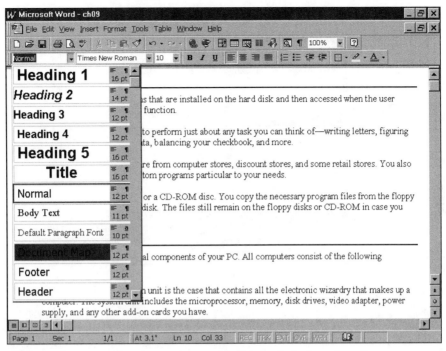

Figure 9-9 New styles you create are added to the Style drop-down list.

3. Click the style you want. Word applies the style to the selected paragraph(s).

Selecting Styles with the Style Command

In previous versions of Word, you saw only the name in the Style drop-down list, so it was hard to tell how the paragraph would look when formatted. Word 97 shows text using the listed style, so you get an idea of how the text will appear when formatted. You don't, however, get an exact sense of how the paragraph is aligned (centered, right-aligned, indented, and so on.)

If you want a more detailed description and want to see both paragraph and character previews, use the following method to apply a style:

1. Select the paragraph(s) you want to format.

2. Select `Format` → `Style`. You see the Style dialog box (see Figure 9-10).

3. Click the style you want in the Styles list. When you select a style, you see a preview in the Character preview and the Paragraph preview. Check these areas to see whether you like the style.

4. Click the Apply button. Word applies the style and closes the dialog box.

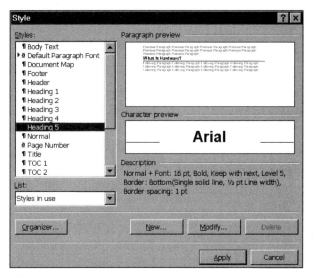

Figure 9-10 Select the style you want to use.

 If the style is not listed, click the down arrow next to the List drop-down list. Then select which styles you want listed: all styles, styles in use, or user-defined styles.

 You can apply some of Word's predefined styles with shortcut keys:

Ctrl+Shift+N	Normal style
Alt+Ctrl+1	Heading 1
Alt+Ctrl+2	Heading 2
Alt+Ctrl+3	Heading 3

No, I Like It That Way

As mentioned, one of the benefits of using a style is how simple it is to make a change and update all the paragraphs formatted in that style. Maybe you decide you don't want a border underneath your headings. Or maybe your boss decides that all report headings should be in italics. Whatever the reason, you simply update the style, and Word updates the document.

To modify a style, follow these steps:

1. Open the Format menu and select the Style command. You see the Style dialog box.

2. Click the <u>M</u>odify button. You see the Modify Style dialog box, which is similar to the New Style dialog box but some options are not available. You can change neither the style which your style is based on nor the style type (see Figure 9-11).

Figure 9-11 Modify the style using the options in this dialog box.

3. Click the F<u>o</u>rmat button and select the type of formatting you want to change: <u>F</u>ont, <u>P</u>aragraph, <u>T</u>abs, <u>B</u>order, <u>L</u>anguage, Fra<u>m</u>e, or <u>N</u>umbering. (Only some options are available for character styles.) Word displays the appropriate dialog box. For instance, if you select <u>F</u>ont you see the Font dialog box.

4. Make the selections you want and click the OK button.

5. Follow steps 3 and 4 for each change you want to make.

6. When you are finished making changes, click OK to return to the Style dialog box.

7. To apply the new style to the selected paragraph, click the <u>A</u>pply button. To close the dialog box without applying the style, click the Close button.

Don't Like It at All

If you have styles that you don't use, you can delete them. All paragraphs formatted with the deleted style will be formatted with the Normal style.

Follow these steps to delete a style:

1. Open the | **Format** | menu and select the | **Style** | command. You see the Style dialog box.

2. Click the style you want to delete.

3. Click the <u>D</u>elete button. You are prompted to confirm the deletion.

4. Click the <u>Y</u>es button. Word deletes the style and reformats paragraphs with that style.

BONUS

Using AutoFormat

Another timesaving formatting feature is AutoFormat. I've covered it here in the Bonus section because I don't find the changes it makes useful. AutoFormat searches through the document and makes style recommendations based on the document type (general, letter, fax). For instance, if Word finds what it thinks is a title, it suggests adding the title style. The same is true for headings, bulleted lists, and numbered lists in your document. Word also replaces certain characters — "1st" with "1st," "1/2" with "$^1/_2$," and so on.

You can use AutoFormat to format the entire document. Most of the changes are made as you type. You can choose to accept or reject all of the changes, or you can go through each change and accept or reject it.

To me, it is just as time consuming to go through these changes as it is to make them myself. Still, AutoFormat may be more useful to you and more pertinent to the documents you create.

To use AutoFormat to format your document, follow these steps:

1. Open the **Format** menu and select the **Auto Format** command. You see the AutoFormat dialog box (see Figure 9-12).

Figure 9-12 Select whether you want to review or go ahead and make changes.

2. Select how you want AutoFormat to work. If you want to go ahead and make all of the changes without being prompted, select AutoFormat now. Follow steps 3 and 4 and skip the rest.

   To review and accept or reject each change, select AutoFormat and review each change. Follow all the remaining steps.

3. Select the document type from the drop-down list. You can select General document, letter, or e-mail message.

4. Click the OK button. Word formats the document and displays another AutoFormat dialog box.

5. To accept all changes, click the <u>A</u>ccept All button. To reject all changes, click the <u>R</u>eject All button. To review the changes, click the Review <u>C</u>hanges button.

6. If you accept the changes, the dialog box is closed, and your document is reformatted with the selected formats. Skip the rest of the steps.

7. If you reject the changes, the dialog box is closed, and your document is unchanged. Skip the rest of the steps.

8. If you selected to review the changes, you see the Review AutoFormat Changes dialog box. Word displays in red and strikes through any text recommended for deletion. New text appears in blue and is underlined. Paragraph marks may appear in blue when a new format is suggested for that paragraph. You also see a description of the change.

9. Move to each change using the <u>F</u>ind Next or F<u>i</u>nd Previous button. To accept a change, just move on to the next change. To reject a change, click the Reject button. To undo the last change, click the <u>U</u>ndo button.

10. When you are finished, click the Cancel button. You see the Review AutoFormat Changes dialog box.

11. Click the <u>A</u>ccept All button to accept the formatting. Word makes the accepted changes.

Summary

This chapter covered some shortcuts you can use to format your document: copying formatting, styles, and AutoFormat. These features are especially important if you create a lot of desktop-published documents. You can save a lot of time by using styles.

The next chapter covers another nifty Word feature — tables. If you need to include any kind of columnar list, use a table. You will be impressed with the features for setting up and formatting a table.

WORKING WITH TABLES

Forget the old-fashioned method of creating a table — setting up tabs, typing a few words, pressing Enter, typing the next line, and hoping that when you get to the end the table is somewhat aligned. If you have to add or delete something, even the "somewhat" alignment goes out the window.

Word makes creating a table much easier. You select the number of columns and rows you want, and Word creates the table. You type your entry within each little cubbyhole (called a *cell*) in the table. You can enter a single word, a line, a paragraph, or several paragraphs in the cell, and Word keeps the text aligned.

This chapter not only covers how to set up a table but also explains some of the editing and formatting changes you can make. You'll probably never press Tab again once you see how cool tables are.

Document for Two

As you might have guessed, you can set up a table using one of several methods. The simplest way to create a table is to use the Insert Table button. This method works when you want a table with equal column widths using the default border (a thin line).

You can also draw a table, drawing the outside border and then each column and row. Use this method to set up a table with different row and column sizes. You can also easily select a different table border.

Which method is best? Take a look at the two tables in Figure 10-1. The first table shows what you get when you use the Insert Table button. You can change how this table looks, as covered in the section "Add Some Spice," but this is the starting point. The second table demonstrates what you can do when you draw a table. With this method, you basically do the formatting as you create the table. As for which one is the best, you can select whichever method appeals to you.

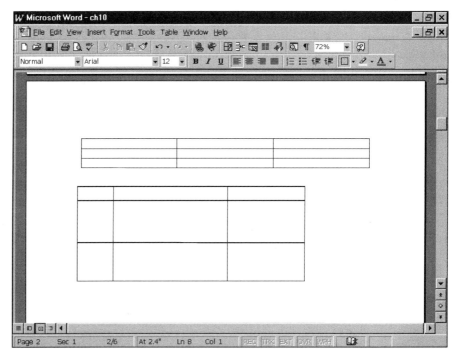

Figure 10-1 You can create a table using the default style or draw one in the style and size you want.

Creating a Simple Table

Follow these steps to set up a simple, default-styled table:

1. Click ▦. You see a drop-down palette of cells (see Figure 10-2).

2. Drag across the number of columns and rows you want to include. For example, to create a table with three columns and two rows, drag across three columns and down two rows. Word displays the dimensions at the bottom of the palette.

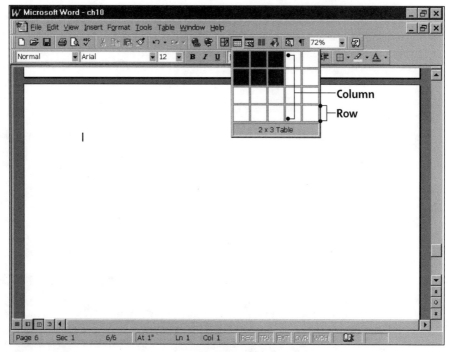

Figure 10-2 From this palette of rows and columns, drag across the number of rows and columns you want to include in your table.

3. Release the mouse button. Word displays the table, a grid of columns and rows (refer to the first table in Figure 10-1). By default, each cell includes a border. You can change the look of this border or delete it, as covered later in this chapter.

Drawing a Table

FEATURE FOCUS Drawing tables is a new feature in Word 97.

If you are more of a visual sort, you can draw a table in your document.

Follow these steps:

1. Click [⊞]. You see the Tables and Borders toolbar (see Figure 10-3).

2. Display the Line Style drop-down list and select the style of border you want to use for the table.

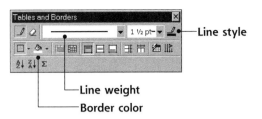

Figure 10-3 Use this toolbar to select a border and draw the table.

Line style

Line weight

Border color

3. Display the Line Weight drop-down list and select the thickness of the line. You can also display the Border Color drop-down palette and select a different color.

4. Move the insertion point into the document area. Notice that it looks like a pencil.

5. Click and drag to draw the outside border of the table (see Figure 10-4).

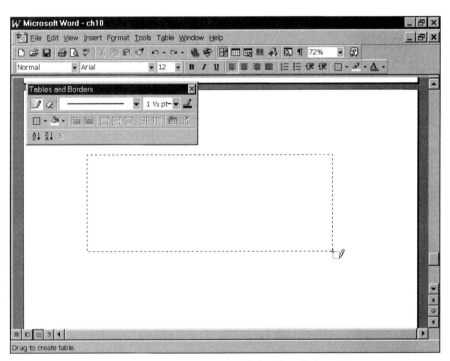

Figure 10-4 Use the pencil to draw the outside border of the table.

6. Draw each column and row you want to add. You can draw columns down the table and rows across. You can make them any size you want. Word uses the selected line style, width, and color displayed in the toolbar. You can use a different line by selecting the options you want before you draw the line.

Word draws the table on-screen. Figure 10-1, shown previously in the chapter, shows an example of a table created with this method.

The Meat of the Table

No matter how you create your table, you follow the same method for entering text in the table. Basically, the table is a grid of columns and rows, and the intersection of a row and a column is a *cell*. Word places the insertion point in the first cell in the table.

To type something in the table, move to the cell you want and type. You can click in the cell or use the arrow keys to move to the cell you want. You can also press Tab to move forward through the cells or Shift+Tab to move backward through the cells.

You can type any amount of text you want. If you type a long entry, you don't have to worry about pressing Enter to keep the text within the cell. When you reach the cell border, Word will wrap the text to the next line and expand the cell downward. You can press Enter if you want to create a new paragraph within the cell. Figure 10-5 shows a table with entries in the first row. Notice how the text in the second column wraps within the cell.

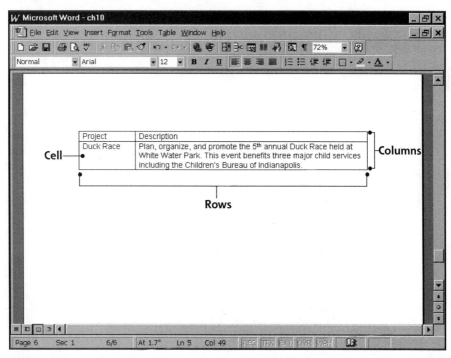

Figure 10-5 If the entry is longer than the cell, Word wraps the text automatically.

You can use any of the editing and formatting features you learned in the preceding chapters. For instance, you can make the headings bold, use Cut or Copy to rearrange table entries, shade cells, and so on. Each cell is a paragraph, so you can also use paragraph formatting options, such as setting tabs, indenting text, or changing the alignment.

In a table, you can use any of the editing and formatting features you learned in the preceding chapters.

Picking the Parts

As when formatting or editing text, you often need to select part of a table — a cell, a column, a row — even the entire table. For example, to delete a row, you first select it. To add a column, you begin by selecting the column next to where you want the new one to appear. The following checklist explains how to select different table elements:

* To select text within a table, drag across the text as you would in a normal document.

* To select a row, put the insertion point within the row and then select the Table → Select Row command. Or click within the left margin area in front of the row you want to select.

* To select a column, put the insertion point within the column and then select the Table → Select Column command. Alternatively, move the pointer just above the column. When the pointer looks like a downward arrow, click the button to select the entire column.

* To select the entire table, put the insertion point within the table and then select the Table → Select Table command or press Alt+Num 5.

Don't see these commands? If most of the commands in the Table menu are dimmed, it probably means your insertion point is not within the table. The commands are available only when the insertion point is within the table. Put the insertion point somewhere in the table and try again.

Oops! Forgot Something

It's sometimes hard to tell how many rows and columns you need for your table. You might need to add a row or even a column. If you'd set up tabs, you'd be stuck with your original format. If you've set up a table using either method described, you can easily add rows or columns, as described in this section.

Adding a Row to a Table

You don't need to worry about guessing the number of rows exactly because it is easy to add a row. The simplest way to add a row is to press Tab in the last row and last column of the table. Word adds a new row.

You can also add a row between two existing rows.

To do so, follow these steps:

1. Put the cursor in the row that is below where you want your new row .

2. Open the `Table` menu and select the `Insert Rows` command. Word inserts the new row.

TIP **Don't worry about getting the rows into a particular order. You can always sort the rows, as covered in the Bonus section of this chapter. You can also sort by any of the columns.**

If the Tables and Borders toolbar button is displayed, you can also use this to draw a new row. To do so, select the line style you want and then draw the new row within the table.

Inserting a Column

Most of the time the rows include the data in a table, and the columns are the categories. Kind of like a minispreadsheet or database. For instance, you might have a price table with columns for the product and price. You might then decide to add another column for the product description.

You can easily add columns to your table by following these steps:

1. Select a column using the `Table` → `Select Column` command. The new column will be inserted to the left of this column. Figure 10-6 shows a selected column.

CAUTION **Be sure to select the column. You can't just put your insertion point within the column. You must use the command to select the entire column.**

2. Open the `Table` menu and select the `Insert Columns` command. (If you don't see this command, you didn't select the entire column.) Word inserts a new column (see Figure 10-7).

You can also draw a new column within the table. To do so, be sure the Tables and Borders toolbar is displayed. (If it is not, click the Tables and Borders button.) Then draw the line where you want to add the new column. You can only add new columns within the current table outline — not at the end or outside of the table.

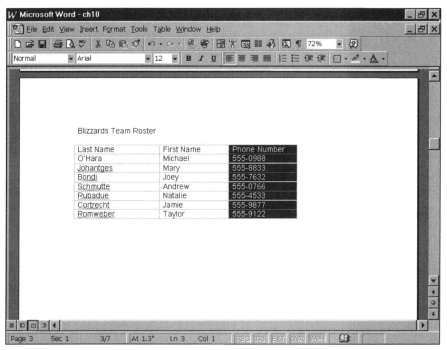

Figure 10-6 To insert a column, start by selecting a column.

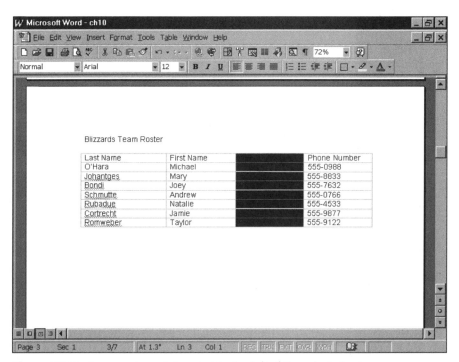

Figure 10-7 A new column is inserted to the left of the selected column.

Get Outta Here

Just as you can add rows and columns, you can also delete them. But when you delete a row or column that contains data, you also delete all the entries. In addition to covering how to delete rows and columns, this section tells you how to delete the entire table. (You can't just select it and press Delete. Doing so deletes the data but leaves the table skeleton.)

Deleting a Row

If you have rows that you no longer want to include, you can delete them. Remember that, if a row contains data, you also delete all the entries in that row.

Follow these steps to delete a row:

1. Select the row you want to delete using the Table → Select Row command. If you just put the insertion point in the row, you can delete only the cell, not the entire row. Be sure to highlight the entire row. Figure 10-8 shows a row selected for deletion.

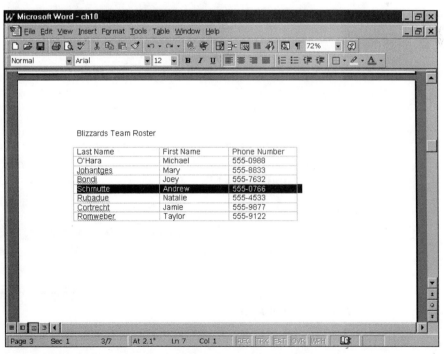

Figure 10-8   Select the row you want to remove.

2. Open the Table menu and select the Delete Rows command. The row (along with any data in the row) is deleted (see Figure 10-9).

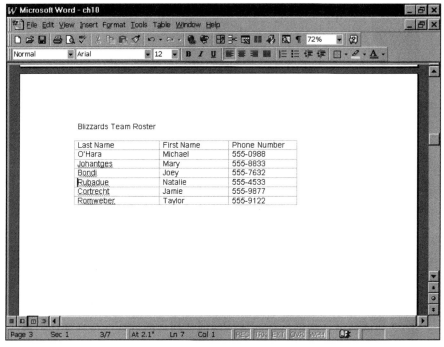

Figure 10-9　The row (including its data) is removed from the table.

TIP　If you want to keep the row but simply clear its contents, select the row by dragging across it. Then press the Delete key.

Deleting a Column

If there's a column that's empty or that just includes text you don't need anymore, you can delete it. If you delete a column that contains text, you delete both the column and the text.

Follow these steps:

1. Select the column you want to delete using the `Table` → `Select Column` command. You can't just put the insertion point within the column; you must select the entire column.

2. Open the `Table` menu and select the `Delete Columns` command. Word deletes the column.

Deleting the Entire Table

Deleting a table is tricky. You might think that you just drag across it and press Delete. This deletes all the entries in the table but leaves the table structure. Arg! How do you get rid of the entries and the table?

Do so by following these steps:

1. Select the table using the `Table` → `Select Table` command.

2. Open the `Table` menu and select the `Delete Rows` command. Word deletes the entire table.

Add Some Spice

YOu have a lot of control over how the table looks. One common change is to resize the columns. When you create a table, it's unlikely that data items in each column will occupy the same amounts of space. Some columns may contain just a word or two. Some may contain longer entries. To balance out the table, you can adjust column widths.

You may also want to use different borders for the table. And you can change the alignment of the text within a cell. You can make these changes and more, as covered in this section.

Fatter! Skinnier! Changing the Column Width

When you create a table using the Insert Table button, Word bases the column width on the size of the page margins and the number of columns you have. Each column is the same size. You can adjust the column width if necessary.

Follow these steps:

1. Place the mouse pointer on the right border of the column you want to change. The pointer should look like two vertical lines with arrows on either side (see Figure 10-10).

2. Drag the border to resize the column width. Drag to the left to make the column smaller. Drag to the right to make the column wider.

Note: You can also use the Table → Cell Height and Width command to set the column width. Use this method when you want to enter precise measurements for each column.

Make Them All the Same Size

Another size option is to have Word make selected rows or columns the same size.

To make this change, follow these steps:

1. Select the rows or columns you want to resize. To resize all rows or columns in the table, select the entire table.

2. To make all columns even, click the Distribute Columns Evenly button in the Tables and Borders toolbar or open the Table menu and select the Distribute Columns Evenly command. Figure 10-11 shows two versions of the same table. The columns in the second table have been distributed evenly.

To make all rows even, click the Distribute Rows Evenly button in the Tables and Borders toolbar or open the Table menu and select the Distribute Rows Evenly command.

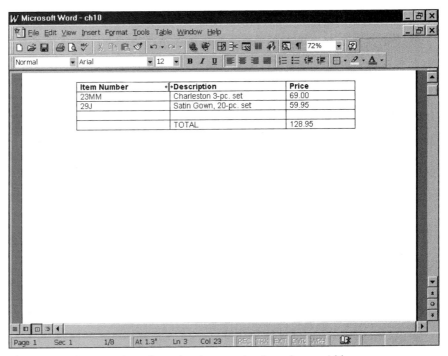

Figure 10-10 Drag the column border to resize the column width.

Lazy-Man Formatting

You can take the time to format a table — aligning the headings, adding borders, possibly shading certain rows or columns — before you take the long route, try the short one. Word provides several predefined table formats. You can use these formats to quickly create a professional-looking table. If none of these work, you can then use the manual method, as covered in the next section.

To try one of the AutoFormats for a table, follow these steps:

1. Click in any cell in the table. To access table commands, your insertion point must be within the table.

2. Open the [Table] menu and select the [Table AutoFormat] command. You see the Table AutoFormat dialog box, shown in Figure 10-12.

3. In the Formats list, click the format you want to use. You see a preview of a sample table formatted with this style.

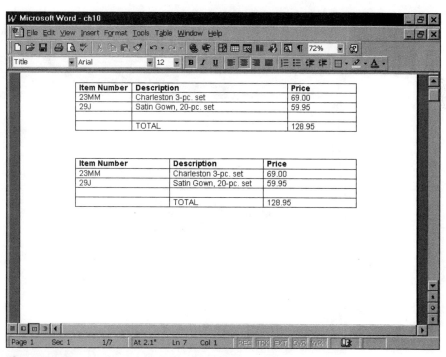

Figure 10-11   You can make selected rows or columns the same size.

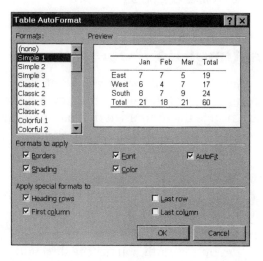

Figure 10-12   Select an AutoFormat for the table.

4. If you want to use some but not all of the format options, uncheck the options you don't want in the Formats to apply area: Borders, Shading, Font, Color, or AutoFit.

5. Check which rows and columns you want specially formatted: Heading rows, First column, Last row, or Last column.

6. Click the OK button. Word formats the table with the selected AutoFormat. Figure 10-13 shows a table formatted with the Contemporary format.

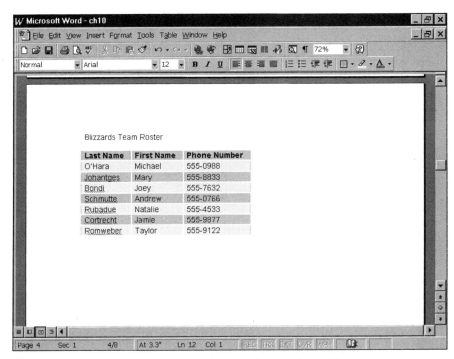

Figure 10-13 Use AutoFormat to apply several formatting options at once.

Hard-Work Formatting: Do It Yourself

If the AutoFormats don't give you exactly what you want, you can also format the table yourself. You can use any of the formatting toolbar buttons and commands to make text bold, change the font, use a different alignment, and so on. The Tables and Borders toolbar also includes some buttons for formatting the table. You can do any of the following:

* To change how the text is aligned vertically (top to bottom), click the Align Top, Center Vertically, or Align Bottom buttons. Figure 10-14 shows examples of each of these alignments.

* To change how the text reads in a cell (across, down, up), click the Change Text Direction button until you get the direction you want. Figure 10-15 shows examples of different text orientations in the cell.

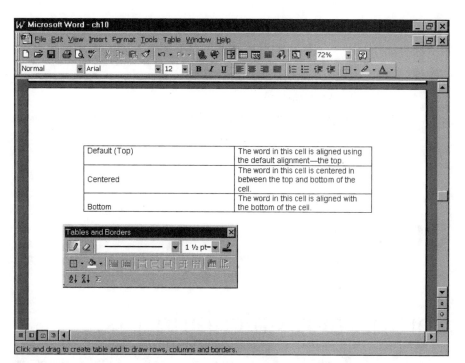

Figure 10-14 You can select different vertical alignments for the table entries.

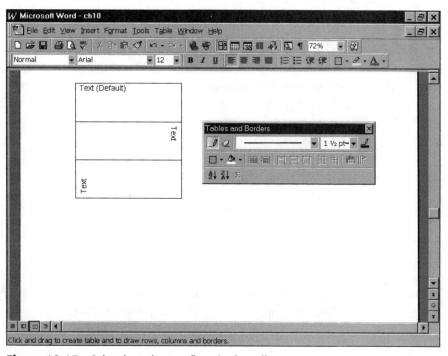

Figure 10-15 Select how the text flows in the cell.

- To use a different line style, thickness, or color, select the style, thickness, and color you want using the Line Style, Line Weight, and Border Color drop-down lists. Then use the pencil to draw across the border you want to change. You can also select where the line appears by using the Outside Border button.

- To apply shading to a cell, a row, or a column, select what you want to shade. Then click the Shading Color button and select the color or pattern you want.

BONUS

Sorting and Calculating

W ord includes several other handy table features, including sorting table entries (or just plain paragraphs) and automatically adding up all the entries in a column. You can use these shortcuts to save time when creating a table.

A to Z: Sorting Text

If you need to keep the table entries in a certain order, don't worry about typing them in order. Type them any way you like and then sort the list. You can use this feature to sort table entries or ordinary text paragraphs. The text does not have to be within a table, even though the placement of the Sort Text command may lead you to think so.

Follow these steps to sort text or a table.

1. To sort text, select the text you want to sort.

   To sort a table, put the insertion point someplace within the table.

2. Open the Table menu and select the Sort Text command. You see the Sort dialog box. If you've selected text, Paragraph is selected as the Sort by option. If you are sorting a table, the Sort by list displays the first column in your table, as shown in Figure 10-16.

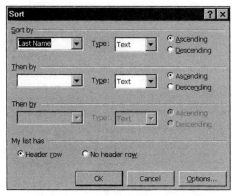

Figure 10-16 Select how to sort the text or table.

* If a table includes headings, you don't want to sort these items. Word can usually tell when you have a header row. If you don't have a header row, change the No header row option.

* Word also reviews the selected text and selects an appropriate type: Text, Date, or Numbers.

3. Click the sort order you want: Ascending or Descending.

4. If you are sorting more than one column in the table, display the Then by drop-down list and select the next field you want to sort. You can also use the next Then by list to select another sort field.

5. Click the OK button. Word sorts the selected text or table.

Calculating a Total

Many times a table includes numeric entries, and you may want to calculate a simple total. You can do so quickly by using the AutoSum button.

Follow these steps:

1. Click where you want the total to appear.

2. In the Table and Borders toolbar, click the AutoSum button. Word totals all the numeric entries in that column and displays the total (see Figure 10-17).

If you change any of the entries included in the total, you can recalculate the total. Select the total (which is really a field). Then press F9. The total is recalculated.

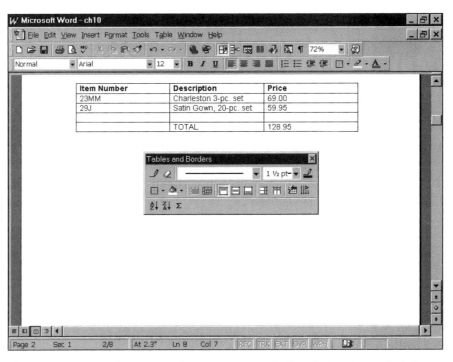

Figure 10-17 Use the AutoSum button to automatically calculate the total of all entries in a column.

X-REF   If you have a lot of numeric entries to include and you have Excel, consider inserting a worksheet in the document instead of a table. You can find information on inserting worksheets in Chapter 15.

Summary

This chapter explained how you can use tables to more easily include a list of entries in your document. You learned not only how to set up a table, but also how to make editing and formatting changes. The next chapter covers another special type of element you might include in a document: graphics. You learn how to insert special characters, drawings, and clip art into your document.

CHAPTER ELEVEN

ADDING GRAPHICS

IN THIS CHAPTER YOU LEARN THESE KEY SKILLS:

Have you ever gotten a memo from someone about, say, your (401)k plan and it's decorated with little cats everywhere? Or maybe you get a newsletter with each little article illustrated with some kind of clip art image — even if that image has nothing to do with the article. You're reading about the annual fund drive, and there's a picture of a mouse driving a car next to the article. Clip art makes it easy to add images to your document, and you probably remember all the *bad* examples of pictures in a document.

But you have better sense than that, don't you? You know that a well-placed graphic can enhance a document. You know that by reading this chapter you'll learn all the ways you can add images to your document. Read on, then.

Symbols (#$!)

As mentioned in Chapter 6, some fonts are actually collections of symbols. For instance, the Symbol font is — guess what — a font full of different symbols. Another popular symbol font is Wingdings. You can use these or any other symbol font you have on your system to insert special characters into your document. You can insert a trademark symbol ™, a copyright symbol ©, a club ♣, an arrow ←, and more.

Inserting a Symbol

To insert a trademark, a Greek letter, a mathematical device, an arrow, or any other special symbol in your document, follow these steps:

1. Open the `Insert` menu and select the `Symbol` command.

2. If necessary, click the Symbols tab. You see the Symbol dialog box, which lists all the symbols in the Symbol font (see Figure 11-1).

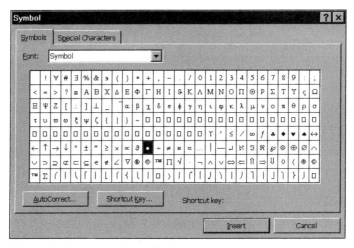

Figure 11-1   Select the symbol you want to insert.

3. To display the symbols in another symbol font, display the Font drop-down list and select the font you want.

4. Click the symbol you want to insert. Word shows a bigger picture of the symbol.

5. Click the Insert button. Word inserts the symbol in your document.

6. Click the Close button to close the dialog box.

To delete the symbol, select Edit → Undo immediately. Or delete it as you would any other character: press Backspace or Delete.

Inserting a Special Character

You can insert special characters, including typographical characters such as em dashes, en dashes, or ellipses with the special characters tab. You can also insert some symbols, such as trademark and copyright symbols.

To insert a special character, follow these steps:

1. Open the `Insert` menu and select the `Symbol` command.

2. If necessary, click the Special Characters tab. Word displays a list of special characters, along with the associated shortcut keys (see Figure 11-2).

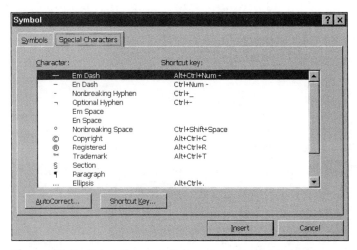

Figure 11-2   Select the special character you want to insert.

TIP   **Some special characters are inserted automatically with AutoCorrect. For instance, if you type two dashes (--), Word automatically replaces them with an em dash (—). Some characters have shortcut keys assigned. You can press the shortcut key to insert the special character.**

3. Click the character that you want to insert.

4. Click the Insert button.

5. Click the Close button. Word inserts the special character in the document.

A Picture Is Worth . . .

Special characters can enhance the text of a document, but when you want something a little more substantial, you can insert a picture. Word enables you to insert several types of pictures. You can use one of the many clip art images provided with Word. (A *clip art* image is a canned drawing that anyone can use.) If you have other clip art images or picture files (such as bitmap or PCX files), you can insert them. You can also insert an AutoShape, such as a circle, a smiley face, or a lightning bolt. These types of pictures are for all the nonartists (like me!) out there.

If you are more artistic, you can use some simple drawing tools provided with Word to create your own drawing. This topic is covered later in this chapter.

Inserting a Clip Art Image

Maybe you're like me — I can draw a pretty good stick figure, but that's about it. If I include any sort of artwork in my document, I can guarantee it isn't something I drew myself. I prefer the predrawn clip art images to dress up my documents. Word includes quite a nice collection of images in several categories, including animals, buildings, electronics, flags, food, maps, nature, people, plants, signs, sports, travel, and more.

To use one of these images, follow these steps:

1. Place the insertion point where you want the picture. You can always move the picture around if necessary, but at least start in the general area.

2. Open the Insert menu and select the Picture command. From the submenu that appears, select Clip Art. You see the Microsoft Clip Gallery.

3. In the category list, click the category you want to view. Word displays the images in that category in the middle of the dialog box. Figure 11-3 shows the clip art images for the Places category.

Figure 11-3   Select the category you want to view, then select the image you want to insert.

4. Click the image you want to insert.

5. Click the Insert button. Word inserts the image in the document. It is sized to its "ideal" size, but you can also change the size.

Inserting Your Own Pictures

In addition to inserting the clip art images that come with Word, you can insert other images that you may have. You can insert any type of image file you may have available, such as TIFF files, PCX files, and BMP files. For instance, you can purchase additional clip art packages, or you can scan in photos or other illustrations.

To insert a picture from a file that you have, follow these steps:

1. Place the insertion point where you want the picture.

2. Open the **Insert** menu and select the **Picture** command. From the submenu that appears, select **From File**. You see the Insert Picture dialog box (see Figure 11-4). This dialog box lists the available picture files in the current folder.

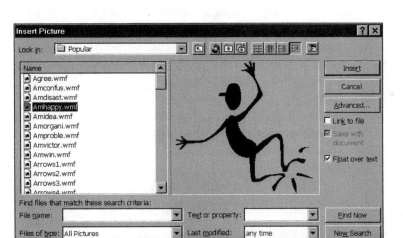

Figure 11-4   Change to the folder and drive that contain the graphics file you want to insert.

3. To change to another drive, display the Look in list and select the drive you want. To change to another folder, double-click it in the Name list. If you don't see the folder listed, use the Up One Level button to move up through the folder structure until you find the folder you want. Then double-click it.

4. When you see the picture file you want, click it. Word displays a preview of the selected file. You can also type the name in the File name text box as an alternative to clicking it.

TIP By default, all picture file types are listed. If you want to view just a particular file type, you can do so. To change the types of files that are displayed in the dialog box, display the Files of type drop-down list and select the file type you want. You can select Windows Enhanced Metafile, Windows Metafile, JPEG, Bitmap, PC Paintbrush, Kodak Photo CD, TIFF, GIF, and several other popular graphics file formats.

5. Click the Insert button. Word inserts the image in the document. It is sized to its "ideal" size, but you can also change the size, as covered later in this chapter.

Adding an AutoShape

If what you want to insert in your document is a basic shape (square, rectangle, triangle, and so forth), an arrow, a flowchart symbol, a star, a banner, or a callout, try AutoShape. This feature includes several styles of commonly used shapes. You can use any of the shapes in your document.

To insert an AutoShape, follow these steps:

1. Open the **Insert** menu and select the **Picture** command. From the submenu that appears, select **AutoShapes**. You see the AutoShapes toolbar, which you can use to insert a shape. The Drawing toolbar is also displayed.

2. Click the shape type that you want. You see a drop-down palette of available choices, as shown in Figure 11-5.

3. When you find a shape you want, click it.

4. Click and drag within the document area to draw the shape. Word adds this shape to your document. Figure 11-6 shows some of the various AutoShapes you can add to your document.

Playing Picasso

The easiest course for me, an artistic simpleton, is to add artwork using someone else's handiwork. You, on the other hand, may have more talent. You may want to try your hand at drawing your own shapes and squiggles. If so, you can read this section to find out all about the drawing tools available in Word.

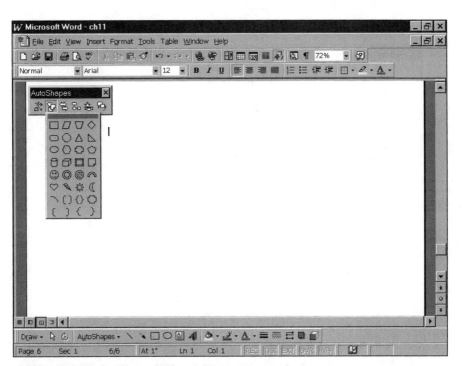

Figure 11-5 Select the AutoShape that you want to insert.

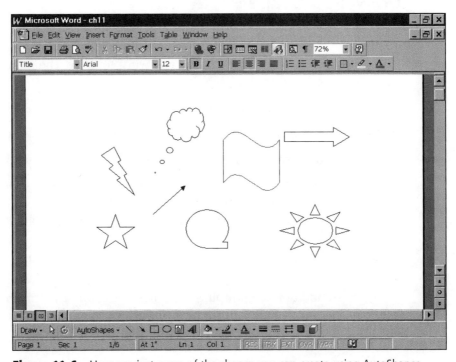

Figure 11-6 Here are just some of the shapes you can create using AutoShapes.

Getting Out Your Palette, the Drawing Toolbar

Your palette of tools is called the Drawing toolbar, and you display this palette of tools by clicking the Drawing button on the Standard toolbar. Word displays the toolbar on-screen, usually along the bottom of the screen. Table 11-1 identifies the tools you use to draw objects. You learn more about the other tools in the sections "Hanging Your Artwork" and "Fine Touches," later in this chapter.

TABLE 11-1   The Tools for Drawing Objects

Button	Name	Description
	LINE	Draws a line.
	ARROW	Draws an arrow.
	RECTANGLE	Draws a rectangle or square.
	OVAL	Draws an oval or circle.
	TEXT BOX	Draws a text box.

Drawing a Shape

When you want to draw something, you follow the same basic steps:

1. Click the button for the shape you want to draw. The mouse pointer changes to a small crosshair.

2. Click within the document and drag to draw the object.

When you draw objects, keep these pointers in mind:

✳ To draw a straight line, hold down the Shift key as you drag.

✳ You can change the line style, color, thickness, and so on. See the section "Fine Touches."

✳ To draw a square, use the Rectangle button and hold down the Shift key as you drag.

✳ To draw a circle, use the Oval tool, but hold down the Shift key as you drag.

✳ In addition to changing the line style, color, and thickness of the outside of a rectangle or circle, you can also add a fill or color, use a shadow, or apply a 3-D effect. See the section "Fine Touches."

GROUPING OBJECTS

Most of the time a simple drawing is actually several shapes combined. When you get the drawing just right, you should group the objects so that you can move and format them as a whole. If you haven't done this and you want to move the drawing, you have to move each individual part.

To group a set of objects, follow these steps:

1. Click the first object you want to group.

2. Hold down the Shift key and click the next object you want to select. Do this for each object you want to select. Each object has its own set of selection handles, indicating it is selected.

3. Click the Draw button. From the menu that appears, select `Group`.

Word groups all the selected drawings into one object. Notice that the selection handles are around the entire set of objects.

To ungroup the objects, select the object. Then click the Draw button and select the Ungroup command.

Drawing a Text Box

Sometimes you may want to insert text in a certain spot in a document. Perhaps you want to include a pull quote or a minitable in the document's margin. You can try to set up this element within the main document and then use the paragraph and other formatting options to get it positioned just right, but you'll probably struggle a lot to get it to work. Instead, create a text box. Text boxes are flexible: you can draw them anywhere within the document and also move them if needed.

To draw a text box, follow these steps:

1. Click the Text Box button in the Drawing toolbar. Or open the `Insert` menu and select the `Text Box` command.

2. Point to the spot in the document where you want to add the text box.

3. Click and drag to draw the text box. After you draw the box, Word displays the insertion point within the text box.

4. Type the text you want to include. You can also make any formatting changes to the text. Figure 11-7 shows a text box with text added.

5. Click outside the box to return to the document.

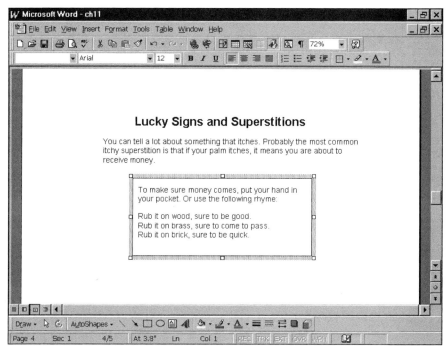

Figure 11-7 Type the text you want to include in your text box.

Hanging Your Artwork

The great thing about adding a graphic is that you aren't stuck with its size and location. Making a change is as simple as dragging it around. You can also delete an image that you don't think works or no longer need. The procedures in this section work for any type of graphic you have added: clip art images, pictures inserted from a file, AutoShapes, and shapes you've drawn yourself.

Moving a Graphic

When you first draw the object, you may not get it in the exact spot you want. Don't worry. You can easily drag the object to a new location.

Simply follow these steps:

1. Click the object to select it.

2. Point to the center of the object — anywhere but on one of the selection handles (see Figure 11-8). When the mouse pointer is in the right spot, it changes to show a four-headed arrow.

3. Drag the object to a new location.

Resizing a Graphic

When you insert an AutoShape or clip art image, Word uses the size it thinks is best for the image. You can, if you want, make the image larger or smaller. Keep in mind that you may mess up the ratio of the image (make it look stretched or smooshed, for instance).

To resize an image, follow these steps:

1. Click the object to select it. Selection handles appear along the edges of the object, as shown in Figure 11-8.

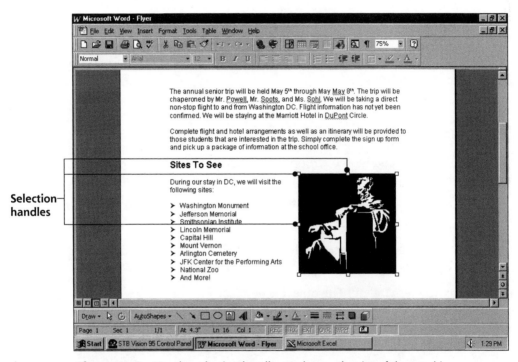

Figure 11-8   Use the selection handles to change the size of the graphic.

2. Put the mouse pointer on one of the selection handles. If you want to make the image taller or shorter, use one of the handles on the top. To make the image wider or narrower, use one on the side. To change both the height and the width, use one of the selection handles in the corners. When the mouse pointer is in the right spot, it changes to a two-headed arrow.

3. Drag the selection handle to resize the object. Word resizes the object.

Copying a Graphic

If you want to use the same shape or image again in the document, don't go to the trouble of inserting or drawing it again. Instead, simply copy it.

Follow these steps:

1. Click the object to select it. You should see selection handles around the graphic.

2. Click 📋 or open the **Edit** menu and select the **Copy** command.

3. Click 📋 or open the **Edit** menu and select the **Paste** command.

4. Drag the copy to the location where you want it to appear.

TIP You can also hold down the Ctrl key and drag a copy off of the original one.

Deleting a Graphic

Sometimes you'll go overboard and add way too many graphics. Or maybe you are just experimenting and have added something by mistake.

Whatever the reason, you can always delete an image you have added by following these steps:

1. Click the object to select it. You should see selection handles around the graphic.

2. Press Delete. The object is deleted.

Controlling How Text Flows around the Picture

How the text and image flow together varies depending on the type of image you insert. When you insert a clip art image, the image is inserted, above or below all of the text. When you draw a shape, the shape is placed above the text; the text doesn't flow around it. You can change how the text flows, selecting from several different options.

To control how the text flows around the picture, follow these steps:

1. Click the object you want to change.

2. Open the **Format** menu and select the **AutoShape** command for shapes you've drawn or the **Object** command for clip art images. You see the Format Object (or AutoShape) dialog box.

3. Select the Wrapping tab. You see the different options you can use for text wrapping (see Figure 11-9). The one currently in use is highlighted.

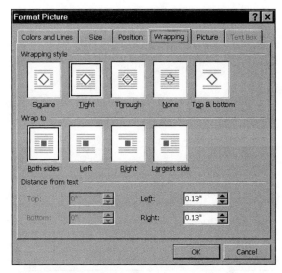

Figure 11-9 Select how you want text to wrap around the graphic.

4. Select the wrapping style you want. You can select Square, Tight, Through, None, or Top & Bottom. The pictures of each option are pretty self-explanatory.

5. For Square, Tight, and Through, select where you want to wrap to: Both sides, Left, Right, or Largest side. Again, the pictures in the dialog box give you a good idea of the effects of each option.

6. Click the OK button. Word wraps the text accordingly.

Fine Touches

You may have noticed that the Drawing toolbar included several other little buttons. What are these buttons for? They are used to format or change how the shape or picture looks. Table 11-2 identifies each button, and the rest of this section explains the changes you can make.

TABLE 11-2 The Tools for Formatting Objects

Button	Name	Description
(icon)	FREE ROTATE	Use to rotate an object.
(icon)	FILL COLOR	Use to fill an object with a color or pattern.
(icon)	LINE COLOR	Use to select a line color.
(icon)	FONT COLOR	Use to select a font color (available for only objects, such as text boxes, that have text).
(icon)	LINE STYLE	Use to select a line style.
(icon)	DASH STYLE	Use to select a dash style.
(icon)	ARROW STYLE	Use to select a style and placement for arrows.
(icon)	SHADOW	Use to add a shadow.
(icon)	3-D	Use to select a 3-D effect.

Changing the Lines

If a drawing includes lines — and most do — you can change their color, style, and thickness. Think of this as selecting just the "brush" you want for your artwork.

Follow these steps:

1. Click the object to select it. If you select a line, Word changes just that line. If you select a rectangle or oval, Word changes the borders or outline of that object.

2. To change the color of the line, click the Line Color button. From the palette that appears, click the color you want.

3. To change the line thickness, click the Line Style button and select a style (see Figure 11-10).

Figure 11-10 Select a thickness for the line.

4. To use dashes in the line(s), click the Dash Style button and select the dash style you want (see Figure 11-11).

Figure 11-11 You can draw a dashed line using any of these dash styles.

5. If you selected an arrow for step 1 and want to change the arrow style, click the Arrow Style button and select the arrow style you want (see Figure 11-12).

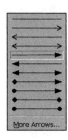

Figure 11-12 If you draw an arrow, you can select a style and placement for the arrow.

Word makes the appropriate changes to the selected object.

Adding Colors, Shadows, and 3-D

For some shapes, you can apply a shadow or 3-D effect. (If you select a shape and click the button and no shadow or 3-D effects are available, you can't do this for the shape you've selected.) You can also fill squares, rectangles, circles, and ovals with color. For clip art images, you can add a background color. Here are the basic procedures for these changes:

✳ To apply a shadow, select the object you want to change. Click the Shadow button and then select the shadow effect you want.

✳ To use a 3-D effect, select the object you want to change. Then click the 3-D button and select the 3-D effect you want.

✳ To fill an object, select the object. Then click the down arrow next to the Fill Color button. Select the color you want from the palette that appears.

✳ To add a background color to a clip art image, click the image to select it. Then click the down arrow next to the Fill Color button. Select the color you want from the palette that appears.

Rotating an Object

You can rotate shapes you've drawn (including AutoShapes). The easiest way is to use the Free Rotate button.

Follow these steps:

1. Select the object you want to rotate.

2. Click the Free Rotate button. Notice that there are round handles around the object.

3. Put the pointer on one of the round selection handles and drag to rotate. As you drag, you see an outline of the image as it is rotated. When you release the mouse button, the object is rotated.

BONUS

Adding Word Art

I f you aren't impressed with the graphic features in Word yet, try this section. Here you learn how to use WordArt, a cool feature for applying special effects to text. Basically, you create a graphic image — a picture — of your text. You can place the text anywhere on the page and select from different colors, shapes, slants, and so on.

Entering Your WordArt Text

To add WordArt text, follow these steps:

1. Open the Insert menu and select the Picture command. From the submenu, select WordArt. You see the WordArt Gallery, displaying the many graphic effects you can try (see Figure 11-13).

2. Select the text effect you want and then click the OK button. You see the Edit WordArt Text dialog box (see Figure 11-14). Here you type the text you want to use.

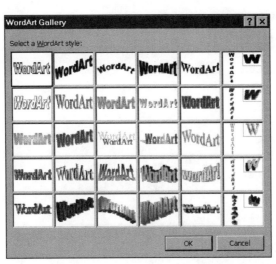

Figure 11-13 Select how you want the text to appear.

Figure 11-14 Type the text you want.

3. Type the text you want to include.

4. To change the font, display the Font drop-down list and select a font. You can also display the Size drop-down list and select a size. To make the text bold, click the Bold button. You can also click the Italic button to make the text italic.

5. Click the OK button. Word adds the text to the document (see Figure 11-15). Keep in mind that this is just like a picture or shape you've drawn. You can move it, resize it, and so on, as covered in the section "Hanging Your Artwork."

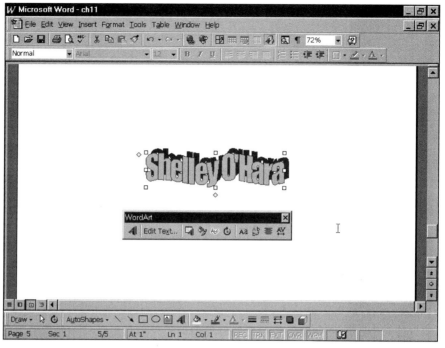

Figure 11-15 You can select and then move, resize, or modify the WordArt object.

Changing the WordArt Text

If you don't like the effect you get with the text, you can make a change using the WordArt toolbar. To display this toolbar, select the WordArt object. Table 11-3 describes the changes you can make using this toolbar.

TABLE 11-3 WordArt Toolbar Buttons

Button	Click . . .	To . . .
	WORDART	Create a new WordArt object.
Edit Text...	EDIT TEXT	Edit the text. Make any changes to the text and then click the OK button.
	WORDART GALLERY	Create another WordArt style from the gallery. Select the style you want and click the OK button. (Don't confuse this with the WordArt button. If you click the WordArt button, you create a new WordArt object.)

Button	Click . . .	To . . .
	FORMAT WORDART	Display a dialog box with options for changing the colors, lines, size, position, and wrapping of the object.
	WORDART SHAPE	Change the shape of the text. Click the WordArt Shape button and select the shape you want.
	FREE ROTATE	Rotate the text. See the section "Rotating an Object."
	WORDART SAME LETTER	Make all the letters the same height.
	WORDART VERTICAL TEXT	Make the text go vertically rather than horizontally.
	WORDART ALIGNMENT	Select an alignment. Click the WordArt Alignment button and then select the alignment you want.
	WORDART CHARACTER SPACING	Select a character spacing (very tight, tight, normal, loose, very loose, or custom).

Summary

Word really includes a lot of neat graphic features. You don't even need any artistic talent to take advantage of them. You just need to read this chapter to find out how to use some of the artwork provided. If you use Word to create published documents, you'll appreciate all the graphics capabilities. You'll also want to check out the next chapter, which explains some special desktop publishing features such as columns and sections.

WEB PATH For a list of clip art sites, try the Yahoo! page,

http://www.yahoo.com/Computers/Multimedia/Pictures/Clip_Art/

CHAPTER TWELVE

DESKTOP PUBLISHING TECHNIQUES: COLUMNS AND SECTIONS

IN THIS CHAPTER YOU LEARN THESE KEY SKILLS

12

One of the biggest joys (and complaints) about word-processing with some of the advanced features these programs now include is that it enables anyone to become a desktop publisher, whether or not they have any design skill or talent. That's great for you! You can create a newsletter about your favorite hobby. You can create flyers. You can create invitations. You can publish articles, pamphlets, even entire books. You can create anything you want.

On the other hand, others can create their own publications and submit them for your reading pleasure. Your neighbor, for instance, can send you his latest version of "Paramilitary Maneuvers for North Central Avenue." Your sister can send you her brochure on the "Uses for Lawn Clippings." Your coworker can force on you his booklet of poems "Angst in the Coffee Room."

This chapter discusses setting up your document for different desktop publishing effects, different numbers of columns, or varied page setups.

Setting up Columns

For certain documents, you may want to vary the look of the page by using columns. For instance, you may want to set up a newsletter that includes columns. Or you might create a page for a catalog, also suited for columns. You can create two, three, four, or more columns of the same size or different sizes. You can set up the columns first and then type the document. Or you can format an existing document into columns.

If you want four columns or fewer, all the same size, the fastest method is to use the toolbar. If you want to set up more than four columns or if you want to set up different sizes from the start, use the menu command. (You can always use the toolbar to modify the columns you have set up — change the size, for instance.)

Quick, Equal Columns

Follow these steps to divide a document into equal columns:

1. Switch to page layout view using the `View` → `Page Layout` command. If you forget this step, Word prompts you to change to this view. Click the OK button in the alert box.

2. Click ▦. You see a drop-down palette of columns (see Figure 12-1).

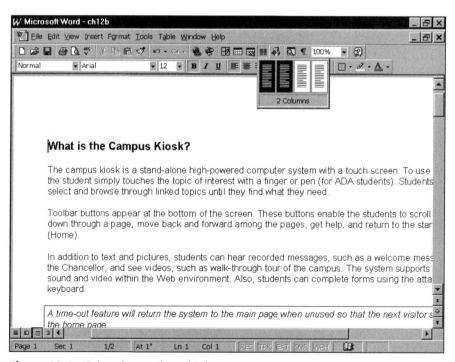

Figure 12-1 Select the number of columns you want.

3. Click the number of columns you want.

If you are formatting a document you have already created, you see the text formatted into columns. Figure 12-2 shows a two-column document.

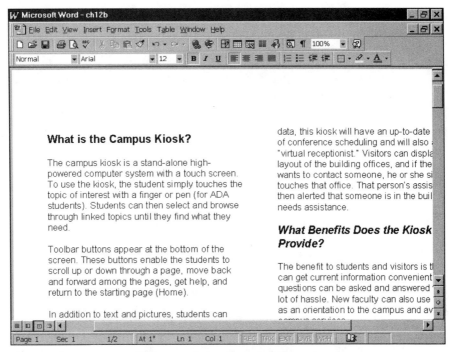

Figure 12-2 You can format an existing document into columns.

CREATING COLUMNS FOR JUST PART OF THE DOCUMENT

If you want, you can format just part of a document into columns. For instance, you can have text that spans the entire page, have a section with two columns, and then have another section with three columns. To do so, you divide the documents into sections (covered later in this chapter). But you don't have to worry about setting up the sections yourself. *Instead, you can do the following:*

1. Select the text you want to format into columns.

2. Click the Columns button and select the number of columns you want.

Just the selected text is formatted into columns. Word also sets up sections and inserts appropriate section breaks, but you don't need to worry about them. If you want more information about sections, see "More Bang for Your Doc" later in this chapter.

If you have not typed text, you may have a hard time telling that the document is now formatted into columns. Notice that the Col indicator appears in the status bar. The next section, "Plugging It In," explains how to add text and move around in the document.

More Control with the Columns Command

If you want to use more than four columns or if you want to use columns of unequal widths, use the Columns command to format a document into columns. You can also use this command when you want to change the columns you have created with the toolbar.

Follow these steps to set up columns with the Columns command:

1. Open the **Format** menu and select the **Columns** command. You see the Columns dialog box (see Figure 12-3).

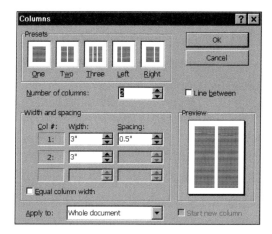

Figure 12-3 Use this dialog box to select the number and size of the columns.

2. To use one of the preset column formats, click the one you want in the Presets area: One, Two, Three, Left, Right. Skip to step 5.

To set the number of columns manually, enter the number of columns you want in the Number of columns spin box. Follow the remaining steps.

TIP If you aren't sure how the columns will affect the document, check the preview in the dialog box. It gives you an idea of how the selected options will look when used in your document.

3. To use the same width for all columns, check the Equal column width check box and then enter the width you want in the Width spin box. Word uses this width for all columns.

To create columns of unequal widths, uncheck the Equal column width check box. Click in the Width spin box for the column you want to change and enter a new width. Do this for each column width you want to change.

4. To change the spacing between columns, click in the Spacing text box for the column you want to change. Enter a new width or use the spin arrows to select the value you want. Do this for each column you want to change.

5. To add a line between the columns, check the Line between check box.

6. Click the OK button.

Word reformats the document into the number of columns you have selected with the column width and spacing as you entered it. Figure 12-4 shows a document with two unequal columns and a line between them.

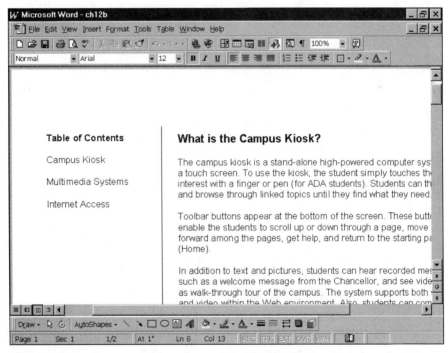

Figure 12-4   You can vary the column size and add a line between the columns.

Plugging It In

I f you set up columns first, you then need to type the text for the document. You also need to know how to move around and insert breaks to move to the next column. This section covers these tasks.

Typing in Columns

If you set up columns in a blank document, you can simply start typing to create the document. Word keeps the text aligned within the columns. If you fill up one column, Word automatically moves you to the next column. Continue typing until you complete the document. You can use any of the editing and formatting features covered in this book. You can copy, move, delete, or add text. You can change the font, apply styles, make text bold, add borders, insert graphics, and so on.

To make an editing change, use the mouse to position the insertion point and then edit as you normally do. You can also use the keyboard to move through the document, but keep in mind that pressing the right arrow key will *not* move you to the next column. You have to go to the end of that column and then up to the top to move through the document. It's faster to use the mouse.

TIP You can move between the tops of two columns using Alt+↑ or Alt+↓.

CAUTION I don't see my columns! In Normal view, the columns are shown in one single column down the page. Normal view is most efficient when you are typing because Word doesn't have to constantly adjust the columns and redisplay the screen. When you are formatting the document and want to see the columns side-by-side, change to page layout view using the View → Page Layout command.

Inserting a Column Break

If you want to start the next column, you may be tempted to press Enter until you jump to the column. But you shouldn't do this because these blank returns will mess up the breaks if you add or delete text. Instead, insert a column break when you want to force a column break.

Follow these steps:

1. Open the Insert menu and select the Break command. You see the Break dialog box (see Figure 12-5).

Figure 12-5 Select Column break to insert a column break.

2. Click the Column break option button.

3. Click the OK button.

Word inserts the column break and moves the insertion point to the next column. In Normal view, you see a dotted line with the words "Column Break" in the center. In Page Layout view, you see the actual break.

Making Them Look Nice

The important part of any document is the content (unless you are someone who believes in style over substance). So when you first create the document, you probably are concerned mostly with the words.

Once the words are OK, you can turn to the look of the document. In a multicolumn document, you may need to make some adjustments. You may want to change the column size, add lines, or add a heading that spans all columns. These topics are covered here.

Changing the Column Size

When you created the columns, you decided the column size. If you used the Columns button to set them up, all columns are the same size. (The size is determined by the number of columns and the margins.) If you used the Columns command, you entered the size and space you wanted between the columns. You can always make a change.

 TIP **If you have a lot of columns, change to landscape orientation using the File → Page Setup command. This orientation gives you more room across the width of the page.**

You can make a change using the Columns dialog box. Select the Format → Columns command and then make any changes. See the section "More Control with the Columns Command." Or you can use the ruler and visually make a change.

Follow these steps:

1. If the ruler is not displayed, open the View menu and select the Ruler command. This step displays the ruler on-screen. Notice in Figure 12-6 that you can see the margins for each column as well as the space between the margins.

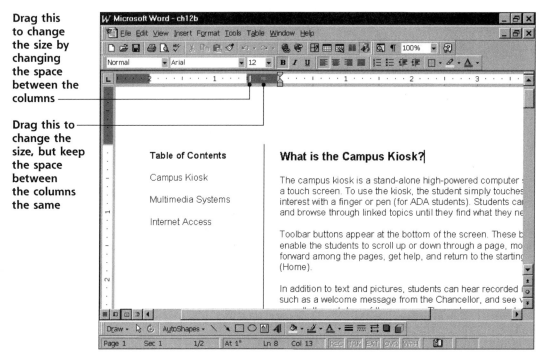

Drag this to change the size by changing the space between the columns

Drag this to change the size, but keep the space between the columns the same

Figure 12-6 Drag the column border you want to resize.

2. To make a change, put the pointer on the column border or area you want to change. To change the width by increasing the space between the columns, put the pointer directly on the border. To change the width but keep the space between the columns the same, put the pointer directly on the gray area indicating the space between columns.

3. Drag the border or area to change the column width.

Keep in mind that there's only so much room on the page. When you increase the size of one column, you leave less room for other columns. To get more room, you can make the left and right page margins smaller. You can also decrease the amount of space between the columns.

Adding a Line between Columns

You can use any text and formatting paragraph options within the columns. For instance, you can create numbered lists, bulleted lists, indents, and so on. You can make the text bigger, use styles, and so on. One change you may want to make is to add a line between each column.

You can do this by following these steps:

1. Open the Format menu and select the Columns command. You see the Columns dialog box (refer to Figure 12-3).

2. Check the Line between check box.

3. Click the OK button. Word adds a line between each column.

Adding a Heading across All Columns

Often you will want to include a banner or heading that spans all the columns.

You can do this by following these steps:

1. Select the text you want to use as the banner.

2. Click ▦ and select one column. The text is formatted as one column and goes across all the columns, as shown in Figure 12-7.

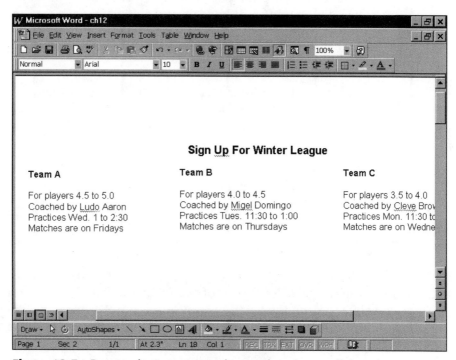

Figure 12-7 Format a banner as one column to have it span all the columns.

Technically, you set up two sections — one for the heading in a one-column format and one for the rest of the document, which is two or more columns. You learn more about sections in the next section.

More Bang for Your Doc

A s you get more and more skilled, you may create more complex documents and in doing so, you may need to vary the page formats for the
document. Here are some examples:

* You may want to have a title page that is one column (that is, it spans
  the entire page). You may want to format the rest of the document using
  two columns.

* You may create a newsletter with a banner that spans the entire page
  but with the text for that page formatted in two columns. You may
  decide that the second page should be broken into three columns.

* You may have a long document that is broken into sections. You may
  want to use different headers and footers for each section.

* You may want to format the title page and most report pages in portrait
  orientation. For some pages — those including wide tables — you may
  want to use landscape orientation.

* For the first page of a document, you may want to have big page
  margins — lots of white space. For the remaining pages, you may want
  to use smaller margins.

These examples give you some idea of ways you may want to vary formatting
from page to page. When you want to do so, you set up a section for each part of
the document with distinct formatting. A section may be just part of the page, a
page, or several pages. Here, you'll learn how to set up and format sections.

Creating Sections

Whenever you vary formatting, such as column width, you need to set up sections. You can do so using one of two methods. You can create sections automatically by selecting the text you want to format. For instance, select the text you
want to have different margins. Then use the command to make the formatting
change. Word applies the formatting to just that marked block and creates the
appropriate sections. You don't have to mess with setting the breaks manually.

As the other method, you can manually insert section breaks to break up the
document. You can then move to each section and format it as you want.

To insert a section break, follow these steps:

1. Place the insertion point where you want the new section.

2. Open the Insert menu and select the Break command. You see the
   Break dialog box (refer to Figure 12-5).

3. In the Sections breaks area, select the type of break you want:

To have the new section start on a new page, select <u>N</u>ext page.

To keep the section on the same page, select Con<u>t</u>inuous.

To have the section start on the next odd-numbered page, select <u>O</u>dd page.

To have the section start on the next even-numbered page, select <u>E</u>ven page.

4. Click the OK button.

Word inserts the section break. On-screen, the break appears as a dotted line with the words "End of Section" in Normal view. In Page Layout view, you see the effects of the break.

To delete a section break, place the insertion point immediately after the break and press Backspace, or place it immediately before the break and press Delete.

 Just as paragraph formatting is stored in the paragraph marker, section formatting (margins, columns, and so on) is stored with the section break. If you delete the section break, the section takes on the formatting of the following section.

Formatting Sections

Once you have created the section breaks, you can format each section the way you want. Here are some of the changes you can make:

* Most of the Page Setup options (margins, orientation, vertical alignment) can apply to the entire document or to just a section. When you select the appropriate tab, use the <u>A</u>pply to drop-down list to select whether to apply the change to the whole document or just this section (see Figure 12-8).

* You can set up sections with different numbers of columns, as covered previously in this chapter.

* You can create distinct headers and footers for each section. To do so, start in the section to which you want to add a header or footer. Create the header or footer as you normally would using the `View` → `Header and Footer` command. Use the Show Previous and Show Next buttons to move among the different section headers. Check the header outline to keep track of which header or footer you are creating. Figure 12-9 shows setting up a header for the second section in a document.

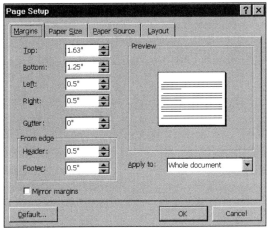

Figure 12-8 You can apply page setup options to the entire document or just the current section.

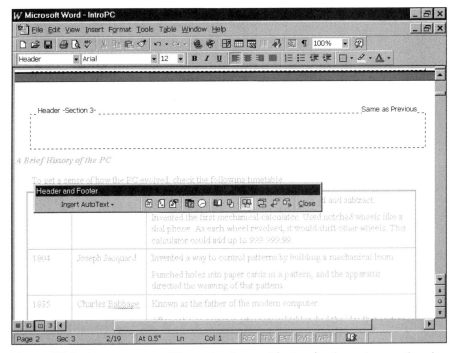

Figure 12-9 You can set up different headers and footers for the various sections in a document.

✳ You can also use different page numbering for each section. For instance, you may want to start numbering each section with the number 1. To do so, insert the page number using the `Insert` → `Page Numbers` command. In the Page Numbers dialog box, click the Format button. In the Page Number Format dialog box, click in the Start at option button and then enter the number you want to start with. Click OK twice.

BONUS

Creating a Brochure

Another desktop publishing technique you can try is to create a brochure. Basically, this is a "regular" document in landscape orientation and set up in three columns. You can then fold the paper to get your brochure. Figure 12-10 shows an example of a brochure in Print Preview.

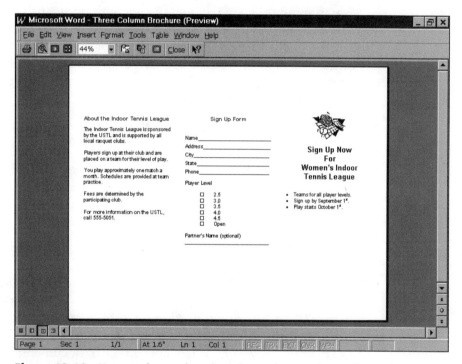

Figure 12-10 You can change the orientation and set up three columns to create a brochure.

To create a brochure, follow these steps:

1. Open the **File** menu and select the **Page Setup** command. Here you can change the paper orientation.

2. Click the Paper Size tab.

3. Click the Landscape orientation.

4. Click the Margins tab and make any margin changes. The default margins are probably too big. So that you can fit as much text on the page as possible, you may want to create smaller left and right margins.

5. Click the OK button. Now divide the document into three columns.

6. Click the Columns button and select three columns. Now you can type the text for the document.

7. Type the text for the column. You can use any of the editing and formatting features to set up this panel. When you want to move to the second panel, insert a column break. Do this for each of the panels of the brochure.

   Keep in mind that you will fold the paper to create the brochure. Be sure to type the panels in order. For the outside page, type the contents of the back panel, the middle panel, and the then front panel (3, 2, 1 order). For the inside page, type the contents of the panels in order: 1, 2, 3. You may want to fold a piece of paper into threes and number them to be sure you set up the panels correctly.

8. Insert a page break and create the next three columns (panels) for the brochure.

9. Print the two pages and then photocopy double-sided. Fold and voilà, you have a brochure.

Summary

This chapter covered some special techniques you may want to try as you create more complex documents. These features — columns and sections — help turn Word into a mini desktop publishing program. You can use them to create various document types.

The next chapter covers another special type of document: a template. You can use a template, basically a predesigned document, to save time.

CREATING SPECIAL DOCUMENT TYPES

THIS PART CONTAINS THE FOLLOWING CHAPTERS

CHAPTER **13** USING TEMPLATES

CHAPTER **14** CREATING FORM LETTERS

CHAPTER **15** INCLUDING DATA FROM OTHER PROGRAMS

This part covers some special documents you can create. The first two chapters cover documents that can save you time. Chapter 13 covers templates, which are predesigned documents in which the text and formatting are already set up. You start with the template and then fill in the blanks to create a new document. Chapter 14 covers form letters. Try this feature when you want to send the same letter to several people. You create one letter and one list of recipients and then merge the two to create personalized letters. Chapter 15 explains how to combine data from several programs into your Word document.

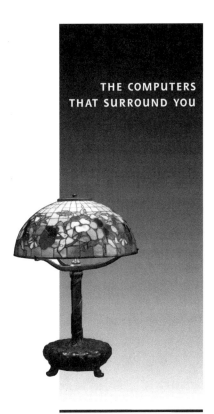

How many times have you heard someone express reluctance or even fear in using a computer?

People are often reluctant when using a computer or an application for the first time. But as users become more familiar with computers and software applications, they usually see the computer and technology in a whole new light. Their reluctance usually dissipates into a new respect for the speed and efficiency of the computer and even an enthusiasm for using the machine.

Take a moment to think about the number of computers that surround you in your day-to-day life. We're not talking only about the computer that runs Word 97 in your office or at home. That computer is known as a general-purpose computer, and it can run a variety of software applications. We're also talking about all of the special-purpose computers that surround you.

Special-purpose computers perform specific tasks. Many of these computers operate within common devices that you use every day. You use products with these "embedded" computers for entertainment, education, communication, transportation, and many other purposes.

For example, do you have a color television? The fine-tuning system for many newer models is a specialized computer that samples information about the signal of the stations and adjusts itself according to that data. Your VCR sports the same type of computerized system for tuning in stations, as does your audio system.

The heating and cooling system in many homes also contains a specialized computer. Again, the system samples information about the temperature in many homes and adjusts it until it matches the temperature you want.

What about the communication you use at home? Your telephone may be capable of redialing the telephone number of the last person who called your home. Thanks to an embedded, special-purpose computer, you might even be able to see the person who is calling you.

Next time you get in your car, think about the computers that it probably contains. If your vehicle is a recent model, it has a computerized ignition system, a computerized fuel-injection system, and numerous other computerized systems. Some newer cars even include computers that monitor the air pressure in the tires and alert you about any problems.

We are surrounded by computers — both general-purpose and special-purpose computers. Word 97 runs on a general-purpose computer. As you continue your discovery of the ways that Word 97 can help you become more productive, think about the embedded computers that are enriching your life in so many other ways.

CHAPTER THIRTEEN

USING TEMPLATES

IN THIS CHAPTER YOU LEARN THESE KEY SKILLS:

WHEN TO USE TEMPLATES   PAGE   225

HOW TO USE A WIZARD   PAGE   229

HOW TO USE A TEMPLATE   PAGE   232

HOW TO CREATE YOUR OWN TEMPLATE   PAGE   234

So far you have learned how to save time entering text into your document. You've also learned shortcuts for using the same set of formatting options. What if you want to do both — save time typing text and save time formatting? Then consider a template.

This chapter starts by defining what a template is and then tells you some cases when you might want to use this feature. You also learn how to use a fancy template, called a wizard. Then the chapter tells you how to use some of the templates provided with Word. Finally, you learn how to create your own templates.

What Is a Template?

Think of one type of document you create again and again. Say something simple like a memo. Each time you create this type of document, you most likely include the same text: the memo heading and the To, From, Date, and Subject lines. You probably also format the text the same way. Perhaps you make the memo header centered and bold. Maybe you also set up tabs for the To, From, Date, and Subject lines and make them bold. If you create a lot of memos, you do these same monotonous tasks.

When you find yourself creating the same document frequently, you should think *template*. A template is a document that includes text and formatting already set up. You simply open the template and then add the text you want to include to complete the memo. You can think of a template as a fill-in-the-blanks document. Figure 13-1 shows, for instance, a simple memo template. This is what you'll get each time you use this template. Figure 13-2 shows the template after text has been added to complete the document.

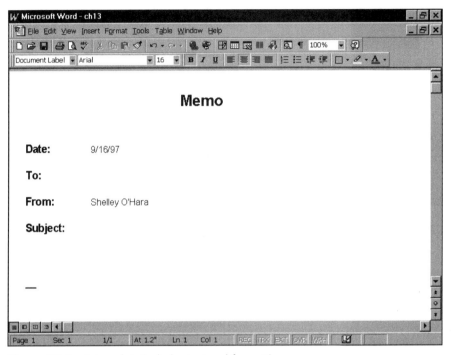

Figure 13-1   A template includes text and formatting.

When you save the document, it is saved and named as a regular Word document. The template remains unaltered so that you can use it again.

Why Use a Template?

You can use a template for any type of document. As discussed above, a memo is a good type of document for a template. You might also use a template for letters, reports, invoices, fax cover sheets, press releases, newsletters, and so on. For instance, I have a template for invoices, faxes, and my letterhead. Each one includes some text that I always want included in the template. The document is also formatted just the way I want. When I use one of these templates, I don't have to enter the same stuff over and over again. I just have to fill in the "blanks" in each document.

To start, you may want to check out some of the templates provided with Word. You may find one that meets your needs. If not, you can always set up your own template.

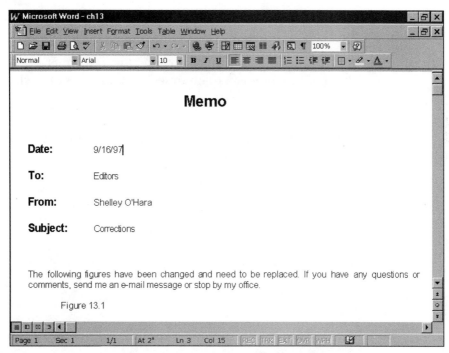

Figure 13-2   You add text to the template to complete the document.

Templates Versus Wizards

Word provides two types of predesigned documents: wizards and templates. The difference is in how they work. A wizard is an automated document. When you use a wizard, Word leads you through the process step by step, prompting you to make selections and enter text. You follow each step, and when you are finished you have a completed document. Word provides wizards for many document types — faxes, letters, mailing labels, envelopes, legal pleadings, newsletters, résumés, and more.

When you use a template, you first select the template you want. You then see a new document based on the template, basically a document skeleton, which includes the text and formatting appropriate for that document type. You add your own text (and make any formatting and editing changes) to complete the document. Word provides many templates that you can use to create a professional-looking document.

Before you begin creating and using the templates, you may want to just get an idea of what's available.

To view the available templates and wizards, follow these steps:

1. Open the File menu and select the New command. Notice that the New dialog box includes tabs for different document types.

2. Click the tab for the type of document you are interested in. For instance, click the Letters & Faxes tab to see the templates and wizards for this category (see Figure 13-3).

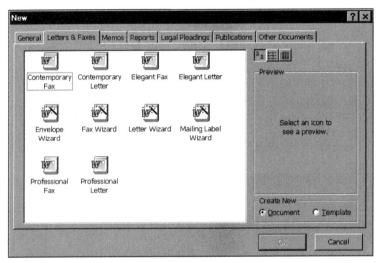

Figure 13-3   You can view the available templates and wizards in the New dialog box.

3. You can see a preview of a template, giving you some idea of the format and layout of the document. To do so, click the template you want. Figure 13-4 shows a preview of the Professional Letter template. You cannot view a preview of wizards.

4. Click the Cancel button to close the dialog box without making a selection.

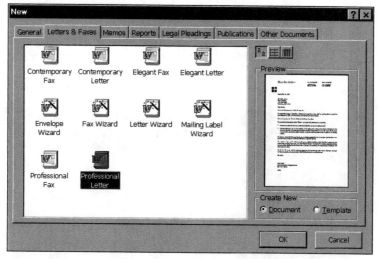

Figure 13-4 You can preview a selected template.

Alakazam! Instant Document

I f you like the step-by-step approach to creating a document, try one of the many wizards provided with Word. Here are just a few:

* Envelope Wizard
* Fax Wizard
* Letter Wizard
* Mailing Label Wizard
* Resume Wizard
* Memo Wizard
* Newsletter Wizard
* Pleading Wizard
* Web Page Wizard

To use a wizard, follow these steps:

1. Open the File menu and select the New command. You see the New dialog box. The default tab, General, is selected.

2. Click the tab for the document type you want to create. You see the available templates and wizards for that document category. You can tell which ones are wizards because they say "Wizard."

3. Click the wizard you want and then click the OK button.

Each wizard has a distinct series of dialog boxes. The first dialog box gives you an overview of the process and steps you follow. For instance, Figure 13-5 shows the opening dialog box for the Memo wizard.

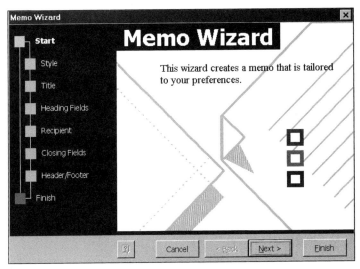

Figure 13-5   The first dialog box for the wizard gives you an overview of all the steps.

4. Follow the instructions in the dialog box. After you complete the step, click the Next button to display the next step (dialog box).

X-REF   **If you make a mistake or change your mind, click the Back button to go back through your selections and make changes. To get help, click the Help button.**

At some steps, you are prompted to enter or select the text to include, as shown in Figure 13-6. At other steps, you are prompted to select a style for the document, as shown in Figure 13-7.

5. Continue moving through the dialog boxes, making selections, until the final one appears.

6. Click the Finish button to complete the document. You see your finished document on-screen. Figure 13-8 shows a document created using the memo wizard. As you can see, some text is already entered, and the document is pretty much formatted for you.

7. Enter the text for the document. You can replace the text in brackets with the appropriate text for your document. Here, for instance, you need to enter the To, CC, and Subject lines for the memo. You also need to type the contents of the memo.

8. Save and print the document. When you use [File] → [Save] to save the document, the document is saved as a separate file, with the name you assign. You can open and edit this document as needed. The original template remains on disk untouched so that you can use it again.

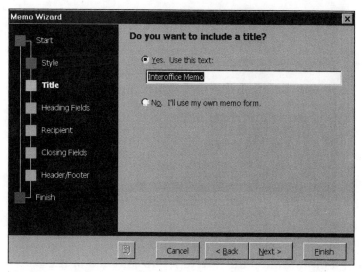

Figure 13-6 At some steps, you enter the text for the document.

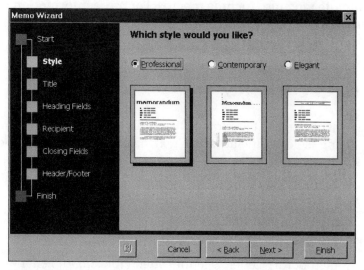

Figure 13-7 At some steps, you select the style or look of the document.

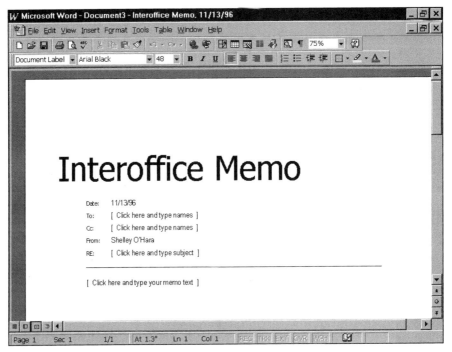

Figure 13-8 Complete the document.

TIP Most templates include a style set up for each of the document elements. You can use these styles for other text in the document. You can also modify the styles. For more information on styles, see Chapter 9. The template may also include macros. For more information on macros, see Chapter 17.

Fill in the Blanks

As mentioned, a template is like a fill-in-the-blank document. The document skeleton includes the text and formatting, and you fill out this skeleton to complete the document. Word includes many different templates. You can select from several document types as well as different styles of each type. Here are a few of the templates included with Word:

* Blank Document (the default)
* Contemporary Fax, Elegant Fax, Professional Fax
* Contemporary Letter, Elegant Letter, Professional Letter
* Contemporary Memo, Elegant Memo, Professional Memo
* Contemporary Report, Elegant Report, Professional Report

* Blank Web Page
* Contemporary Résumé, Elegant Résumé, Professional Résumé

To use a template, follow these steps:

1. Open the **File** menu and select the **New** command. You see the New dialog box.

2. Click the tab for the document type you want to create. You see the available templates and wizards for that document category.

3. Click the template you want to use. You see a preview of the selected template. Figure 13-9, for instance, shows a preview of the Contemporary Fax template.

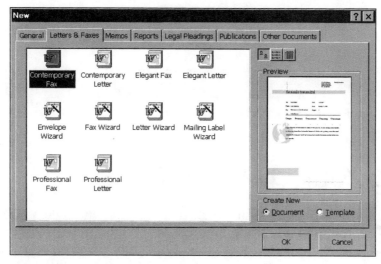

Figure 13-9 Select the template you want to use.

4. Click the OK button. Word displays the document on-screen (see Figure 13-10). Some text is included, such as the document title, subject fields, and date for the fax. Other text is in brackets, indicating your need to replace the "filler" text with your "real" text.

5. Click the text you need to replace and type the actual text. Do this for each section of text that needs to be completed.

You can make any editing and formatting changes to the document, as needed.

6. Save and print the document. This new document is saved as a separate file; the template remains unchanged.

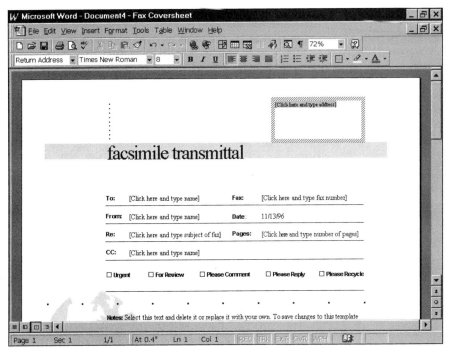

Figure 13-10 Complete the bracketed text to create your document.

Using Your Own Templates

E ach person and business has a unique flair and style. You may not like the formatting and text of the "canned" templates. Also, you may have other documents pertinent to your work or home life that aren't included in any of the templates. For instance, you may have forms that you want to set up as templates. If so, you can create and save your own templates and make them available for you (or others to use).

Creating Your Own Template

It's easy to create a template. You just create the document as you normally would and then use a special procedure to save the document as a template.

Follow these steps:

1. Start with a blank document and then type the text you want and format the template document as you want.

   All new documents based on this template will include all the formatting and text you include. Therefore, include in the template only the elements you want in all documents based on this template. For example, if you are creating a letterhead, you might include your company name in a header and the address in the footer. You might include a field to insert the date. You might also set up the margins you want for the page and any other formatting you want to include.

You wouldn't, on the other hand, include any specific text such as "Dear John" in the letter. You will add this text for the actual document when you use the template.

TIP **You can start a template with a document you have already created and formatted. If you do so, be sure to delete any text that you don't want included in the template.**

2. When you have completed the template, open the [**File**] menu and select the [**Save As**] command. You see the Save As dialog box.

3. Display the Save file as type drop-down list and click Document Template as the type. Word automatically selects the Templates folder — where you must place your templates to make them available. Notice that you can select the folder (tab) in which you want the template to appear (see Figure 13-11).

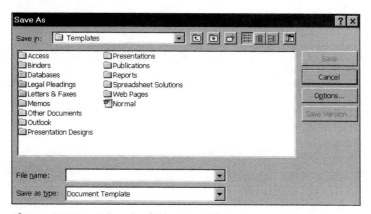

Figure 13-11 Select the folder in which you want to place the template.

4. Select the folder in which you want to place this template. You can place it within any of the existing folders.

5. In the File name text box, type a name for the template. Use something descriptive that will remind you of the contents and purpose of the template.

6. Click the Save button. Word saves the document as a template.

Using Your Template

When you want to use a template you have saved, you simply select it from the New dialog box.

Follow these steps:

1. Open the File menu and select the New command.

2. Click the tab for the template. This is the folder where you placed the template when you saved it. You should see your template listed (see Figure 13-12).

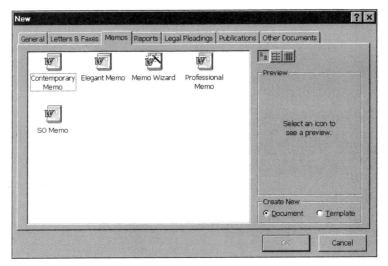

Figure 13-12 Templates you create are also listed in the New dialog box.

3. Click the template name.

4. Click the OK button.

BONUS

Editing Your Template

Getting your template set up exactly right may take some trial and error. As you use the template, you may notice some things you want to change. You may want to get rid of text that isn't appropriate for every document based on that template. Or you may want to add text or formatting that you do want to include.

When you use the template, remember that you are creating a new document. The original template remains unchanged. When you want to actually work on the template, you need to open the template file.

Follow these steps:

1. Open the `File` menu and select the `Open` command. You see the Open dialog box.

2. Change to the folder for templates. This folder is named \Program Files\Microsoft Office\Templates. Use the Up One Level button to move to this folder.

3. Change to the template folder that contains your template. Remember that the templates folder has several subfolders for different document types (memos, reports, and so on). When you saved your template, you selected one of these folders. Select that same folder here.

4. Display the Files of type drop-down list and select Document Templates. You should see your template listed.

5. Click the template you want to edit.

6. Click the Open button. Word displays the template on-screen.

7. Make any editing or formatting changes to the template.

8. Save the template using the `File` → `Save` command. Word saves the template in the same folder with the same name. The next time you use this template to create a document, it will include all the editing and formatting changes you've made. Any previous documents based on the template remain unchanged.

Summary

I n this chapter you learned how to save time by setting up and using "automatic" documents, or templates. You can use any of the existing templates or you can create your own. The next chapter covers another option for saving time creating documents: a special type of letter called a form letter.

CREATING FORM LETTERS

IN THIS CHAPTER YOU LEARN THESE KEY SKILLS

14

'm willing to venture that everyone at sometime or another has received a form letter. You know the letter that reads at least a little like the following:

Dear Bob:

Guess what, Bob! You may already be a winner. Yes, Bob, you might already have won one of the 1,000 fabulous prizes in our grand prize drawing. You may have won a trip to Hawaii or a new car. Isn't that great, Bob?

All you need to do is attend this really, really boring presentation where I or one of my many sales persons will try to pressure you into buying something you don't need, like the world's lightest vacuum cleaner or a timeshare in downtown Burbank. Then you will receive some really lame prize like a box of macaroni and a jar of car wax. If you're lucky.

And Bob, don't think about throwing this away. Because, Bob, we know where you live, and you can expect to receive this same letter next week. Every week, Bob, for the rest of your life. How do you like that, Bob?

OK. Maybe that letter is a little untrue (or maybe a little too true). Form letters mail merge are ways to send the same letter to many people. And even though you may think "junk" mail, these types of letter can come in handy to you or your business.

For instance, if you have a small business, you may want to send a letter to your clients announcing a new product or service. Or you may want to thank a customer for an order. If you are a real estate agent, you may want to send out a letter introducing yourself to your neighbors. If you use Word mainly for family functions, you may want to send a holiday letter to all your friends and family. Or you may be in charge of one of your children's sports teams and need to send the same information to several people. The types of letters you may want to create are endless.

Word provides a convenient way to send the same letter — but personalized — to several people. This chapter starts by giving you an overview of the process and then tells you how to set up and merge the two documents you need.

Two Documents into One

Two files make up a basic merge procedure: the data source and the main document. And you follow three basic steps to create a merge:

* Set up the main document.
* Create the data source.
* Merge the two.

This section gives you an overview of the process and explains what each document contains. The remaining sections tell you specifically how to create each document and then do the merge.

Setting up the Main Document

The main document contains the text of the letter. This is the boilerplate letter that you want to send to everyone. That's the text of your yearly Christmas letter that tells all your friends and family about Jimmy Junior getting released from jail and Little Suzie winning the Little Miss Okra Pageant. You type this text as you would any other letter.

What's special about the letter is that you insert codes for the fields you want to include. For example, a last name field code tells Word to take the specific last name and insert it in that spot in the main document.

You start this document first, then create the data source, and then go back to complete the main document. Kind of out of order, but that's the way it is.

Creating the Data Source

The data source is basically an address list. You use this address list to create personalized letters. You can use an existing data source (such as an address book or a database file), or you can set up a data source.

If you create the data source, you basically create a table. The first row of the table contains the name of the *fields* or variable information you want to insert in the main document. For example, you may have fields for first name, last name, address, city, state, zip, and so on. Each field has a name (called a *field name*) and appears in its own column. Word provides several predefined fields that you can use in the data source. Or you can create your own.

After you've set up the data source, you then enter the specific information for each field. One set of fields (or a row) is called a *record*. For instance, in one row you will have the name and address of a specific person. You next enter the records using a data form — a fill-in-the-blank dialog box where you complete the information for each person. You enter a record for each person to whom you want to send the letter.

Merging the Two

After you create both documents, you then merge the two. Word creates one big document, with a personalized letter for each record in the data source. You can then print or save the resulting document.

Steps 1, 2, 3

To lead you through the process of performing a mail merge, Word provides the Mail Merge Helper, which outlines the three steps you follow.

To display this helper and start the main document, follow these steps:

1. Start with a blank document on-screen. Word makes a connection between the two documents (the main document and the data source). You will create the main document using this blank document later.

2. Open the Tools menu and select the Mail Merge command. You see the Mail Merge Helper dialog box (see Figure 14-1). Notice that the dialog box outlines the three key steps you follow.

    To start you select the type of main document you want to create, although you don't create this document until later. (The steps are kind of misleading.)

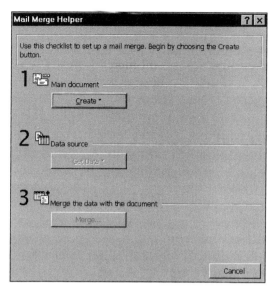

Figure 14-1 The Mail Merge Helper shows you the three steps to perform a merge.

3. Under Main document, click the Create button. You see a drop-down list of the different types of main documents you can set up. You can create form letters, mailing labels (covered later), envelopes, or a catalog.

4. Click Form Letters. You are prompted to use the current window or a new window for the main document (see Figure 14-2).

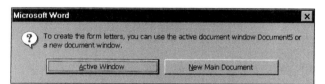

Figure 14-2 Select to use the current window or to create a new window.

5. Click the Active Window button.

Word records the document type (form letters) and document window you are using for the main document. This information is listed in the Mail Merge Helper dialog box, which remains open. The next step is to create the data source, as described in the next section.

The Addresses

You may think that setting up a mail merge is complex because you have to follow a lot of steps, but your hard work will be rewarded once you see the results. Your next task is to create the data source.

Remember that the data source contains the header row with field names for each piece of information you want to include. The data source also includes individual records for each person (or item or event). When you create the data source, you start by defining the fields to include. Then you enter the data.

Setting up the Fields

To start, you set up the fields you want to include. Word includes some commonly used fields such as FirstName, LastName, Company, Title, City, State, HomePhone, and so on. You can use any of these fields. Plus, you can add your own fields.

Which fields do you need? To come up with your list of fields, think about each individual piece of data you want to include. Which of the predefined fields are appropriate? Which additional fields do you need to include? For instance, suppose that you are in charge of organizing the community services program for your company. Part of that involves setting up committees for each activity. You could create a form letter to send to each volunteer. For this data source, you would include all the name and address information for each person, as well as a field for the committee to which that person was assigned.

TIP **You may want to think through the contents of the letter and write down a list of fields you need to include. Remember that you can include other variable information, such as a committee name, a project, a sales representative, a class, and so, on relating to that person. And you can include more than one "added" field.**

To select the fields you want to include in the form letter, follow these steps:

1. Click Get Data in the Mail Merge Helper dialog box. You see a submenu of choices. You can choose to create the data source, open a data source, use the address book, or set header options. Here you will create a data source.

 X-REF **For information on using other data sources — such as an Access database — see the next chapter.**

2. Click <u>C</u>reate Data Source. You see the Create Data Source dialog box (see Figure 14-3). Word sets up some common fields which are listed in the Field <u>n</u>ames in header row list. You can delete any of these fields that you don't want to include and add any additional fields.

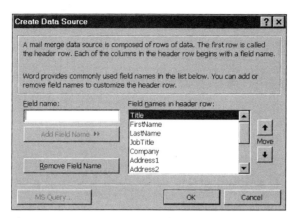

Figure 14-3 Add or remove fields to or from the data source using this dialog box.

3. To remove a field, select it in the Field <u>n</u>ames in header row list. Then click the <u>R</u>emove Field Name button. Do this for each field you want to remove from the predefined list.

4. To add a field, type the name of the field in the <u>F</u>ield name text box and then click the <u>A</u>dd Field Name button. Do this for each field you want to add.

5. When you are finished adding or removing fields, click the OK button. Word displays the Save Data Source dialog box, shown in Figure 14-4. Before you enter records, save the data source.

6. Use the Save <u>i</u>n drop-down list to change to the drive or folder you want. You can also double-click folders listed in the file and folder list. To move up through the folder structure, click the Up One Level button.

7. In the File <u>n</u>ame text box, type the file name. Use a name that will remind you that this is a data source document and of that data source's purpose.

8. Click the <u>S</u>ave button. Word next prompts you to choose whether you want to edit either the main document or the data source (see Figure 14-5). You want to edit the data source, adding the records to your data table. This is the topic of the next section.

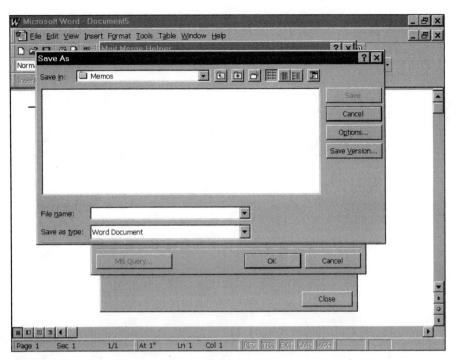

Figure 14-4 Save the data source before you start to enter records.

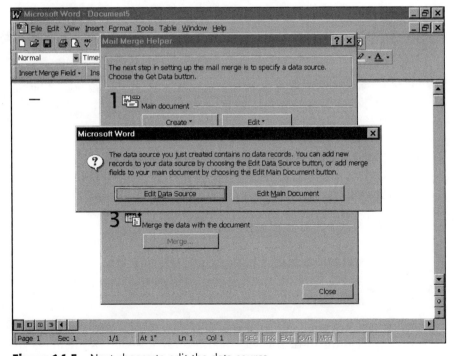

Figure 14-5 Next choose to edit the data source.

If you already have a data source and want to use it with a different letter, you can do so. *Follow these steps:*

1. In the Mail Merge Helper dialog box, click the <u>G</u>et Data button and select <u>O</u>pen Data Source. You see the Open Data Source dialog box.

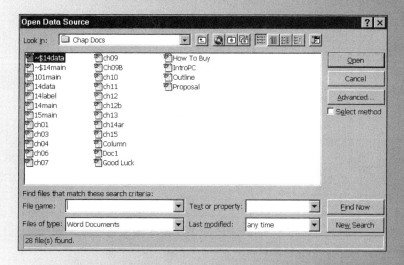

2. Use the Look <u>i</u>n drop-down list to change to the drive that contains the file you want to use.

3. Double-click the folder that contains the file. If needed, use the Up One Level button to move up through the folder structure.

4. When you see the file listed, double-click it. Word lists this filename in the Mail Merge Helper dialog box. You can then create the new main document you want to use.

Entering the Data for the Data Source

After you've set up the fields, you next enter the specific information for each person to whom you want to send a letter. For instance, if you wanted to send out ten letters, you would next enter the specific name and address information for those ten people.

Follow these steps:

1. Click the Edit <u>D</u>ata Source button. You see the Data Form, shown in Figure 14-6. You see an entry box for each of the fields you added in the preceding section. Here you type the information for each of those fields for each person you want to receive the letter.

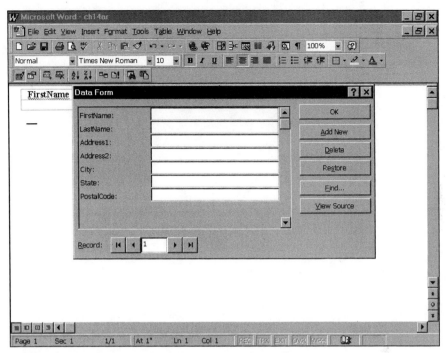

Figure 14-6 Enter the data for each person.

2. Type the information for the first field and press Tab.

TIP If you somehow get off track when completing the data source, you can always go back to setting up the data source or adding records. You can also edit records. See the section "Getting Back on Track" later in this chapter.

3. Continue entering information for all the fields until you complete the record.

4. When you are finished, click the Add New button.

5. Follow steps 2 through 4 for each record you want to add.

6. When you have completed all the records, click the OK button. You see the main document on-screen. The next section describes how to complete this document.

The Letter

Congratulations! You've completed the first step of the mail merge. Now you have reached step 2 — creating the main document. When you finish adding records, Word displays the main document, shown in Figure 14-7.

You can then type the text of the document as well as insert the merge fields.

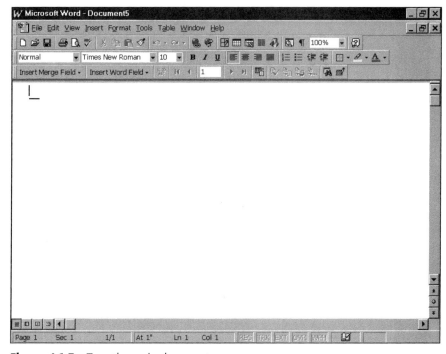

Figure 14-7   Type the main document.

Follow these steps:

1. Type the text of the letter.

2. When you get to a spot where you want to insert variable information (such as the name and address), click the Insert Merge Field button. You see a list of fields you have set up in the data source (see Figure 14-8).

Be sure to include appropriate spaces and punctuation between each of the merge fields. Otherwise, the fields will run together. Instead of John Smith, you'll get JohnSmith.

3. Click the field you want to insert. Word inserts the merge code into the document. You can tell that this is a code rather than regular text because it appears within little brackets.

4. Continue typing and inserting fields until you complete the document. Figure 14-9 shows a document with text for the letter as well as merge codes to merge the information from the data source. Once the main document is complete, you need to save it.

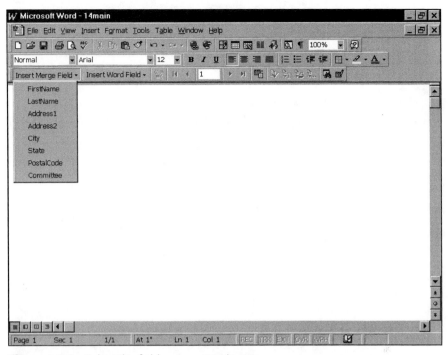

Figure 14-8 Select the field you want to insert.

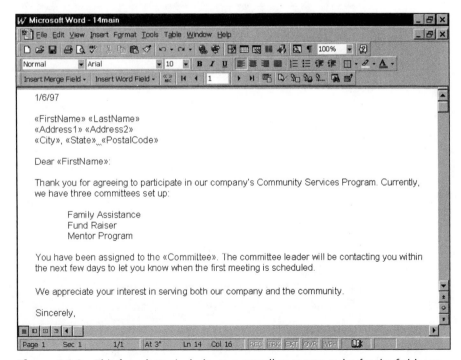

Figure 14-9 This form letter includes text as well as merge codes for the fields you want to include.

You can't just type the merge codes within brackets. You have to insert them using the Insert Merge Field toolbar button.

If you need to return to this document to make changes, you can do so. See the section "Getting Back on Track" later in this chapter.

5. To save the main document, open the File menu and select the Save command. You see the Save As dialog box (see Figure 14-10).

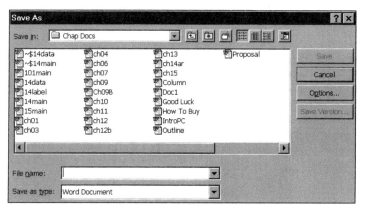

Figure 14-10 Type a filename for the main document.

6. Type the filename and click the Save button.

Now that both documents are complete, you can merge the two.

The Address and the Letter Together

The final step is the easiest. You select a few commands and Word performs the merge. Word takes your main document and pulls the specific information from each record in the data source, creating a custom letter for each record in the data source.

To perform the merge, follow these steps:

1. Open the Tools menu and select the Mail Merge command. You see the Mail Merge Helper dialog box. All the selections you made and filenames for each file are listed, as shown in Figure 14-11.

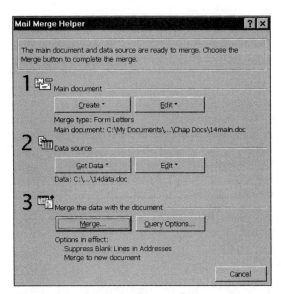

Figure 14-11   The Mail Merge Helper dialog
box keeps track of your progress.

2. Click the <u>M</u>erge button. You see the Merge dialog box, shown in
    Figure 14-12.

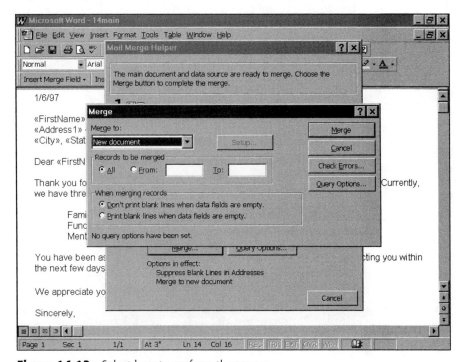

Figure 14-12   Select how to perform the merge.

TIP To merge directly to a new document, click the Merge to New Document button on the Merge toolbar. To merge directly to the printer, click the Merge to Printer button on the Merge toolbar.

3. To merge to the printer, display the Merge to drop-down list and select Printer. You can also select Electronic mail.

4. To merge only selected records, select the From option button and then enter the record numbers you want to use in the merge.

5. If Word encounters a blank field or line, it does not print the line. If you want to print this line, select the Print blank lines when data fields are empty option button.

6. Click the Merge button. Word merges the letters and displays each one on a separate page (if you merged to a new document). Figure 14-13 shows the first page of the merge used throughout this chapter.

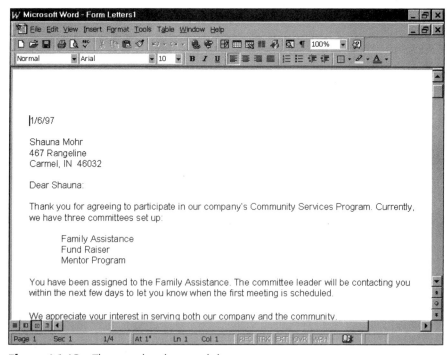

Figure 14-13 The completed merged document.

7. Print the letters using the File → Print command.

Getting Back on Track

A merge is really one long process. You need to follow each step in each section in order to get the merge to work. But there are some steps that can go wrong, and you may get off track. If that happens, use this section to figure out where you are and how you can get back on the 1-2-3 step of the merge.

Forget Where You Are?

If you forget where you are in the merge process, you can always display the Mail Merge Helper, which keeps track of your progress. You can tell a lot from the dialog box, including the names of the main document and data source (see Figure 14-14). You can also use this dialog box to switch to and work on another file.

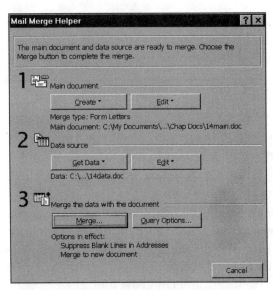

Figure 14-14 Use the Mail Merge Helper to switch to the main document or the data source.

For instance, suppose that you somehow got sidetracked and did not complete your main document. To return to the main document, display the Mail Merge Helper dialog box by selecting Tools → Mail Merge. Then click the Edit button under Main document.

TIP You can also switch between the main document and the data source using the Window menu. Open this menu and then at the bottom of the menu, click the document you want to switch to.

Need to Find or Add Records?

When you are creating the data source, you have a lot of options for working with the records. For instance, you may want to add another field. Or perhaps you prefer a different view of the data. Or maybe you need to edit a record.

To edit the data source, display the Mail Merge Helper dialog box, click the Edit button under Data source, and then click the filename for the data source. You should see the data form displayed (see Figure 14-15). You can then do any of the following:

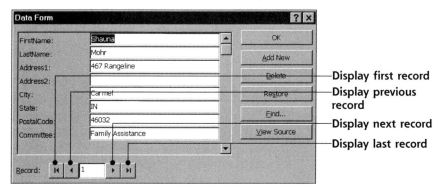

Figure 14-15 Use the Record scroll buttons to move among the records.

✳ To edit a record, use the Record scroll arrows to display the record. Make changes to any field in the record. When you move to another record, the changes are saved.

✳ To delete a record, use the Record scroll arrows to display the record you want. Then click the Delete button.

✳ If you have a lot of records, you may not want to scroll through them individually. Instead, you can search for a record. To do so, click the Find button. In the Find in Field dialog box, enter the text you want to find in the Find what text box. Select which field to search from the In field drop-down list. Then click the Find First button.

✳ If you would rather work in a table view than in the data form, click the View Source button. You see the data source in a table layout (see Figure 14-16). You can use the toolbar buttons to work with the records or change to the main document. To redisplay the data form, click the Data Form button.

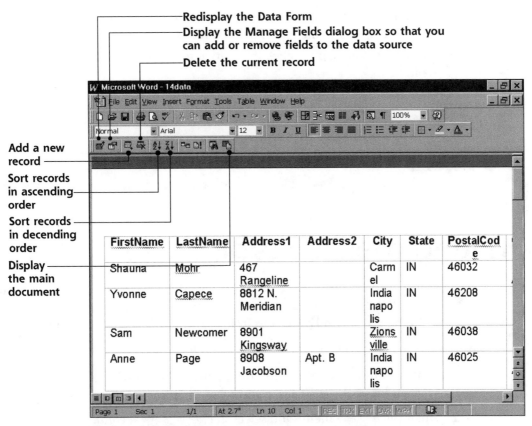

Redisplay the Data Form

Display the Manage Fields dialog box so that you can add or remove fields to the data source

Delete the current record

Add a new record

Sort records in ascending order

Sort records in decending order

Display the main document

FirstName	LastName	Address1	Address2	City	State	PostalCode
Shauna	Mohr	467 Rangeline		Carmel	IN	46032
Yvonne	Capece	8812 N. Meridian		Indianapolis	IN	46208
Sam	Newcomer	8901 Kingsway		Zionsville	IN	46038
Anne	Page	8908 Jacobson	Apt. B	Indianapolis	IN	46025

Figure 14-16 You can view the data source as a table.

I'm Not Done with the Main Document!

If you somehow got out of the main document when you weren't complete, you can switch back to it from the Mail Merge Helper dialog box or from the Window menu. Then you can make any changes. When creating or editing the main document, keep these tips in mind:

* If you make any mistakes while typing, just correct them as you would in any regular document.

* If you insert a field incorrectly, select it and press the Delete key.

* You can use the same field more than once in the document. You don't have to use all the fields you've included in the data source.

* Be sure to include spaces after the merge fields. Otherwise, when you do the merge, the text won't be spaced properly.

* To check on your progress and see how the data will be merged, click the View Merged Data button in the toolbar. You can then use the record

scroll buttons next to the View Merged Data button to move through the records, displaying the letter for each record.

✱ To edit the data source, click the Edit Data Source button in the Merge toolbar.

BONUS

Printing Mailing Labels

Y ou've saved all that time creating the letters, but what about addressing them? Word can save you time there, too. You can set up mailing labels, using the names and addresses in the data source, as covered here.

To print mailing labels for your form letters, follow these steps:

1. Start with a blank document on-screen. You will use this document to set up your labels.

2. Open the Tools menu and select the Mail Merge command. You see the Mail Merge Helper dialog box (refer to Figure 14-1).

3. Under Main document, click the Create button and select Mailing Labels.

4. When prompted to use the current or new window, click the Active Window button. You next open the data source, which you have already created.

5. Click the Get Data button and select Open Data Source. You see the Open Data Source dialog box.

6. Change to the drive and folder that contain the data source. Use the Look in drop-down list to change to another drive. If you see the folder listed, double-click it to open it. You can use the Up One Level button to move up through the folder structure until you find the folder you want.

7. When you see the file listed, double-click it. Word prompts you to set up the main document.

8. Click the Set Up Main Document button. You see the Label Options dialog box (see Figure 14-17).

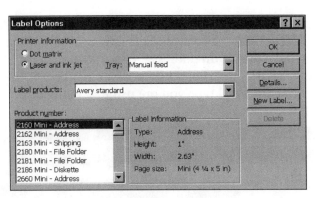

Figure 14-17   Select the type of labels you are using.

9. Display the Label products drop-down list and select the brand of label you are using. The most common types of labels are made by Avery. Many other brands are interchangeable with the Avery labels.

10. In the Product number list, select the name of the labels you are using. Check the label box for the product number.

11. If necessary, make any changes to the printer information. Select the type of printer as well as the tray that contains the labels (for laser and inkjet printers).

12. Click the OK button. You see the Create Labels dialog box (see Figure 14-18). Here you use the merge labels to set up an address.

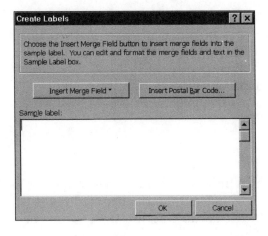

Figure 14-18   Enter the merge codes to create the mailing labels.

13. Click the Insert Merge Field button and select the merge field to include in the address label. Do this for each part of the address.

14. When you have finished setting up the sample label, click the OK button. You are returned to the Mail Merge Helper dialog box. You can now merge your mailing label document with the data source.

15. Click the <u>M</u>erge button and then in the Merge dialog box that appears, click the <u>M</u>erge button again. Word creates a document based on the label size and includes an address for each label. Figure 14-19 shows an example. Keep in mind that your document will look different depending on the label type you are using.

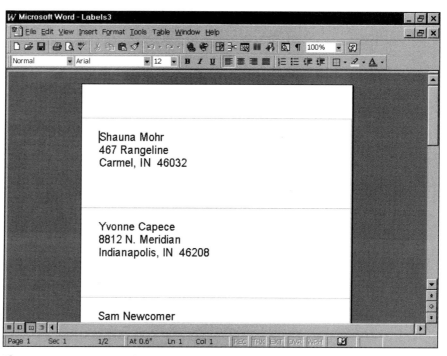

Figure 14-19 You can then print your mailing labels.

16. Insert the labels into the printer, select the `File` → `Print` command, and click the OK button to print the labels.

Summary

This chapter explained how to save time when you want to send the same letter to several people and you want to personalize the letter. You learned how to complete the two documents (the main document and data source) and then merge them.

If you already have a data source, such as a database, you can use the data it contains. You may also want to use other data from other programs, such as a worksheet from Excel or a slide from PowerPoint. The next chapter covers how to use data from several programs in your Word document.

INCLUDING DATA FROM OTHER APPLICATIONS

IN THIS CHAPTER YOU LEARN THESE KEY SKILLS

Y ou or your office may have purchased Word as part of the Microsoft Office package. Or you may just have Excel 97, a spreadsheet program. If so, you probably use these other programs to create other types of documents. For example, you may have created a budget worksheet or a chart showing sales growth. You may keep track of your clients using Access 97, a database program. You may also create presentations using PowerPoint 97.

As you get more skilled, you may want to create a document that incorporates data from these other sources. That's the topic of this chapter. Here you learn first about the different ways you can share data. Then you learn about some specific types of data swapping — worksheets and charts from Excel, slides from PowerPoint, and databases from Access.

NOTE   You can copy and share data among most Windows applications, but this chapter specifically covers how to do so using Office.

15

Share and Share Alike

There are several methods you can use to incorporate data from another program. Which one works best for you depends on the type of document you are creating and the results you want. Here are the three basic ways:

* Copy data. You can simply copy data from one application to another. For instance, you can copy an Excel worksheet and paste it into Word as a table. With this type of data sharing, the two files remain separate. If you change the worksheet in Excel, the data in Word is not updated. You also cannot use any of Excel's commands and features to modify the worksheet once it is placed in the Word document.

* Link data. You can also insert a linked object. With this type of data sharing, the two files remain separate, but if you change the source file, the destination file is updated also. For instance, if you insert a linked Excel worksheet into Word and then change the worksheet in Excel, the worksheet in Word is updated as well. Basically, the Word document includes only the location of the source file and pulls the data from this file.

* Embed data. You can also insert an embedded object. With this type of data sharing, the embedded object becomes part of the destination file. For instance, if you embed an Excel worksheet into Word, that worksheet becomes part of the Word file. You can use the Excel commands and features to modify the worksheet, but if you modify the original Excel worksheet, the embedded worksheet is not updated.

So the key questions are:

1. Do you need to keep the data updated?

2. Do you want to be able to modify the data using commands and features from the other program?

If the answer to both questions is no, just copy the data. If the answer to both question is yes, link the data. And if the answer to the first one is no and the second is yes, embed the data. This section explains briefly how to copy, link, and embed data. The rest of the chapter gives you some specific examples of sharing data using Microsoft Office programs.

Copying Data

Copying and pasting data is the simplest way to share data. Use this method when you don't need to update the information and when you want the data inserted as part of the Word document.

Follow these steps:

1. Move to the document that contains the data you want to copy. To switch among applications, click the application you want in the taskbar.

2. Select the data you want to copy. Figure 15-1 shows Excel data selected. If you aren't sure how to select data in that program, check the online help for that program.

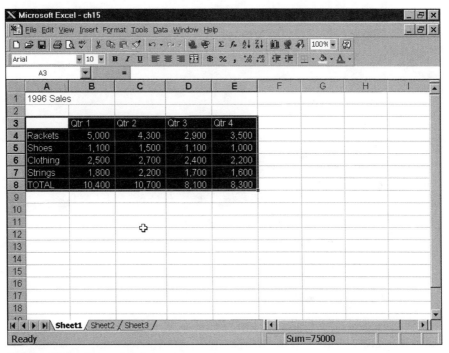

Figure 15-1 Select the data you want to copy.

3. Open the Edit menu and select the Copy command. The data are copied to the Windows Clipboard.

4. Move to the Word document where you want to paste the data. Again, you can use the taskbar to switch applications.

5. Move the insertion point to where you want to paste the data.

6. Open the Edit menu and select the Paste command or click 🖹. The data are pasted into the document. In Figure 15-2 you see the results of pasting Excel data. Notice that this set of data is pasted as a table. Depending on what you copy, you'll get different results. Data such as Excel worksheets and Access data are pasted as a table. Pictures such as Excel charts or PowerPoint objects are pasted as objects by default.

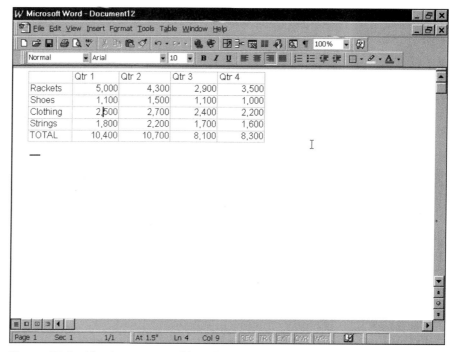

	Qtr 1	Qtr 2	Qtr 3	Qtr 4
Rackets	5,000	4,300	2,900	3,500
Shoes	1,100	1,500	1,100	1,000
Clothing	2,500	2,700	2,400	2,200
Strings	1,800	2,200	1,700	1,600
TOTAL	10,400	10,700	8,100	8,300

Figure 15-2 The data are pasted into the document.

You can use any of Word's editing and formatting features to modify the data. For instance, you can adjust the width of the columns or make the column headings bold.

Linking Data

Sometimes the data you insert will change, and you will want to keep the Word document updated. For instance, you may include a sales worksheet in a sales report in Word. To ensure that the sales worksheet is the most recent, you can link the data.

Follow these steps to insert a linked object:

1. Move to the document that contains the data you want to link. To switch among applications, click the application you want in the taskbar.

2. Select the data you want to link.

3. Open the Edit menu and select the Copy command. The data are copied to the Windows Clipboard.

4. Move to the Word document where you want to paste the data. Again, you can use the taskbar to switch applications.

5. Move the insertion point to where you want to paste the data.

6. Open the [Edit] menu and select the [Paste Special] command. You see the Paste Special dialog box (see Figure 15-3). Here you can paste the data as just regular data or as a link.

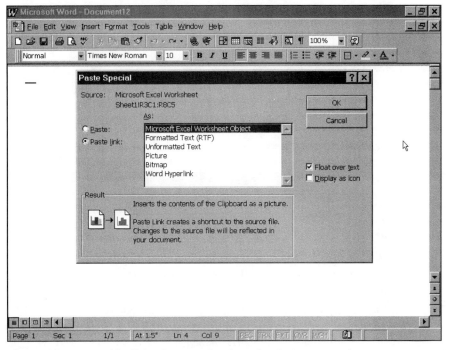

Figure 15-3   Use this dialog box to select how the data are pasted.

7. Select the Paste link option. You can then select how the object is pasted: as an object, formatted text, unformatted text, a picture, a bitmap, or a hyperlink. For Excel worksheets, choose the Microsoft Excel Worksheet Object option.

8. Select what you want the object pasted as and click the OK button. The data are pasted into the document and linked to the source. Figure 15-4 shows a worksheet object pasted into Word. If you make a change to this worksheet in Excel, the Word document is updated.

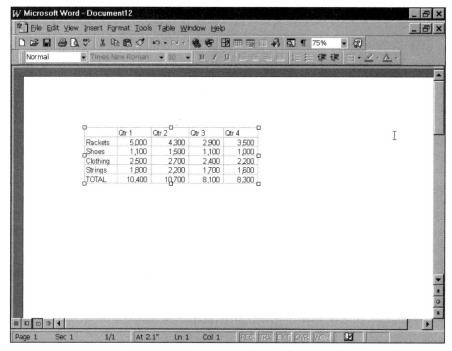

Figure 15-4   You can paste linked data into a document.

If you paste the data as an object, that object is like a picture. You can move it around within the document, but you cannot adjust the columns or edit the data from within Word. If you want to make a change, you can double-click the object. Double-clicking in this case opens the originating application and displays that file. You can then make a change and go back to the Word document. Contrast this with double-clicking an embedded object, covered next.

Embedding Data

In some cases you will want to be able to manipulate the data using the program you used to create the data. But you won't need to keep two separate files. In that case, you can embed the data as an object into the document.

Follow these steps:

1. Move to the document that contains the data you want to embed. To switch among applications, click the application you want in the taskbar.

2. Select the data you want to embed.

3. Open the Edit menu and select the Copy command. The data are copied to the Windows Clipboard.

4. Move to the Word document where you want to paste the data. Again, you can use the taskbar to switch applications.

5. Move the insertion point to where you want to paste the data.

6. Open the **Edit** menu and select the **Paste Special** command. You see the Paste Special dialog box (refer to Figure 15-3). Here you can paste the data as an embedded object. (Notice that this process is similar to pasting a link, only you do not select the Paste link option.)

7. Select Microsoft Excel Worksheet Object.

8. Click the OK button. The data are pasted into the document.

Figure 15-5 shows a worksheet object pasted into Word. Although the results look the same as when you've pasted a link, they are not. Unlike with linked data, if you make a change to this worksheet in Excel, the Word document is *not* updated. Also, you can double-click the worksheet to edit it. Rather than go to that source file, you see the Excel commands and toolbars and a miniworksheet within the Word document (see Figure 15-6). There are not two separate files when you embed data. The worksheet is saved with the Word document.

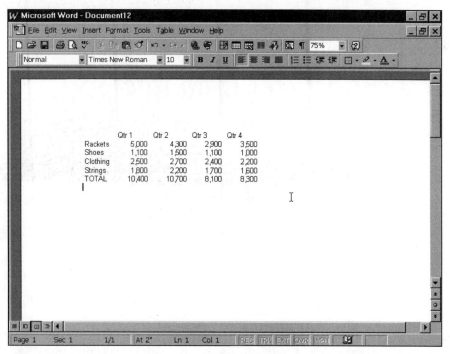

Figure 15-5 You can embed an object from another application into a Word document.

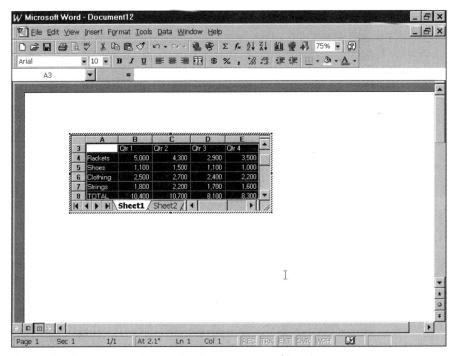

Figure 15-6 The embedded object becomes part of the document.

Inserting Excel Data into Your Document: Fun with Numbers

Now that you know your choices, you can use these skills to try some specific cases. This section covers how to insert Excel data into a document. If you are creating a report, you may want to include some of the worksheets you have created in Excel — sales, budgets, expenses, income, and so on. You can insert the data in any of the three ways covered in the last section:

* As a table. To do so, just use a straight copy and paste. The data will not be updated if you change the original worksheet.

* As a linked object. To do so, use the Paste Special command to paste the data and select Paste link option. Here you have two separate files. If you change the source file (the Excel worksheet), the destination file (the worksheet object in the Word document) is updated.

* As an embedded object. To do so, use the Paste Special command and paste the data as an Excel Worksheet Object. Here you have just one file — the Word document. If you change the worksheet in Excel, the worksheet in Word is *not* updated.

For specific steps, refer to the preceding section. That section uses pasting Excel data as its example.

Charting Your Progress

In addition to Excel worksheets, you can also insert Excel charts into your Word document. You might include a pie chart showing sales, a line chart of expenses, a bar chart showing income. You can keep the chart linked or simply embed it as an object.

To insert an Excel chart into a Word document, follow these steps:

1. Move to the Excel document that contains the chart. To switch among applications, click the application you want in the taskbar.

2. Select the chart you want to insert by clicking it. You should see selection handles around the chart (see Figure 15-7).

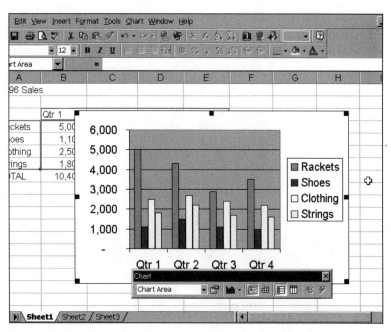

Figure 15-7 Select the chart you want to insert into Word.

3. Open the **Edit** menu and select the **Copy** command. The chart is copied to the Windows Clipboard.

4. Move to the Word document where you want to paste the chart. Again, you can use the taskbar to switch applications.

5. Move the insertion point to where you want to paste the chart.

6. To paste the chart as an embedded object, open the Edit menu and select the Paste command.

To paste the chart as a linked object, open the Edit menu and select the Paste Special command. In the Paste Special dialog box, select Paste link and click the OK button.

Both charts look the same when inserted into Word (see Figure 15-8). But the linked object will be updated if you change the original. The embedded object will not. If you double-click the linked object, you open the application and that separate document file. If you double-click the embedded object, you have access to all the Excel commands, but you are not working in a separate Excel file. The worksheet is saved as part of the Word document.

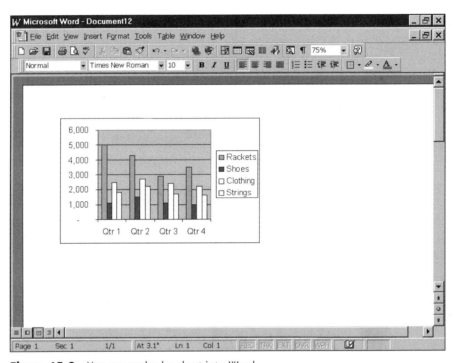

Figure 15-8   You can embed a chart into Word.

You can move the object around and also change how text flows around the object. This object is just like a picture you've inserted. Refer to Chapter 11 for more information on formatting and working with objects.

"Sliding" into Word

If you do a lot of presentations, you may use PowerPoint, the presentation program included with Microsoft Office. You may want to include some of the slides from a presentation in your Word document. You can paste the slide as a picture (which you cannot edit with PowerPoint) or as a Microsoft PowerPoint Slide Object (which you can edit with PowerPoint). You can also choose to paste it as either an embedded object or a linked object.

Follow these steps to copy a slide from PowerPoint to Word:

1. Move to the PowerPoint presentation that contains the slide. To switch among applications, click the application you want in the taskbar.

2. If necessary, switch to Slide Sorter view so that you can select the entire slide.

3. Click the slide you want to copy to Word. You should see a black border around the selected slide (see Figure 15-9).

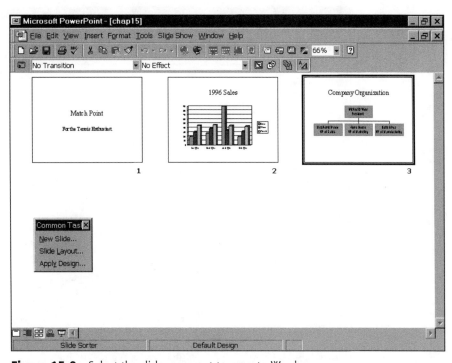

Figure 15-9   Select the slide you want to copy to Word.

4. Open the `Edit` menu and select the `Copy` command. The slide is copied to the Windows Clipboard.

5. Move to the Word document where you want to paste the slide. Move the insertion point to where you want to paste the slide.

6. To paste the slide as an embedded object, open the `Edit` menu and select the `Paste` command.

To paste the slide as a linked object, open the `Edit` menu and select the `Paste Special` command. In the Paste Special dialog box, select Paste link and click the OK button.

To paste the slide as a simple picture, open the `Edit` menu and select the `Paste Special` command. In the Paste Special dialog box, select Picture and click the OK button.

Figure 15-10 shows a slide pasted as a picture. You can use any of the picture formatting options included with Word, but you cannot edit the slide using PowerPoint.

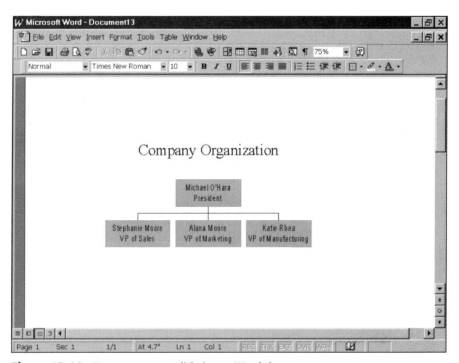

Figure 15-10 You can paste a slide into a Word document.

X-REF You can move the object around and also change how text flows around the object. For information, see Chapter 11.

Accessing Addresses

If you have to keep track of a lot of data, you may use a sophisticated database program. For example, you may use Access, the database program included with Microsoft Office. If you track names and addresses, you may want to use the data to create form letters with Word.

You can do so by following these steps:

1. Start in Word with a blank document on-screen.

2. Open the [Tools] menu and select the [Mail Merge] command. You see the Mail Merge Helper dialog box.

X-REF **For complete information on performing mail merges, refer to Chapter 14.**

3. Under Main document, click the <u>C</u>reate button and select Form Letters. You can also use the database and set up labels or envelopes.

4. When prompted to use the current window or a new window for the main document, click the <u>A</u>ctive Window button.

5. Click the <u>G</u>et Data button and select <u>O</u>pen Data Source. You see Open Data Source dialog box.

6. Display the Files of <u>t</u>ype drop-down list and select MS Access Databases as the file type. Then use the Look <u>i</u>n drop-down list to change to the drive that contains the file you want to use. Also, change to the folder that contains the Access database. You should see your database file listed (see Figure 15-11).

Figure 15-11   Select the database you want to use.

7. When you see the file listed, double-click it. Word lists this filename in the Mail Merge Helper dialog box. Word also establishes a DDE (Dynamic Data Exchange) link so that the data are linked. (This may take a while.)

When the links are established and the data records read, you are prompted to set up the main document.

8. Click the Edit Main Document button. You see the main document on screen.

9. Type the text of the letter.

10. When you get to a spot where you want to insert variable information from the Access database, click the Insert Merge Field button. You see a list of fields from the Access database (see Figure 15-12).

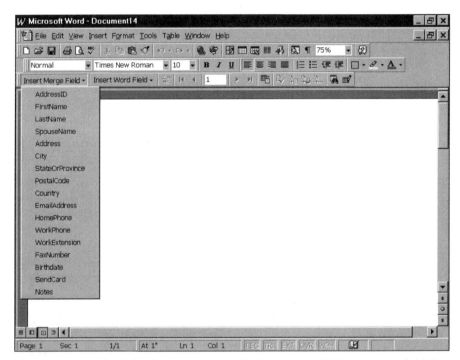

Figure 15-12　The fields from your Access database are available as merge fields in your Word merge document.

11. Click the field you want to insert.

12. Continue typing and inserting fields until you complete the document.

13. To save the main document, open the [File] menu and select the [Save] command. Enter a name and location for the main document. You can now merge the two.

14. Open the [Tools] menu and select the [Mail Merge] command. You see the Mail Merge Helper dialog box, which lists all the file information. Notice that the data source is an Access table (see Figure 15-13).

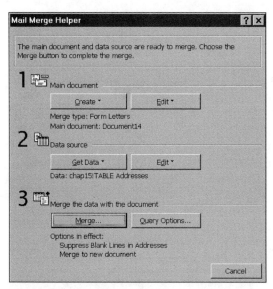

Figure 15-13   The Mail Merge Helper dialog box lists the Access database as the data source.

15. Click the Merge button. You see the Merge dialog box. (For information on selecting options in this dialog box, see Chapter 14.)

16. Make any changes to how you want the merge performed and then click the Merge button. Word merges the letters and displays each one on a separate page (if you merged to a new document). Word uses the data from the Access database for the letters. Figure 15-14 shows one of the letters from a merge.

17. Print the letters using the [File] → [Print] command.

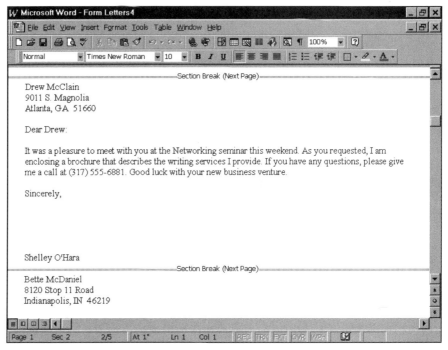

Figure 15-14 The merged letter pulls data from your Access database.

SIDE TRIP

You can also include Access data as a simple table in Word. *To do so, follow these steps:*

1. In Access, display the database in Datasheet view.

2. Select the records you want to copy.

3. Open the Edit menu and select the Copy command.

4. Move to the Word document where you want to paste the data.

5. Open the Edit menu and select the Paste command. The Access data are pasted as a table.

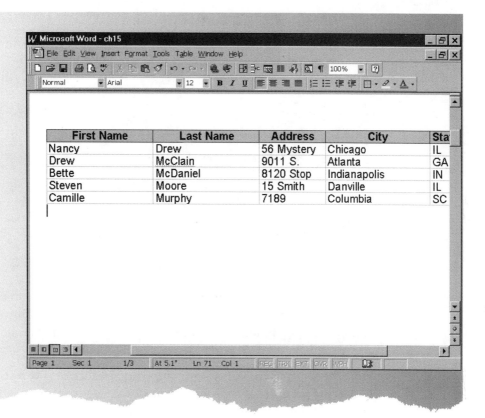

First Name	Last Name	Address	City	Sta
Nancy	Drew	56 Mystery	Chicago	IL
Drew	McClain	9011 S.	Atlanta	GA
Bette	McDaniel	8120 Stop	Indianapolis	IN
Steven	Moore	15 Smith	Danville	IL
Camille	Murphy	7189	Columbia	SC

BONUS

Embedding a New Object

I f you haven't already created the embedded object, you can create it from within Word. You can create several different types of objects (as long as you have those applications). For instance, you can insert an Excel chart, an Excel worksheet, an organizational chart, a graph, a picture, and so on.

Follow these steps:

1. Open the Insert menu and select the Object command. You see the Object dialog box.

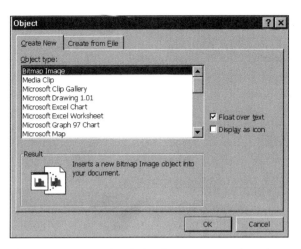

Figure 15-15 In this dialog box, you can select the type of object you want to embed.

2. Select the type of object you want to create. (Notice that you can also use the Create from File tab to insert an object from a file you have created. This process is similar to copying the data, but instead you insert the entire file.)

3. Click the OK button. Word starts that application, and you see a blank document for that application. For instance, if you chose to insert an Excel worksheet, you see a blank worksheet.

4. Create the object using any of the tools from that application.

5. When you are finished creating the object, open the **File** menu and select the **Close & Return to document** command. (The command will list the document name.) The object you just created is inserted into the Word document. When you save the Word document, this object is saved as well.

Summary

If you use a lot of programs, you may want to use bits and pieces from each application. You can combine the data to create a document with varied sorts of information. This chapter explained the various ways you can share data. The next part moves on to the topic of customizing Word. Here you learn how to make the program work just the way you want. The next chapter covers how to set up folders and manage the documents you create using Word.

CHANGING HOW WORD WORKS

Word can work the way you want it to. Practically every option and feature can be tinkered with a little so that it suits how you work or how you compose documents. This part covers some of the changes you may want to make.

"I think that street newspapers might play a big part in helping poor people improve their lives," says Tim Harris, founder and director of Seattle's *Real Change* homeless newspaper.

Real Change was the first online newspaper to focus on the needs of homeless people. Homeless street vendors sell the printed version. Vendors buy their papers, up front, from *Real Change* for a cost of 25 cents per paper. The vendor then sells the paper to the public for one dollar and keeps the 75 cents in profit. This provides a source of income to the vendor, and the 25 cents contributes toward the expenses of *Real Change*.

Harris says that the expenses for the Web site are negligible. *Real Change* trades advertising for the cost of hosting the site. Harris creates the HTML, and volunteers create the CGI scripts. The annual budget amounts to around $100,000, and it is covered by sales to vendors (60 percent), donations, subscriptions, advertising, and proceeds from special events.

The homeless people involved with *Real Change* do more than just sell the papers. They contribute poetry, artwork, and relevant articles to help bring about social change in attitudes toward homelessness. They also serve on the editorial committee,

deciding the content of each monthly issue. An excellent list of volunteers and two paid staff members round out the organization's work group.

The articles for *Real Change* are written using Microsoft Word, and PageMaker is used for the layout. Then a professional printer prints the newspaper.

Harris was inspired to start his own homeless newspaper when he saw a copy of *Street News* in New York several years ago. In 1992 he started his first paper, *Spare Change*, in Boston. After approximately a year of struggling and facing various problems, he disassociated himself from that project. He then moved to Seattle, armed with knowledge from past mistakes, and founded *Real Change*.

"I think the basic appeal of homeless newspapers is that people like to see people doing something to help themselves," says Harris. "The explosion in personal computers and especially the accessibility of desktop publishing has made it easier to publish a newspaper. With a computer, a space to operate, and the energies of one or two dedicated people, you could start a successful newspaper in your own city."

You can visit the Web site of *Real Change* at `http://www.speakeasy.org/realchange/arc.home.html`.

CHAPTER SIXTEEN

MANAGING YOUR WORD FILES

IN THIS CHAPTER YOU LEARN THESE KEY SKILLS

When you start using Word 97, you'll probably have just a few documents. You'll easily recognize each one, and you'll know exactly where each one resides. Think of this as moving into a nice new office and having about four or five sheets of paper to keep track of.

Now fast-forward a few months. You have about fifty documents to keep track of — maybe more — and your nice new office isn't so nice and new anymore. Where is everything? What the heck is this file named MXTOFF97? Why can't you find anything?

As you create more documents, you will want to learn some skills for organizing and keeping track of these documents. That's the topic of this chapter. Here you learn some additional ways to save documents as well as how to organize your documents into folders. You learn how to move, copy, rename, and delete documents you have saved. This is your housekeeping chapter.

Save a Lot

Chapter 2 covered the basics of saving a document — how to name it and assign a folder the first time, how to save it again, and how to save it with a new name or in a different folder. These skills are critical to using Word.

16

Word also includes some other save options applicable in different situations. For instance, you may want to save other key information to remind you of the contents of the file. Or you may have a different word-processing program at home and want to save your Word document as a different file type. You may want to set up a default folder that Word uses to store your files. This section discusses these and other save options.

More about the File: Saving File Summaries

When you have a gazillion files on your computer, sometimes knowing what a file contains by the name — even if it is descriptive — is difficult. You may want to keep and review other information about the document, such as a title or a keyword.

If so, you can save summary information by following these steps:

1. Display the document for which you want to add summary information.

2. Open the File menu and select the Properties command.

3. If necessary, click the Summary tab. You see the Properties dialog box for the document (see Figure 16-1). You see the several pieces of information you can save (and then review) for the document, including a title, a subject, an author, a manager, a company name, a category, keywords, and comments. Notice that Word automatically completes some fields, such as the author field. Word may also suggest entries for other text boxes. You can change any of the entries.

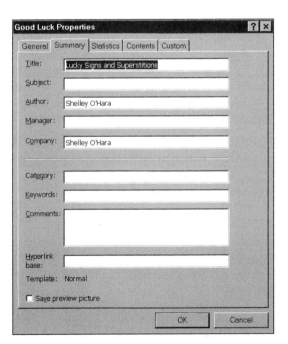

Figure 16-1 Use this dialog box to save other key information about a document.

4. Type or edit the entries in any of the text boxes.

5. Click the OK button.

TIP You can also use this dialog box to display other information about the document — such as document statistics, general file information, and so on. To do so, click the appropriate tab.

If you want, you can be prompted to enter this information each time you save. See the section "Adding a Password and Other Save Options" later in this chapter.

Changing the Default Folder

Each time you select the <u>S</u>ave command, you may be surprised to see a different folder listed. In fact, it's easy to put a document into the wrong folder because you may not realize which folder is the current one.

When you first use Word and then save a document, the My Documents folder is selected as the default folder. You can then change to any other folder to save the document. The next time you save, Word goes back to the folder you most recently selected. For instance, the first time you use the <u>S</u>ave command, you see My Documents. Suppose that you change to a folder on your computer called Memos and save the document in this folder. The next time you use the <u>S</u>ave command, Word will display the Memos folder. It's easy to get confused.

You can do two things to avoid misplacing documents. First, you should always check that the appropriate folder is selected when you save. Second, you can select the default folder you want to use for saving documents.

To set the default folder, follow these steps:

1. Open the **Tools** menu and select the **Options** command.

2. Click the File Locations tab. You see the default folders for the different file types (see Figure 16-2).

3. Select Documents and then click the <u>M</u>odify button. You see the Modify Location dialog box (see Figure 16-3).

4. Select the folder you want to use. You can double-click any folders listed to open and select them. You can use the Up One Level button to move up through the folder structure. You can also use the Look <u>i</u>n drop-down list to change to a different drive.

5. Click the OK button twice.

TIP Just because you've changed the default folder, that doesn't mean you have to save all documents to that folder. You can always select a different folder when you save. Also, Word will not go back to this folder each time — just the first time you select <u>S</u>ave.

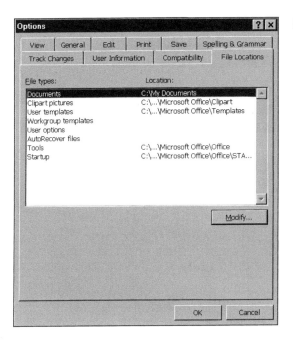

Figure 16-2 You can select the default folder used for these different file types.

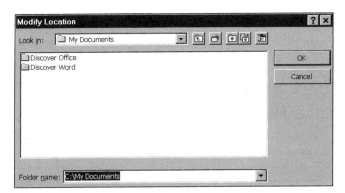

Figure 16-3 Select the folder you want to use to save documents.

Saving a Document as Another File Type

If you work in an office, you may not use the same word-processing program at home. Or perhaps you have an older version. Or you may need to share a document with a friend or coworker who uses a different program. If so, you can use Word to save the document as another file type. You can select from lots of different formats including just plain text, Word 2, WordPerfect, Windows Write, Word for DOS, Works, and several others. Just find out the file format needed.

Then follow these steps to save the document as that type of file:

1. Open the document you want to save as another file type.

2. Open the ▢ **File** ▢ menu and select the ▢ **Save As** ▢ command. You see the Save As dialog box.

3. Display the Save as type drop-down list. You see a list of the different file formats, as shown in Figure 16-4. Note that there are several available; you can scroll the list to see additional formats.

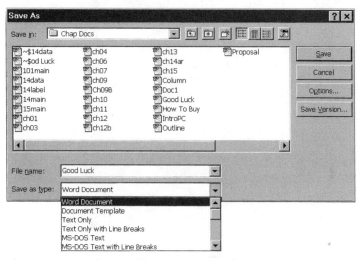

Figure 16-4 Select the file type you want from this list.

4. Click the type of file format you want.

5. If necessary, select the drive and folder where you want to save the new file. Also, you can type a new name in the File name text box.

6. Click the OK button. Word saves the document in the new format.

If you need to share documents between different word-processing programs, you can use Word to save the document as another file type.

Adding a Password and Other Save Options

As with most options, you can control how saves are carried out. You can change, for instance, how often the file is automatically saved. You can add a password if needed.

To make a change, follow these steps:

1. Open the **Tools** menu and select the **Options** command.

2. Click the Save tab. You see the various options you can use for saving documents (see Figure 16-5).

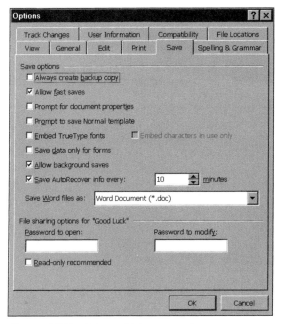

Figure 16-5   Select which save options to use from this dialog box.

3. To turn on an option, check its check box. For example, if you want to be prompted to save file summary information, check the Prompt for document properties check box. If you are not sure what an option does, right-click it and then select **What's This?** to view a pop-up explanation of the option.

4. To set a password for opening or modifying the file, type the password in the Password to open or Password to modify text box.

5. Click the OK button.

6. If you've added a password, you are prompted to confirm it. Retype the password and click OK. Word uses the save options you have set.

Housekeeping on Your PC

You'd be surprised at how many people just save all their documents in one folder. That's the equivalent of having one big filing cabinet and just throwing all the papers into it without any organization. Are you guilty of this sin? If so, take a look at this section for help on keeping those documents organized.

Creating a New Folder

To better manage your documents, you should set up folders and store similar documents together. You can use any organizational scheme you want. For instance, you may want to set up different folders for each type of document you create — memos, letters, reports, and so on. Then when you create a memo, you can save it in the memo folder. And when you want to find a memo, you know to look in the memo folder. Or you may want to set up folders for projects or use some other organizational scheme that makes sense to you and works in your situation.

You can use Windows to create and manage folders, but you may not think of setting up the folders until you are ready to save. In that case, you can use Word to create a new folder.

Follow these steps:

1. If you are saving a new document, open the **File** menu and select the **Save** command. If you are resaving a document, open the **File** menu and select the **Save As** command. You see the Save As dialog box.

2. Change to the folder where you want the new one placed. You can place folders within other folders. You can use the Up One Level button to move up to a higher folder. You can double-click any folder listed to select and open that folder. And you can use the Save in drop-down list to change to a different drive.

3. To create a new folder, click the New Folder button. You see the New Folder dialog box shown in Figure 16-6.

4. Type a name for the folder and click the OK button. Word creates the new folder. You should see it listed in the Save As dialog box.

5. To change to this folder, double-click it in the folder list. You can then use the Save button to save the current document in this folder. If you want to close the dialog box without saving, click the Cancel button.

New folder button

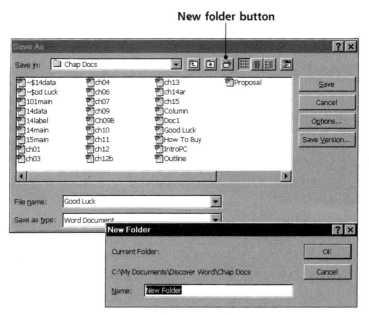

Figure 16-6 Type the name for the new folder.

Using "Favorite" Folders

If you are a "good" saver, you probably have several folders that you use. These may be scattered all over your system — on different drives, within different folders. Rather than navigate through your drives and folders to change to these folders, you can set up a list of your favorite folders and then quickly change to these folders to save or open a document.

TIP Keep in mind that these favorite folders work for other Office applications and Windows. For instance, you can set up a favorite folder for your Excel folders.

To add a favorite folder to the list, follow these steps:

1. Open the **File** menu and select the **Open** command. You see the Open dialog box, shown in Figure 16-7. (The Add to Favorites button is not available in the Save dialog box.)

2. Display the folder you want to add to your favorites list. You can use the Up One Level button to move up to a higher folder. You can double-click any folder listed to open and select that folder. And you can use the Look in drop-down list to change to a different drive.

Look in Favorites button ─┐ ┌─ Add to Favorites button

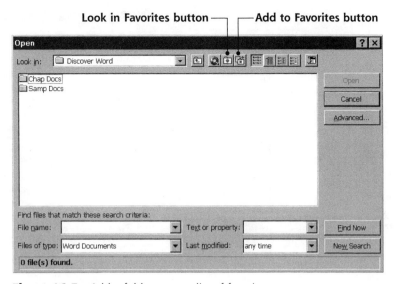

Figure 16-7 Add a folder to your list of favorites.

3. Select the folder.

4. Click the Add to Favorites button. Word adds this folder to your list of favorites.

5. If you want to open a document, change to that folder and double-click the document. To close the dialog box without opening a document, click the Cancel button.

When you want to save a document to one of your favorite folders or open a document in one of these folders, you can use the Look in Favorites button to quickly display the folders and files in the favorites list.

Follow these steps:

1. To open a document, open the [File] menu and select the [Open] command. To save a document, open the [File] menu and select the [Save] command. You see the Open or Save As dialog box.

2. Click the Look in Favorites button. Word displays the folders in your favorites list (see Figure 16-8).

3. Double-click the folder you want to open.

4. If you are opening a file, double-click the file you want to open. To save a file, type a filename and click the Save button.

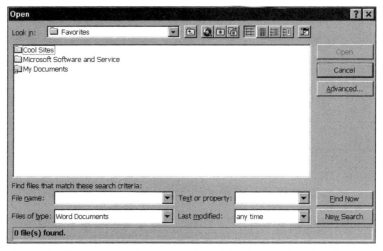

Figure 16-8   You can select any of the folders in your favorites list.

SIDE TRIP

FIGURING OUT FILES

When you are opening a document, you can change how the files are listed to help identify the file you want. To do so, use the buttons in the Open dialog box:

List   Displays a list of folders and files (the default view).

Details   Displays a detailed list, including file size, type, modify dates, etc.

Properties   Displays file summary information about the selected document.

Preview   Displays a preview of the selected document.

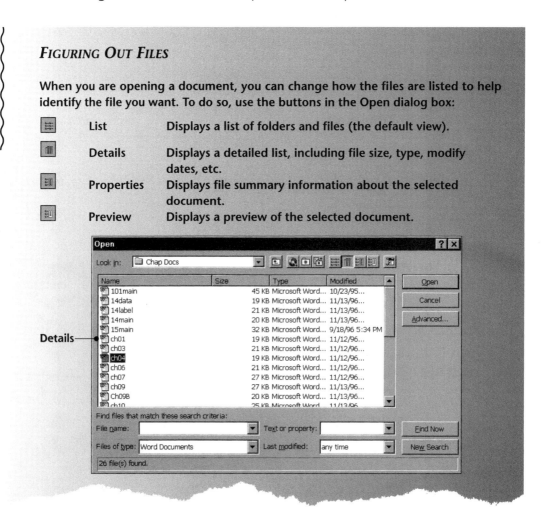

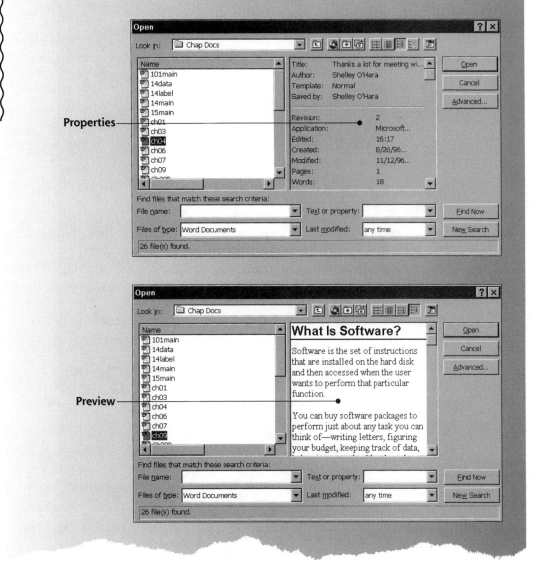

Properties

Preview

Fun with Files

Windows 95 brought a lot of changes to file management. First, with Windows 95 you are no longer restricted to the eight-character filename. You can type up to 255 characters, including spaces. You can use something descriptive like December Expense Report — decoding names like DECEXREP. Remember that if you are sharing files with users of Windows 3.1 or Macintosh computers, their operating systems won't be able to decode the long filenames and they'll get cut off. Your December Expese Report will look something like dec~1.doc.

Also, you no longer have to use a separate file-management program to work with files. All Microsoft programs enable you to work with files within the Open and Save dialog boxes. Say you wanted to delete a document. With previous versions, you would have to know the document name and location. You could then exit Word and use a program like File Manager or File Find to find and then delete that document. Then go back to Word. Ugh!

With the new versions of Word (both Word 95 and Word 97), you can make changes to the file right from within Word. You can delete, rename, copy, and move files from both the Open and Save As dialog boxes, as covered in this section.

Deleting a Document

Do you save every scrap of paper no matter what its significance or importance? Do you have every magazine you've ever received, starting with that *Highlights for Children* kids' magazine? If so, you are probably a pack rat on your PC too. You probably have every document you've ever created. Sooner or later, though, you are going to run out of room. And you are going to need to do a little housekeeping. You should periodically go through your documents and delete those you don't need.

It's a good idea to make periodic backups of your work. Then if something goes wrong, you can use these backup files. You also don't have to worry so much when you delete something because you can always use your backup copy.

Keep in mind that Murphy's Law is always in effect. The minute you think you don't need a document is the minute you do. The next section tells you how to undelete files. You might also consider backing up a document before you delete it.

To delete a document from within Word, follow these steps:

1. Display the Open or Save As dialog box. You can do so by selecting File → Open or File → Save As .Either dialog box is OK.

2. Right-click the document you want to delete. You see a pop-up menu with commands for working with files (see Figure 16-9).

3. Select the Delete command. You are prompted to confirm the deletion.

4. Click the Yes button to delete the document.

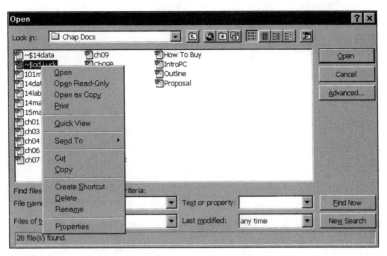

Figure 16-9 You can use these commands to delete, copy, move, and rename your documents.

Undeleting a Document

Make a mistake? Delete a file by accident? Don't panic. Windows doesn't really delete documents; it simply moves them to a temporary holding area called the Recycle Bin. As long as the Recycle Bin has not been emptied, you can retrieve your document from the "trash."

To do so, follow these steps:

1. Go to the Windows desktop. You can minimize the Word window by clicking the Minimize button. You may also need to minimize other open programs. You should see an icon named the Recycle Bin.

2. Double-click the Recycle Bin icon. You see the contents of this bin — any program, document, file, shortcut, or what-have-you that you have deleted recently.

3. Right-click the file you want to undelete. You see a pop-up menu (see Figure 16-10).

4. Select the **Restore** command. Word removes the document from the Recycle Bin and puts it back in its original spot.

5. Click the Close button to close the Recycle Bin window.

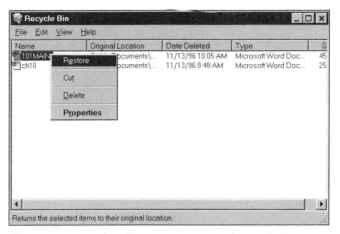

Figure 16-10 Select the R̲estore command to undo the deletion.

SIDE TRIP

EMPTYING THE TRASH

What if you have a document you *really* want to get rid of? Say a letter you wrote telling your boss that he is an ignoramus. You don't want anyone snooping through your trash getting ahold of this letter. When you want to, you can empty the trash. All documents are deleted and cannot be restored. The contents of the Recycle Bin take up disk space, so you should clean it out periodically as well to recover that space.

Follow these steps to empty the Recycle Bin:

1. Double-click the Recycle Bin icon. Check the contents to be doubly sure there's nothing you want to retrieve. Once you empty the trash, you cannot get the document back. (Not without special software and some outside expertise.)

2. Open the File menu and select the Empty Recycle Bin command. You are prompted to confirm the deletion.

3. Click the Y̲es button. Windows permanently removes all the contents of the bin.

4. Click the Close button to close the Recycle Bin window.

Renaming a Document

I can't always decide what I want to name a document. Because I have been using a computer for so long, I have a hard time *not* limiting my filenames to those eight characters. Either I use a name like RPTMTTOM that isn't descriptive enough or I go overboard and use a name like Report on Tuesday's Meeting with

Tom about the IUPUI Project. Luckily for me (and you too), you can easily rename a document.

Simply follow these steps:

1. Display the Open or Save As dialog box. You can do so by selecting File → Open or File → Save As . Either dialog box is OK.

2. Right-click the document you want to rename. You see a pop-up menu with commands for working with files (refer to Figure 16-9).

3. Select the Rename command. Word highlights the current name and displays a box around it (see Figure 16-11).

Figure 16-11 Type or edit the filename.

4. Type a new name and press Enter. The file is renamed.

Copying a Document

As mentioned in Chapter 2, you can use the Save As command to make a copy of a document. You can also use the Copy and Paste commands to copy a document. Use this method when you are reorganizing files and moving them from folder to folder. As another option, you can use the Send To command. Use this command when you are copying the document to a floppy disk to take with you or to keep as a backup copy.

COPYING AND PASTING A DOCUMENT

Just as when you are copying and pasting text, you can use the Copy and Paste commands to copy a document.

Follow these steps:

1. Display the Open or Save As dialog box. You can do so by selecting **File** → **Open** or **File** → **Save As** . Either dialog box is OK.

2. Right-click the document you want to copy. You may need to change to another folder to find the document you want. You see a pop-up menu with commands for working with files (refer to Figure 16-9).

3. Select the **Copy** command.

4. Change to the folder where you want to place the copy of the document.

5. Right-click a blank area of the dialog box and select the **Paste** command. Word copies the document to that folder.

Be sure to right-click a blank area of the folder list. If you right-click a document, you see the pop-up menu for working with that file.

SENDING A DOCUMENT TO A FLOPPY DISK

You may want to keep an extra copy of important documents on a floppy disk for safekeeping. Or you may need to put a document on disk to take with you to your home or another business site. The fastest way to copy a document to a floppy disk is to use the Send To command.

Follow these steps:

1. Display the Open or Save As dialog box. You can do so by selecting **File** → **Open** or **File** → **Save As** . Either dialog box is OK.

2. Right-click the document you want to copy. You may need to change to another folder to find the document you want. You see a pop-up menu with commands for working with files (refer to Figure 16-9).

3. Select the **Send To** command.

Be sure to insert a floppy disk in the drive before you select this command.

4. From the submenu, select your floppy disk drive. Word copies the document to this disk.

Moving a Document

When you save a document, you may accidentally save it in the wrong folder. To make sure it winds up in the right location, you may want to move it to the right folder. Or you may decide to change how you are organizing your documents and move them to other folders. Whatever the reason, you can use the Cut and Paste commands to move a document from one location to another.

Follow these steps:

1. Display the Open or Save As dialog box. You can do so by selecting File → Open or File → Save As . Either dialog box is OK.

2. Right-click the document you want to move. You may need to change to another folder to find the document you want. You see a pop-up menu with commands for working with files (refer to Figure 16-9).

3. Select the Cut command.

4. Change to the folder where you want to place the document.

5. Right-click a blank area of the dialog box and select the Paste command. Word moves the document to that folder.

WORKING WITH SEVERAL FILES

For most commands, you can work with several files at once. For instance, you can select several files and copy them or move them at once. You can also print or delete several files. You cannot rename more than one file at a time.

To select several files that are next to each other, click the first file you want to select and then hold down the Shift key and click the last file. The first and last file and all files in between are selected.

To select files that are not next to each other, click the first file. Then hold down the Ctrl key and click the next file you want to select. Do this for each file you want to select.

Once the files are selected, you can then right-click any of the selected files and select the command you want.

BONUS

Finding a Document

There's nothing more frustrating than *knowing* that you saved a document but not being able to find it. Where is that document hiding? Did that gremlin inside the PC move your file again? Are you losing your mind? You can try looking through folders on a scavenger hunt, or you can search for the document using Word, a much better prospect.

Word offers several ways to search for a file. This section covers the most common. You can try some of the others on your own or consult online help for information.

I Know the Filename . . .

If you know part or all of the filename but just can't remember which folder you saved the file in, you can search by filename.

Follow these steps:

1. Open the `File` menu and select the `Open` command. You see the Open dialog box.

2. In the File name text box, type the name of the file you want to find. You can type all or part of the filename. For example, if you know you named the file something that started with *ch*, you can type *ch**. Use the asterisk (*) wildcard to indicate any number of characters in that spot. Use the question mark (?) wildcard to indicate a single wildcard character in that spot.

   If you have a lot of files in the current folder, you may want to simply search it. But you probably could find the file if it was in the current folder, so most of the time, you will want Word to search through the subfolders too. If so, follow the next step.

3. If you want to search this folder and any other folders within this folder, click the Commands and Settings button and select the Search Subfolders command.

   Keep in mind that Word searches down — not up — through the folders. If you think the folder might be somewhere outside the current folder branch, select a higher folder. Here's an example. Suppose that you have three main folders for your Word documents: LETTERS, MEMOS, and

REPORTS. Within each of these folders, you may also have several subfolders. For instance, within REPORTS, you may have a folder for SALES and one for MARKETING. If you start within REPORTS, Word searches that folder as well as SALES and MARKETING, but *not* MEMOS and LETTERS. If you want to search MEMOS and LETTERS, you have to start at the top-level folder.

4. If necessary, click the Find Now button. (If you decide to search subfolders, you don't need to click this button.) Word displays the results of the search. In Figure 16-12 you see the results of searching for a filename that starts with *ch* in the Discover Word folder and all its subfolders.

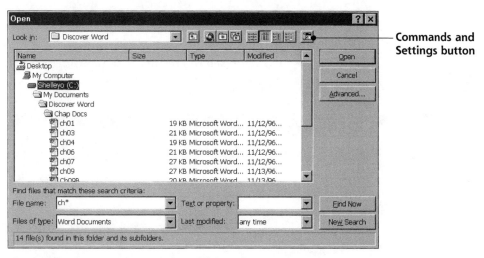

Commands and Settings button

Figure 16-12 You can search for a file by its name.

5. If you want to open a found file, double-click it. To close the dialog box without opening a file, click the Cancel button.

I Know What's in the File . . .

OK. Say you can't even remember the filename, but you do remember what the document said. In that case, you can search for the file based on its contents.

To do so, follow these steps:

1. Open the File menu and select the Open command. You see the Open dialog box.

2. Leave the File name text box empty. If it contains an entry, delete it.

3. If you want to search this folder and any other folders within this folder, click the Commands and Settings button. If you don't see a checkmark next to the Search Subfolders command, select this command.

TIP **Word keeps the Search Subfolders command on until you turn it off. You can tell whether this command is on by clicking the Commands and Settings button and looking at the command. If there's a checkmark next to it, it's on. (You can turn it off by selecting the command again.)**

4. In the Text or property text box, type the text that's in the file you want to find. Type a unique word or phrase. If you type something too common, you'll get too many matches and will never be able to find the file.

5. If necessary, click the Find Now button. Word displays the results of the search. In Figure 16-13 you see the results of searching for a file with the text *kiosk* in the Discover Word folder and all its subfolders.

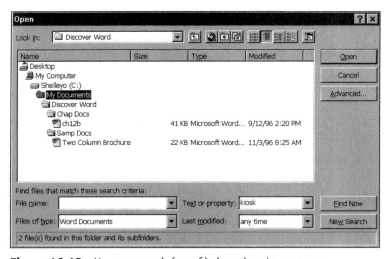

Figure 16-13 You can search for a file based on its contents.

6. If you want to open a found file, double-click it. To close the dialog box without opening a file, click the Cancel button.

I Remember When I Last Worked on the File . . .

If you still can't find the file, but you *know* that you worked on it sometime last week, you can try searching based on when the file was last modified.

Follow these steps:

1. Open the `File` menu and select the `Open` command. You see the Open dialog box.

2. Leave the File name text box empty. If it contains an entry, delete it.

3. If you want to search this folder and any other folders within this folder, click the Commands and Settings button. If you don't see a checkmark next to the Search Subfolders command, select this command.

4. Display the Last modified drop-down list and select the date range you want to search: yesterday, today, last week, this week, last month, this month, or any time.

5. If necessary, click the Find Now button. Word displays the results of the search.

6. If you want to open a found file, double-click it. To close the dialog box without opening a file, click the Cancel button.

Summary

This chapter covered how to set up your folders in just the way you want. You also learned some techniques for working with the documents you have stored on your computer. The next chapter continues the topic of customization and covers some changes you can make to how Word works.

MAKING WORD WORK THE WAY YOU WANT

IN THIS CHAPTER YOU LEARN THESE KEY SKILLS

Think about how you perform a task such as cooking a meal. Do you have everything going at once? Or do you make each meal item one thing at a time? Do you clean up as you go? Or do you leave it all for the end? Do you use a food processor? Or do you chop by hand? Now think about how your mother or your aunt or your spouse or your neighbor cooks the same meal. It's likely each person does the same task differently.

The same is true for creating documents. If several people are creating the same type of document, most likely each does that job in a different way.

The makers of Word needed a way to accommodate how most people work. That's why certain options have defaults that work in the most common situations. The makers of Word also needed to make Word flexible so that if the defaults didn't work for a user's particular work habits or situation, the user could make a change. This chapter discusses some of the changes you may want to make to how Word works.

Arranging the Word Tools

You can think of Word as your desktop, equipped with all the tools you need to write, edit, and change the look of your text. If you don't have the tools you need handy, you can make them handy, as described here.

Hiding Toolbars

If you don't use the toolbars, you can close them so that they do not appear. Doing so will give you some extra room for your document text.

To hide a toolbar, follow these steps:

1. Open the ⬚ **View** ⬚ menu and select the ⬚ **Toolbar** ⬚ command. You see a list of the available toolbars (see Figure 17-1). Toolbars with checks next to their names are displayed.

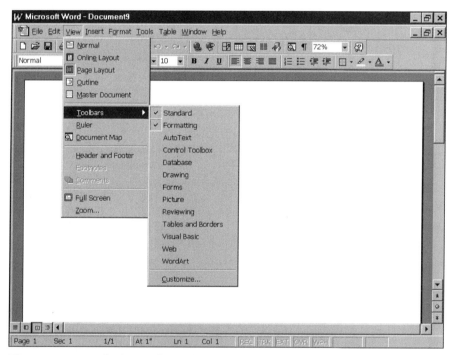

Figure 17-1   Uncheck a toolbar to hide it.

2. To hide a toolbar, select it. Figure 17-2 shows the screen with both the standard and formatting toolbars turned off.

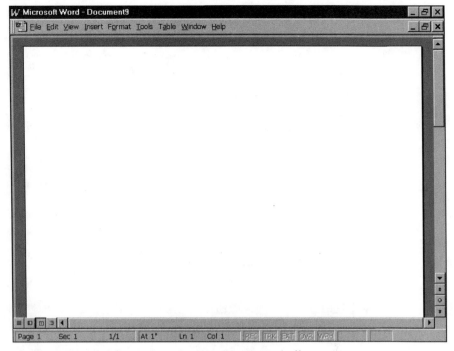

Figure 17-2 This figure shows both toolbars turned off.

Displaying Other Toolbars

By the same token, if you really like the toolbars, you may want to display other toolbars. In addition to the standard and formatting toolbars, Word includes several other toolbars: WordArt, AutoText, databases, drawing, picture, and tables and borders. (Some of these toolbars are displayed automatically. For instance, if you insert an AutoShape, the Drawing toolbar is displayed.)

To display other toolbars, follow these steps:

1. Open the **View** menu and select the **Toolbar** command. You see a list of the available toolbars (refer to Figure 17-1).

2. Select the toolbar you want displayed. Word displays the toolbar. Figure 17-3 shows some of the different toolbars you can display. Notice that the name of each toolbar appears in the title bar of the toolbar.

X-REF You can move the toolbars around and make other changes. To do so, see the section "Your Own Toolbox!"

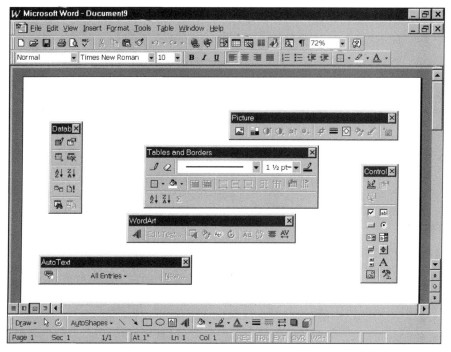

Figure 17-3 You can display other toolbars on-screen.

Hiding Other Stuff

You have a lot of control over what appears on your screen. You can hide or display items such as the status bar, the scroll bars, the ruler, nonprinting characters, and other elements.

To make a change, follow these steps:

1. Open the Tools menu and select the Options command.

2. Select the View tab. You see the View tab, shown in Figure 17-4.

3. In the Show area, select what you want displayed. By default, Word shows drawings, animated text, ScreenTips, and highlighting. You can turn off any of these items by unchecking its check box. You can also choose to display hidden items such as bookmarks, field codes, picture placeholders, text boundaries, or object anchors. To display an item, check its check box.

TIP Not sure what an option does? You can get help by right-clicking the option and selecting the What's This? command.

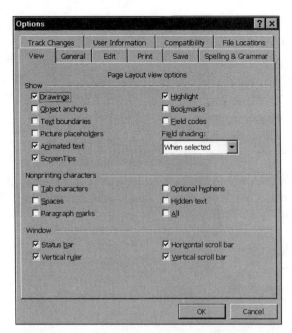

Figure 17-4   Check items you want displayed;
uncheck items you want to hide.

4. In the Nonprinting characters area, select which nonprinted characters you want displayed. You can display characters for tabs, spaces, paragraph marks, optional hyphens, hidden text, or all.

5. In the Window area, all items — Status bar, Vertical ruler, Horizontal scroll bar, Vertical scroll bar — are on. You can hide any of these by unchecking its check box.

6. Click the OK button.

Hiding Everything

If you used a DOS version of WordPerfect, you may like just a plain old blank screen without any toolbars, menu bars, or other distractions. You can make Word kind of like that old blue WordPerfect screen. Even if you didn't use DOS, you may prefer a blank screen, like a big clean piece of paper.

If so, you can hide everything by following these steps:

1. Open the View menu and select the Full Screen command. Everything on-screen is hidden except for a small Full Screen toolbar (see Figure 17-5). You can use this toolbar to return to the regular view.

2. Click the Close Full Screen button in this toolbar to redisplay the on-screen elements.

CHANGING THE LOOK OF THE BUTTONS

You can change how the buttons appear in the toolbar. You can also turn off the ScreenTips — the pop-up names that appear. *To make a change, follow these steps:*

1. Open the Tools menu and select the Customize command.

2. Click the Options tab. You see the Customize dialog box with the Options tab displayed.

3. To display large icons, check the Large icons check box. To turn off the ScreenTips, uncheck the Show ScreenTips on toolbars check box. To display any keyboard shortcuts for the button, check the Show shortcut keys in ScreenTips check box.

4. Click the Close button.

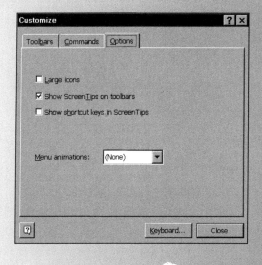

Your Own Toolbox!

Y ou can not only select which toolbars are displayed, as covered in the last section, but you can also move the toolbars where you want, change which buttons are on each toolbar, and even create your own toolbar with your favorite buttons. This section discusses these types of changes.

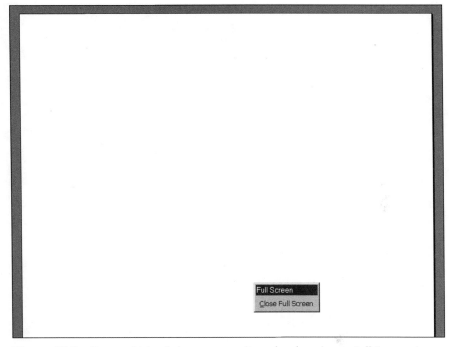

Figure 17-5   You can hide all the on-screen items by changing to Full Screen view.

Moving the Toolbars

When you start Word, the formatting and standard toolbars are displayed right under the menu bar. If you don't like this placement, you can move them to another spot. You can have them float as a palette, or you can dock them next to (butt them up against) the edge of the screen. (When the toolbars aren't docked, you can also resize them.)

To move a toolbar, follow these steps:

1. Point to an area that doesn't include a button. This step can be kind of tricky. You can't put the pointer on a button or you will select that button. Put it right between two buttons.

2. Drag the toolbar to a new location. Word moves the toolbar. Figure 17-6 shows the Formatting toolbar moved. Notice that you can now see the title bar and Close button for the toolbar.

You can do any of the following:

❋   To return the toolbar to a docked position, drag it until it butts up against a window edge.

❋   To resize the toolbar, point to one of the borders and drag.

❋   To close the toolbar, click the Close button.

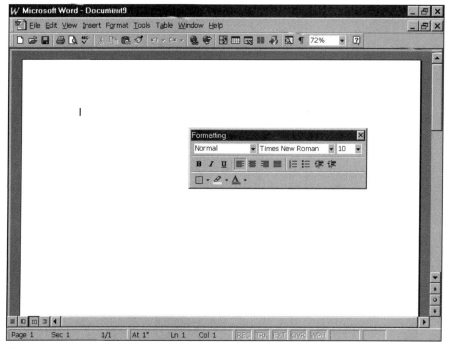

Figure 17-6   You can move a toolbar to another position on-screen.

Adding or Deleting Buttons from a Toolbar

The formatting and standard toolbars each contain buttons for commonly used features. You may find that you use some buttons all the time. You may also find that you don't use some buttons at all. You can make changes to the toolbar if you want, to make it more suitable to how you use it. You can rearrange the buttons, putting them in a different order. You can delete buttons you don't use or add buttons you do want.

To add or delete a button, follow these steps:

1. Display the toolbar you want to customize. You can customize any of the Word toolbars — not just the standard and formatting ones.

2. Open the **View** menu and select the **Toolbars** command.

3. From the submenu, select the **Customize** command. You see the Customize dialog box.

4. Click the Commands tab. Yes, that's the tab you want — not the Toolbars tab. On the left, you see a list of categories. On the right you see the commands in the selected category. For example, Figure 17-7 shows the Insert commands.

5. Once this dialog box is open, you can make changes to the toolbar.

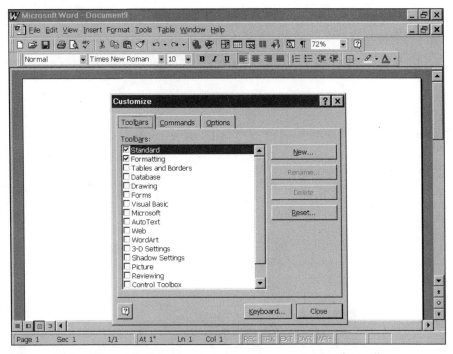

Figure 17-7 When this dialog box is open, you can customize the toolbars.

6. Do any of the following:

✳ To move a button on a toolbar, drag it to a new location on the toolbar. For this action, you only have to have the dialog box displayed. You don't actually do anything in the dialog box.

✳ To delete a button on a toolbar, drag it off the toolbar. Again, you only have to have the dialog box open; you don't need to select anything in the dialog box.

✳ To add a button, select the category you want from the Categories list in the dialog box. Then select the command you want in the Commands list. Drag the command from the Customize dialog box to the toolbar on-screen. Word adds a button to the toolbar. If the command had an icon next to it, that's the icon used for the button. If the command doesn't have an icon, Word just uses a text button. Figure 17-8 shows a button for Insert Page Break added to the end of the standard toolbar.

TIP If you try to add the button to the end, be sure it's right on the toolbar. You can tell when the pointer is in the right spot. If you see a plus sign, the button will be added. If you see an X, you are not on the toolbar.

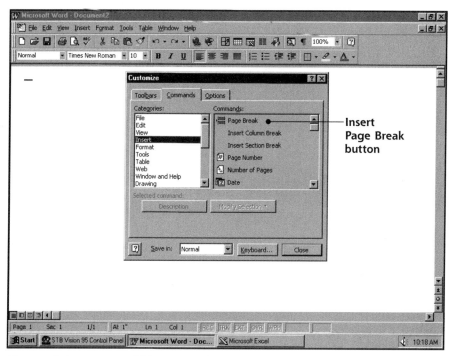

Figure 17-8 You can add buttons to the toolbars.

7. When you are finished adding and deleting buttons, click the Close button.

TIP If you make a lot of changes and want to go back to the default, you can reset the toolbar. To do so, select <u>V</u>iew → <u>T</u>oolbars → <u>C</u>ustomize. On the Tool<u>b</u>ars tab, select the toolbar you want to reset. Then click the <u>R</u>eset button. Word goes back to the default order and buttons. Close the dialog box by clicking the Close button.

Creating Your Own Toolbar

Instead of messing with the standard and formatting toolbars, you may want to leave them as is and create your own little box (in this case, bar) of tools. You can create a new toolbar and then add the buttons you want.

To create a new toolbar, follow these steps:

1. Open the **View** menu and select the **Toolbars** command.

2. From the submenu, select the **Customize** command. You see the Customize dialog box.

3. Click the Tool<u>b</u>ars tab.

310 CHANGING HOW WORD WORKS

4. Click the <u>N</u>ew button. You see the New Toolbar dialog box (see Figure 17-9).

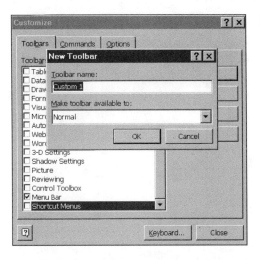

Figure 17-9 Type a name for your toolbar.

5. Type the toolbar name in the <u>T</u>oolbar name text box. Type something that will remind you of the purpose of the toolbar.

6. If you want to make the toolbar available to a specific template, display the <u>M</u>ake toolbar available to drop-down list and select the template you want. The default is Normal.

7. Click the OK button. You see the Customize dialog box and a really small toolbar. You may have to look around to find it (see Figure 17-10).

8. Click the <u>C</u>ommands tab.

9. Select the category you want from the Categories list. You can add buttons from the various menus, and other toolbars, as well as for macros, fonts, AutoText entries, and styles.

10. Drag the command from the Customize dialog box to the new toolbar on-screen. Word adds a button to the toolbar. If the command had an icon next to it, that's the icon used for the button. If the command doesn't have an icon, Word just uses a text button. Do this for each button you want to add.

11. When you are finished adding buttons, click the Close button. Your toolbar is displayed on-screen. You can use any of the buttons. You can move it around. And you can close it by clicking the Close button.

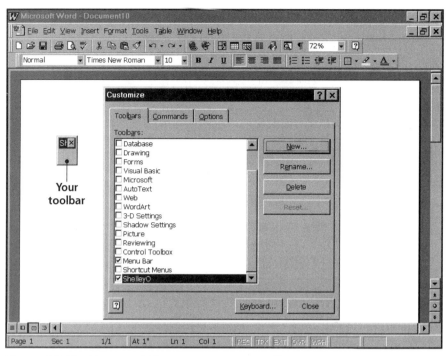

Figure 17-10 You can add buttons to your new toolbar.

SIDE TRIP

DELETING AND RENAMING CUSTOM TOOLBARS

If you don't like the name you used for a toolbar, you can rename it. You can also delete a custom toolbar you no longer need. You cannot delete or rename any of the default Word toolbars.

To rename or delete a toolbar, follow these steps:

1. Open the ⌑ View ⌑ menu and select the ⌑ Toolbars ⌑ command.

2. Select ⌑ Customize ⌑.

3. Click the Toolbars tab.

4. Select the toolbar you want to delete or rename. Notice that the Rename and Delete buttons are available only when you select a custom toolbar.

5. To delete the toolbar, click the Delete button. When prompted to confirm the deletion, click the OK button.

6. To rename the toolbar, click the Rename button, type a new name, and click OK.

7. Click the Close button.

Customize

Toolbars | Commands | Options

Toolbars:

- [ ] Database
- [ ] Drawing
- [ ] Forms
- [ ] Visual Basic
- [ ] Microsoft
- [ ] AutoText
- [ ] Web
- [ ] WordArt
- [ ] 3-D Settings
- [ ] Shadow Settings
- [ ] Picture
- [ ] Reviewing
- [ ] Control Toolbox
- [x] Menu Bar
- [ ] Shortcut Menus
- [x] ShelleyO

New...
Rename...
Delete
Reset...

Keyboard... | Close

Changing the Menus

Just as you can customize the toolbars, you can also customize the menus — rearranging commands, adding new commands, deleting commands. For the most part, changing the menus can cause a big mess; this book, the Word 97 online help, and other users of your computer will assume that all default commands are available. If you make a change, you may end up like a sailor out to sea without a map. Therefore, I am not going to cover how to modify the menus. (If you really want to know, it's similar to customizing the toolbars. You can get more information using the Office Assistant.)

I will show you one cool change you can make: how menus are opened.

To make a change, follow these steps:

1. Open the **Tools** menu and select the **Customize** command.

2. Click the Options tab. You see the Customize dialog box with the Options tab displayed.

3. Display the Menu animations drop-down list and select an animation (see Figure 17-11). You can select Random, Unfold, or Slide. Try them out to see how they differ.

4. Click the Close button. Now try opening a menu. Nifty, huh? It can make you a little dizzy after a while, though. "Slide" slides the menu down like a window shade. "Unfold" unfolds it from one corner to the opposite corner.

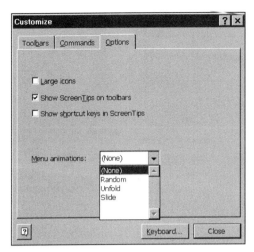

Figure 17-11 Select a menu animation.

FEATURE FOCUS Menu animation is a new feature in Word 97.

More Tinkering under the Hood

Word includes many other program options that you can control. Many have been covered throughout this book. For instance, Save options and setting a default folder using the File Locations tab are both covered in Chapter 16. Spelling and grammar options are covered in Chapter 4.

Follow these steps to review or change some of the other program options:

1. Open the **Tools** menu and select the **Options** command.

2. Select the tab you want to change or review. For example, Figure 17-12 shows the Edit tab options. You can tell what the tab contains by its name. For instance, the Print tab contains options for — guess what — printing. If you aren't sure, just display the tab and then see what options are included.

3. Review or make any changes.

4. Click the OK button.

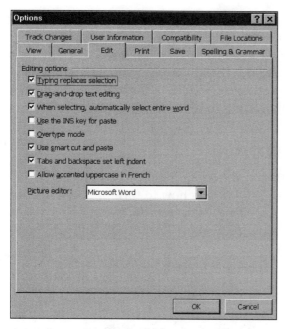

Figure 17-12 Make changes to Edit options using this tab.

You Don't Even Have to Know Programming!

Word includes a lot of features that automate creating a document. You can use AutoText to insert frequently used words or phrases. You can use styles and AutoFormat to speed up formatting. And you can use templates to speed both entering text and formatting. But what if you have some *other* type of task you want to automate? Something else that you do over and over.

The makers of Word couldn't possibly anticipate each type of situation that you would need to automate. Therefore, when there's some task that you do over and over again, and styles, AutoText, AutoCorrect, AutoFormat, or templates don't help you out, you can create a macro.

When you discover that you're performing a task over and over again, you can create a macro to automate that task.

A macro is a set of recorded actions. You can record typing text, selecting commands, moving the insertion point, anything you do in Word. Then once you record these actions, you can play them back. You can select one command (the command to play back the macro) instead of selecting the same set of commands again and again.

This section explains how to record, play back, and edit a macro.

Recording a Macro

If you are worried that you have to be a programmer to create a macro, stop worrying. All you need to know is how to turn on the macro recorder. Then go about your business selecting the commands and actions you want recorded. When you're done, turn off the macro recorder. It's that easy. You don't have to know programming because Word translates your actions into programming instructions.

 TIP Word includes a complex and complete programming language called Visual Basic, which you can use to create more advanced macros. If you are interested in this type of programming, you can use the online help to get information on using the programming language.

WHAT SHOULD I RECORD?

There's no set rule for what types of actions are best suited to a macro. It depends on what you do with Word and what types of tasks you find yourself doing over and over. A little bell should go off in your head when you find yourself repeatedly selecting the same set of commands. When you hear the ding of that bell, you should consider creating a macro.

For instance, when I submit a chapter to my editor, I usually create a folder with the name of the book, the filename, and the page number. I could open each file, select the View → Header and Footer command, switch to the footer, type the text I want to include, and then close the footer, but to save time, I create a macro to do it for me. (I could also have used a template.) As another example, I have to underline the key letter in each Word command. If I did this manually, I would have to select the single character and then either click the Underline button or press Ctrl+U or use the Font dialog box to add underlining. Instead, I recorded a macro that selects the next character, turns on underlining, and then moves the insertion point one character over. These are just some of the macros that work for my situation. Yours will surely be different, but at least you get an idea of when to think macro.

HOW DO I RECORD A MACRO?

Before you record your macro, you should think about what actions you want to perform. Include in the macro only the tasks you want to record. Remember that every key you press, everything you type, every command you select will be included. You may want to jot down some notes so that you don't make a mistake when recording.

It's also a good idea to start in a blank document. Then if something goes wrong, you don't have to worry about messing up that document.

Once you are ready to create the macro, you can follow these steps to turn on the recorder and record your actions:

1. Open the **Tools** menu and select the **Macro** command.

2. From the submenu that appears, select **Record New Macro** . You see the Record Macro dialog box (see Figure 17-13).

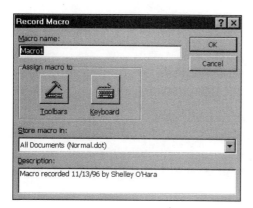

Figure 17-13 Type a name for the macro.

3. Type a macro name in the Macro name text box. Use a name that will remind you of the purpose of the macro.

4. To change which template the macro is stored in and available with, display the Store macro in drop-down list and select the template you want. The default is All documents or the Normal template.

X-REF **You can assign a macro to a toolbar or shortcut key. For help on customizing a toolbar, see the section "Your Own Toolbox!" The Bonus section at the end of this chapter covers how to assign keyboard shortcuts to commands and macros.**

5. If you want, type or modify the description in the Description text box.

6. Click the OK button. You see the current document as well as the Stop Recording toolbar (see Figure 17-14). The mouse pointer represents a cassette tape to remind you that you are recording a macro. From now until you turn off the macro recorder, everything you do — any text you type, buttons you click, commands you select, movements you make — is recorded.

**Stop
Recording button** Stop F ✕ **Figure 17-14** Record your macro actions and then use the
button in the toolbar to stop recording.

7. Perform the actions you want to record. You can type text, select commands, click toolbar buttons, move through the document, and so on. It's best to go slowly so that you don't make a mistake. (A later section tells you how to edit a macro if you do make a mistake.)

8. When you complete all the steps you want to record, click the Stop Recording button.

The macro is saved to the template you selected. You can now play back this macro in any document created with that template. The next section covers how to play back a macro you have recorded.

Playing Back a Macro

After you record a macro, you can easily play it back. All the commands you selected, the text you typed, the buttons you clicked, the actions you performed are carried out just as you recorded them.

Before you try your macro in a "real" document, you may want to test it in a blank document. Then if there are any problems, you can just close the document without saving. Once you know the document is working as you want it to, you can play it in your other documents.

To play back the macro, follow these steps:

1. Open the ⎡ **Tools** ⎤ menu and select the ⎡ **Macro** ⎤ command.

2. From the submenu, select ⎡ **Macros** ⎤. You see the Macros dialog box (see Figure 17-15).

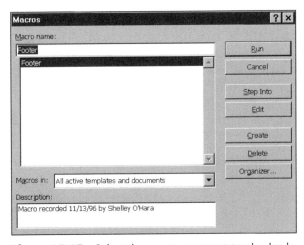

Figure 17-15 Select the macro you want to play back.

3. In the <u>M</u>acro name list, click the macro you want to run. You can also type the macro name.

4. Click the <u>R</u>un button. Word carries out the actions you recorded in the macro.

Deleting a Macro

If you can't get a macro to work or you find you don't need a macro, you can delete it.

To do so, follow these steps:

1. Open the `Tools` menu and select the `Macro` command.

2. From the submenu, select `Macros`. You see the Macros dialog box (refer to Figure 17-15).

3. In the <u>M</u>acro name list, click the macro you want to delete.

4. Click the <u>D</u>elete button. You are prompted to confirm the deletion.

5. Click the <u>Y</u>es button. Word deletes the macro.

6. Click the Close button to close the Macro dialog box.

Editing a Macro

When you first try a macro, you may have a hard time selecting just the commands you want. You may forget something or include something that shouldn't be part of the macro. If you make a mistake, don't worry. You can always correct it.

The easiest way to fix a mistake is to delete the original macro and then rerecord the macro. You can also edit the macro and type the programming commands. To use this method, you should have a good understanding of Visual Basic, Word's programming language. This section covers how to rerecord a macro and tells you how to display and edit a macro.

RERECORDING A MACRO

Many users won't want to take the time to learn how to use Word's programming language. It's not really all that critical to know. If you don't want to open *that* can of worms, you can simply fix a macro by deleting it (covered in the preceding section) and then creating a new macro and rerecording it.

EDITING A MACRO MANUALLY

If you know Visual Basic (a popular programming language), you can edit the macro manually, typing new commands, editing existing commands, or deleting commands you no longer want to include. Word includes a separate Visual Basic editor that includes many commands and features for modifying macros. This topic is too complex to cover in this book. For more information, consult online help or the Visual Basic manual. This section just gives you a peek at the Visual Basic editor.

Follow these steps to edit a macro:

1. Open the **Tools** menu and select the **Macro** command.

2. From the submenu, select **Macros** . You see the Macros dialog box (refer to Figure 17-15).

3. In the Macro name list, click the macro you want to edit. You can also type the macro name.

4. Click the Edit button. Word starts the Visual Basic editor and displays the macro (see Figure 17-16).

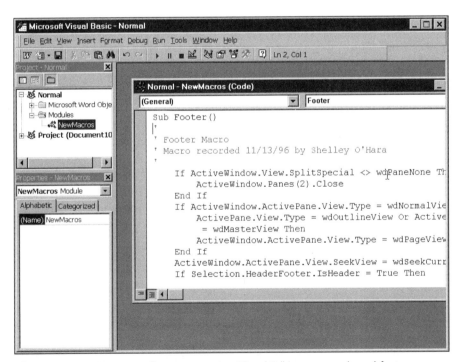

Figure 17-16 You can edit a macro using Visual Basic commands and features.

5. Make any changes to the macro. You should consult the Visual Basic manual for help on the editor and available programming commands.

6. To close the macro and the Visual Basic editor, click the Close button for the window. Any changes you made are saved.

BONUS

Assigning Shortcut Keys

I love shortcut keys. I'm a fast typist, and I don't like to have to move my hand away to the mouse to select a command or click a button. Plus, I learned to use a PC before a mouse was standard equipment and before software was dolled up with all the buttons. To do something more quickly, you *had* to learn keyboard shortcuts.

If you, too, like keyboard shortcuts, you may want to review and even change some of the keyboard assignments. For example, when I write a book, I have to assign styles to the different headings, bulleted lists, and numbered lists. To do so quickly, I assign shortcut keys to the styles I use most frequently. You can assign keyboard shortcuts to styles, macros, AutoText entries, toolbar buttons, fonts, commands, and common symbols.

Here's how to make a change:

1. Open the **Tools** menu and select the **Customize** command.

2. Click the Keyboard button. You see the Customize Keyboard dialog box.

3. In the Categories list, select the category you want to change. As mentioned, you can assign shortcut keys to menu commands, toolbar buttons, macros, fonts, AutoText entries, styles, and common symbols. The Commands list shows the available items. For example, if you select a menu, you see menu commands. If you select styles, you see a list of styles.

4. In the Commands list, select the item (command, button, macro, font, AutoText, style, or symbol) for which you want to assign a keyboard shortcut. You see any current shortcut keys. The Description area displays a short description of the command or item.

5. Click in the Press <u>n</u>ew shortcut key text box and press the keys you want to use as the shortcut. You can press any combination of Ctrl, Alt, Ctrl+Shift, Ctrl+Alt, Alt+Shift, Ctrl+Alt+Shift with any of the number or character keys. If you press a keyboard combination that is already used, you see the current assignment in the dialog box. You can either press Backspace to delete this key combination and then press another key combination, or you can reassign the current one.

6. To assign this shortcut key combination, click the <u>A</u>ssign button.

7. Follow steps 3 through 6 for each keyboard shortcut you want to assign.

8. When you are finished making changes, click the Close button. You see the Customize dialog box.

9. Click the Close button to close this dialog box. You can now use this keyboard shortcut.

Summary

This chapter explained how to change what appears on-screen, modify the toolbars to suit your preferences, create new toolbars, change how menus are displayed, and set other program options. You should feel pretty comfortable with how Word works because you have a lot of control over most features and options.

This chapter also covered how to record and play back macros, a feature you can use to automate routine tasks. The chapter also briefly introduced the Visual Basic editor, which may be of interest to any programmers who use Word.

The next part includes some reference information including a troubleshooting guide, a visual index of document examples, and a glossary.

WEB PATH ➡ **Check out this Web site for information about Word macro viruses and how to protect your files.**

`http://www.datafellows.fi/macro/word.htm`

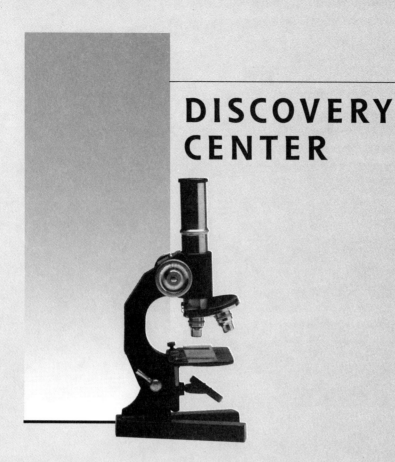

DISCOVERY CENTER

In this section, you'll discover many of the important steps for accomplishing tasks in Word 97. The Discovery Center serves as a handy reference to the most important tasks in the chapters. The quick summaries include page references referring you back to the chapters, if you need more information.

CHAPTER 1

How to Start Word (page 12)

1. Click the Start menu.

2. Select the [Programs] command.

3. If necessary, open the program folder that contains the Word program icon.

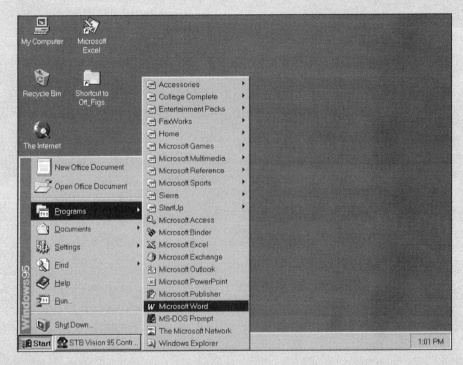

4. Click the program icon to start Word.

How to Select a Menu Command (page 15)

1. Click the menu name to open the menu.

2. Click the command you want.

How to Use Undo (page 18)

1. Select [Edit] → [Undo] or click [✎ ▾].

How to Get Help (page 22)

1. Click the Office Assistant.
2. Type what you want to do.
3. Select the topic you want.
4. Click the Close button.

How to Exit Word (page 26)

1. Save all your documents.
2. Select File → Exit .

CHAPTER 2

How to Type Text (page 31)

1. Press the letters and number keys on the keyboard to type text.
2. When you get to the end of the line, *don't* press Enter. Instead, let Word wrap the text to the end of the line. Do press Enter when you want to insert a line or a paragraph break.

How to Insert a Page Break (page 33)

1. Press Ctrl+Enter.

How to Move Around Using the Mouse (page 36)

1. Move the mouse pointer to where you want to place the insertion point.
2. Click the mouse button.

How to Move Around Using the Keyboard (page 36)

Press any of the following keys:

←	Move left one character
→	Move right one character
↑	Move up one line
↓	Move down one line

Press any of the following keys:

Home	Move to the beginning of the line
End	Move to the end of the line
Ctrl+Home	Move to the top of the document
Ctrl+End	Move to the end of the document

How to Save a Document (page 40)

1. Select **File** → **Save** or click 🖫.

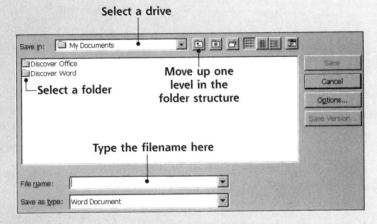

Select a drive

Move up one level in the folder structure

Select a folder

Type the filename here

2. If this is the first time you are saving a document, type a name.
3. Select a folder.
4. Click the Save button.

How to Close a Document (page 42)

1. Save the document.
2. Click Close in the document window or select **File** → **Close**.

How to Open a Document (page 42)

1. Select **File** → **Open**.
2. Open the folder that contains the document.
3. Click the Up One Level button to move up one level.
4. Use the Look in drop-down list to change to another drive.

5. When you see the file listed, double-click it.

How to Create a New Document (page 43)

1. Click 🗋.

CHAPTER 3

How to Select Text with the Mouse (page 48)

1. Click at the start of the text.

2. Hold down the mouse button and drag across the text you want to select.

3. Release the mouse button.

How to Select Text with the Keyboard (page 50)

1. Move the insertion point to the start of the text.

2. Hold down the Shift key and use the movement keys to select the text you want.

3. Release the Shift key.

How to Delete Text (page 50)

1. Select the text you want to delete.

2. Press the Delete key.

How to Move Text (page 51)

1. Select the text you want to move.

2. Select Edit → Cut or click ✂.

3. Move to where you want to paste the text.

4. Select Edit → Paste or click 📋.

How to Copy Text (page 53)

1. Select the text you want to copy.

2. Select ⌜ Edit ⌟→⌜ Copy ⌟ or click 🗐.

3. Move to where you want to paste the text.

4. Select ⌜ Edit ⌟→⌜ Paste ⌟ or click 📋.

How to Find Text (page 55)

1. Select ⌜ Edit ⌟→⌜ Find ⌟.

2. Enter the text you want to find.

3. Click the ⌜ Find Next ⌟ button.

How to Replace Text (page 58)

1. Select ⌜ Edit ⌟→⌜ Replace ⌟.

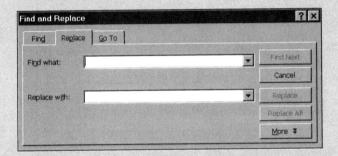

2. Enter the text you want to replace.

3. Enter the text you want to use as the replacement.

4. Click the Find Next button.

5. Word moves to the first match and highlights it. To make this replacement, click the Replace button. To make all replacements, click the Replace All button.

CHAPTER 4

How to Correct a Highlighted Spelling Error (page 66)

1. Right-click the highlighted word.

2. Select the correct spelling.

How to Correct a Highlighted Grammar Error (page 68)

1. Right-click the highlighted word or phrase.
2. Select the correction.

How to Check the Spelling of the Entire Document (page 70)

1. Select `Tools` → `Spelling and Grammer` or click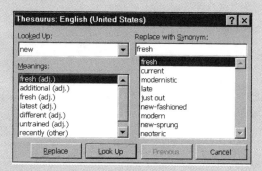
2. To skip this occurrence but stop on the next one, click the Ignore button. To skip all occurrences of this word, click the Ignore All button.
3. To replace the word with one of the suggested spellings, click the spelling in the Suggestions list. Click the Change button to change this occurrence. Click the Change All button to replace all occurrences of the word.
4. If none of the replacements are correct, correct the error by editing the word or phrase in the Not in Dictionary list box. Then click the Change button.
5. Click the Add button to add the word to the dictionary.
6. If you want to add the error and its correction to the AutoCorrect list, click the AutoCorrect button.

How to Look up a Word in the Thesaurus (page 77)

1. Click within the word you want to look up.
2. Select `Tools` → `Language`.

3. To look up synonyms for another meaning, click the meaning you want in the Meanings list.
4. To look up synonyms for another listed synonym, click the word you want in the Replace with Synonym list. Then click the Look Up button.

5. To use one of the listed synonyms, click the word you want to use and then click the Replace button.

CHAPTER 5

How to Preview a Document (page 82)

Select File → Print Preview or click 🔍.

How to View a Document Page by Page (page 85)

Select Tools → Page Layout.

How to Zoom a Document (page 86)

1. Select Tools → Zoom.

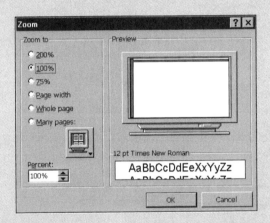

2. Select the view or zoom percentage you want.

How to Print a Document (page 88)

1. Select File → Print or click 🖨.

2. Make any changes to the print options.

3. Click the OK button.

How to Print an Envelope (page 90)

1. Display the letter for which you want an envelope.

2. Select | Tools | → | Envelopes and Labels |.

3. If necessary, click the Envelopes tab.

4. Make any corrections to the Delivery address.

5. Insert the envelope in the manual feed for your printer.

6. Click the Print button.

CHAPTER 6

How to Make Text Bold, Italic, or Underlined (page 98)

1. Select the text you want to change.

   For bold text, click [B].

   For italic text, click [I].

   To underlined text, click [U].

How to Change the Font (page 100)

1. Select the text you want to change.

2. Click the down arrow next to the Font list box.

3. Click the font you want to use.

How to Change the Font Size (page 103)

1. Select the text you want to change.

2. Click the down arrow next to the Font Size list box.

3. Click the font size you want.

How to Change the Text Color (page 105)

1. Select the text you want to change.

2. Click the down arrow next to ☒.

3. Click the color you want.

How to Highlight Text (page 106)

1. Select the text you want to change.

2. Click the down arrow next to ☒.

3. Click the color you want.

CHAPTER 7

How to Align a Paragraph (Center, Left, Right) (page 115)

1. Click within the paragraph you want to change.

2. To center the text, click ☒.

3. To left-align text, click ☒.

4. To right-align text, click ☒.

5. To justify text, click ☒.

How to Indent Text (page 117)

1. To indent a single paragraph, click within it. To indent several paragraphs, select the paragraphs you want to indent.

2. To indent text, click ☒.

3. To unindent text, click ☒.

How to Double-Space a Document (page 119)

1. To indent a single paragraph, click within it. To indent several paragraphs, select the paragraphs you want to indent.

2. Select | Format | → | Paragraph |.

3. If necessary, click the Indents and Spacing tab.

4. Display the Line spacing drop-down list.

5. Click the spacing you want.

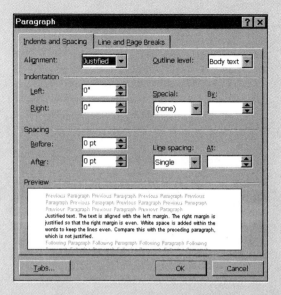

How to Add a Border to a Paragraph (page 126)

1. To indent a single paragraph, click within it. To indent several paragraphs, select the paragraphs you want to indent.

2. Click the down arrow next to ▦.

3. Click the border placement you want.

How to Shade a Paragraph (page 127)

1. To indent a single paragraph, click within it. To indent several paragraphs, select the paragraphs you want to indent.

2. Select `Format` → `Borders and Shading`.

3 Click the Shading tab.

4. Select a fill style.

5. Click the OK button.

How to Create a Bulleted List (page 129)

1. To indent a single paragraph, click within it. To indent several paragraphs, select the paragraphs you want to indent.

2. Click ▤.

1. To indent a single paragraph, click within it. To indent several paragraphs, select the paragraphs you want to indent.

2. Click [≡].

CHAPTER 8

How to Set Margins (page 136)

1. Select [**File**] → [**Page Setup**].

2. Click the Margins tab.

3. Press Tab to move to and highlight the margin you want to change. Type the new value. Do this for each margin you want to change.

4. Click the OK button.

How to Number Pages (page 141)

1. Select [**Insert**] → [**Page Numbers**].

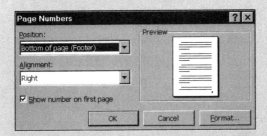

2. Display the Position drop-down list box and select Top of Page (Header) or Bottom of Page (Footer).

3 Display the Alignment drop-down list and select the alignment of the page number.

4. To skip a page number on the first page, uncheck the Show number on first page check box.

5. Click the OK button.

How to Create a Header (page 144)

1. Select [**View**] → [**Header and Footer**].

2. Type the text for the header. Use the toolbar buttons to insert special information:

    ▢   Date

    ▢   Time

    ▢   Page Number

3. Make any formatting changes to the text.

4. Click the Close button.

How to Create a Footer (page 145)

1. Select View → Header and Footer .

2. Click the Switch Between Header and Footer button.

3. Type the footer. Use the toolbar buttons to insert special text:

    ▢   Date

    ▢   Time

    ▢   Page Number

4. Make any formatting changes to the text.

5. Click the Close button.

How to Add a Page Border (page 148)

1. Select Format → Borders and Shading .

2. Click the Page Border tab.

3. Select the type of border you want to add.

4. Select the line style.

5. Select the color.

6. Select the width.

7. To use the same border on all sides, skip this step. To use different borders, click in the diagram where you want the border. Do this for each border you want to add.

8. Click the OK button.

CHAPTER 9

How to Copy Formatting (page 156)

1. Select the text with the formatting you want to copy.
2. Click .
3. Select the text that you want to format.

How to Create a Style (page 162)

1. Format the text/paragraph with the options you want.
2. Highlight the style name in the Style list box: [Heading 5 ▾].
3. Type a new name and press Enter.

How to Apply a Style (page 164)

1. Select the text you want to change.
2. Click the down arrow next to the Style list box.
3. Click the style you want to use.

How to Modify a Style (page 166)

1. Select [Format] → [Style].

2. Click the style you want to modify.

3. Click the Modify button.

4. Click the Format button and select the command. Make your format selections.

5. Click the OK button.

6. Click the Close button.

How to Delete a Style (page 167)

1. Select `Format` → `Style` .

2. Click the style you want to delete.

3. Click the Delete button.

4. Confirm the deletion by clicking the Yes button.

CHAPTER 10

How to Set Up a Table (page 172)

1. Click ⊞ .

2. Drag across the number of rows and columns you want to include in the table.

How to Enter Data in a Table (page 175)

1. Click within the cell.

2. Type the entry.

3. Press Tab to move to the next cell.

How to Select Part of a Table (page 176)

Do any of the following:

* To select text within a table, drag across the text.

* To select a row, put the insertion point within the row and then select `Table` → `Select Row` .

* To select a column, put the insertion point within the column and then select `Table` → `Select Column` .

* To select the table, put the insertion point within the table and then select `Table` → `Select Table` .

How to Add a Row or Column (page 177)

1. Select the row or column where you want the new row.
2. To insert a row, select Table → Insert Rows .
   To insert a column, select Table → Insert Columns .

How to Delete a Row or Column (page 179)

1. Select the row or column you want to delete.
2. To delete a row, select Table → Delete Rows .
   To delete a column, select Table → Delete Columns .

How to Delete the Entire Table (page 180)

1. Select the table using Table → Select Table .
2. Select Table → Delete Rows .

How to Change the Column Width (page 181)

1. Put the mouse pointer on the right border of the column you want to resize.
2. Drag the border to resize the column.

How to Use a Predesigned Set of Formats for the Table (page 182)

1. Put the pointer within the table.
2. Select Table → Table AutoFormat .

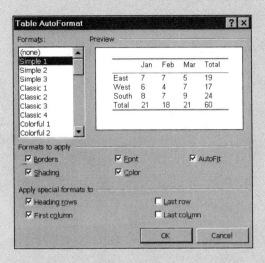

3. Select the format you want.

4. Click the OK button.

CHAPTER 11

How to Insert a Symbol (page 190)

1. Select Insert → Symbol .

2. If necessary, click the Symbols tab.

3. Click the symbol you want to insert.

4. Click the Insert button.

5. Click the Close button to close the dialog box.

How to Insert a Clip Art Image (page 192)

1. Select Insert → Picture → Clip Art .

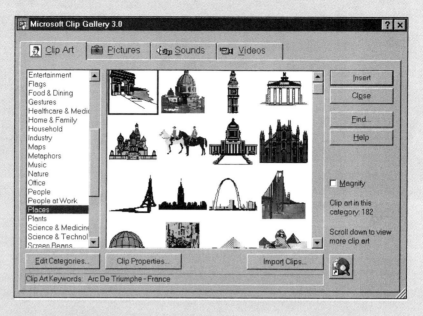

2. Click the category you want to view.

3. Click the image you want to insert.

4. Click the Insert button.

How to Insert an AutoShape (page 194)

1. Select │ Insert │ → │ Picture │ → │ AutoShapes │.

2. Click the shape type that you want.

3. Click the shape you want.

4. Click and drag within the document area to draw the shape.

How to Draw an Object (page 196)

1. Click .

2. Do one of the following:

   ✻ Click to draw a line.

   ✻ Click to draw a rectangle.

   ✻ Click to draw a oval or circle.

3. Click within the drawing area and drag to draw the shape.

How to Move an Object (page 198)

1. Select the object you want to move by clicking it.
2. Drag the object to a new location.

How to Resize an Object (page 199)

1. Select the object you want to resize by clicking it.
2. Drag one of the selection handles to resize.

How to Delete an Object (page 200)

1. Select the object you want to delete by clicking it.
2. Press the Delete key.

How to Change the Look of an Object (page 201)

1. Select the object you want to change.
2. Do one of the following:
   * To change the color of the line, click 🖊. Click the color you want.
   * To change the line thickness, click ▤ and select a style.
   * To use dashes in the line(s), click ▦ and select the dash style you want.
   * For arrows, click ⇄ and select the arrow style you want.
   * To apply a shadow, click ▣ and then select the shadow effect you want.
   * To use a 3-D effect, click ◧ and select the 3-D effect you want.
   * To fill an object, click the down arrow next to ▨.

CHAPTER 12

How to Set Up Columns (page 210)

1. Click ▥.
2. Select the number of columns you want to include.

1. Select $\boxed{\text{Insert}}$ → $\boxed{\text{Break}}$.

2. Click the Column break option button.

3. Click the OK button.

1. Select $\boxed{\text{Format}}$ → $\boxed{\text{Columns}}$.

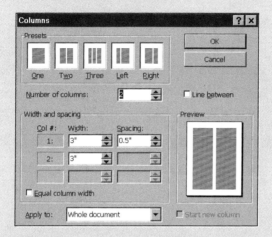

2. Click one of the preset column formats and skip to step 5.

Or

Enter the number of columns you want.

3. To use the same width for all columns, check the Equal column width check box and enter the width you want.

4. To create columns of unequal widths, uncheck the Equal column width check box. Click in the Width spin box for the column you want to change and enter a new width. Do this for each column width you want to change.

5. To change the spacing between columns, click in the Spacing text box. Enter a new width or use the spin arrows to select the value you want. Do this for each column you want to change.

6. To include a line between the columns, check the Line between check box.

7. Click the OK button.

How to Insert a Section Break (page 218)

1 Place the insertion point where you want the new section.

2 Select `Insert` → `Break` .

3 To start the new section on a new page, select Next page.

4. To keep the section on the same page, select Continuous.

5. To have the section start on the next odd-numbered page, select Odd page.

6. To have the section start on the next even-numbered page, select Even page.

7. Click the OK button.

CHAPTER 13

How to Use a Wizard (page 229)

1. Select `File` → `New` .

2. Click the tab for the document type you want to create.

3. Click the wizard you want and then click the OK button.

4. Follow the instructions in the dialog box.

5. Click the Next button.

6. Continue making selections and clicking Next until you reach the final dialog box.

7. Click the Finish button.

8. Enter the text for the document.

9. Save and print the document.

How to Use a Template (page 233)

1. Select `File` → `New` .

2. Click the tab for the document type you want to create.

3. Click the template you want to use.

4. Click the OK button

5. Click the text you need to replace and type the actual text. Do this for each section of text that needs to be completed.

6. Save and print the document.

How to Create Your Own Template (page 234)

1. Create the document including the text and formatting you want to save in the template.

2. Select `File` → `Save As`.

3. Display the Save file as type drop-down list and click Document Template as the type.

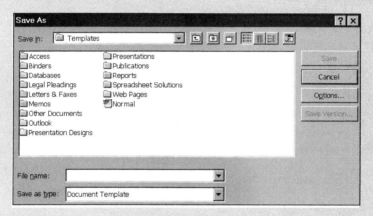

4. Select the folder for the template.

5. Type a name for the template.

6. Click the Save button.

CHAPTER 14

How to Start the Mail Merge Process (page 241)

1. Start with a blank document on screen.

2. Select `Tools` → `Mail Merge`.

3. Under Main document, click the Create button and click Form Letters.

4. Click the New Main Document button.

How to Create the Data Source (page 243)

1. Click Get Data in the Mail Merge Helper dialog box.

2. Click Create Data Source.

3. To remove a field, select it and click the <u>R</u>emove Field Name button.

4. To add a field, type the field name and click the <u>A</u>dd Field Name button.

5. When you are finished adding or removing fields, click the OK button.

6. In the Save As dialog box, change to the drive and folder for saving this file. Type the filename and click the <u>S</u>ave button.

7. Click the Edit <u>D</u>ata Source button.

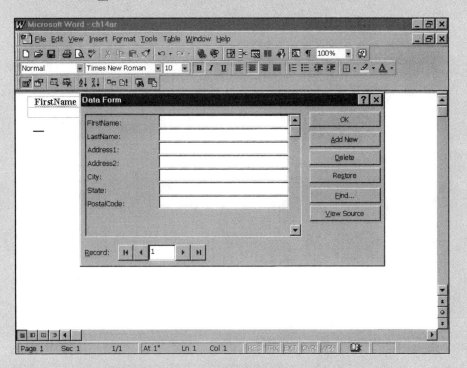

8. Type the information for the first field and press Tab. Do this for each field.

9. When you are finished, click the <u>A</u>dd New button.

10. Follow steps 8 and 9 for each record you want to add.

11. When you have completed all the records, click the OK button.

How to Create the Main Document (page 248)

1. In the main document window, type the text you want the letter to include.

2. When you get to a spot where you want to insert variable information (such as the name and address), click the Insert Merge Field button.

3. Click the field you want to insert.

4. Continue typing and inserting fields until you complete the document.

5. Open the ☐ File ☐ menu and select the ☐ Save ☐ command. Change to the drive and folder in which to save the file. Type the filename and click the ☐ Save ☐ button.

How to Merge the Two Documents (page 250)

1. Select ☐ Tools ☐ → ☐ Mail Merge ☐.

2. Click the Merge button.

3. To merge to all records to a new document and skip blank lines, click the Merge button.

4. Print the letters using the ☐ File ☐ → ☐ Print ☐ command.

CHAPTER 15

How to Copy Data from One Application to Another (page 261)

1. Open the document that contains the data you want to copy.

2. Select the data you want to copy.

3. Select ☐ File ☐ → ☐ Copy ☐.

4. Switch back to Word and move to the Word document where you want to paste the data.

5. Move the insertion point to where you want to paste the data.

6. Select ☐ Edit ☐ → ☐ Paste ☐.

How to Link Data from One Application to Another (page 262)

1. Open the document that contains the data you want to copy.

2. Select the data you want to link.

3. Select ☐ Edit ☐ → ☐ Copy ☐.

4. Switch back to the application where you want to place the linked data.

5. Move the insertion point to where you want to paste the data.

6. Select ☐ Edit ☐ → ☐ Paste Special ☐.

7. Select the Paste link option.

8. Select what you want the object pasted as (an object, formatted text, unformatted text, a picture, a bitmap, or a hyperlink).

9. Click the OK button.

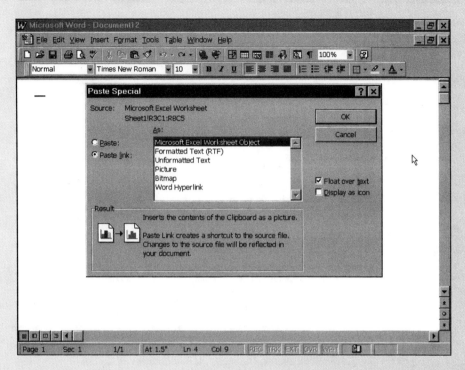

How to Embed Data from One Application in Another (page 264)

1. Open the document that contains the data you want to embed.

2. Select the data you want to embed.

3. Select **Edit** → **Copy**.

4. Switch to the application where you want to embed the data.

5. Move the insertion point to where you want to place the data.

6. Select **Edit** → **Paste Special**.

7. Select Paste.

8. Select the object. The name of the object will vary depending on what you copied.

9. Click the OK button.

CHAPTER 16

How to Create a New Folder (page 285)

1. In the Save As dialog box, click the New Folder button.
2. Type the name for the new folder.
3. Click the OK button.

How to Add a Folder to the Favorite List (page 286)

1. In the Save As or Open dialog box, select the folder you want to add to the list.
2. Click the Add to Favorites button.

How to Open a Favorite Folder (page 287)

1. In the Save As or Open dialog box, click the Look in Favorites button.
2. Double-click the favorite folder you want to open.

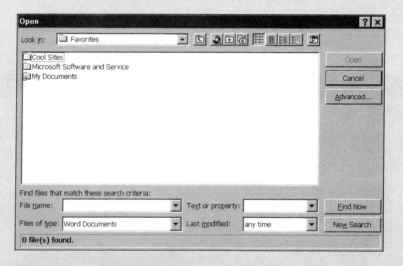

How to Delete a File (page 290)

1 In the Open or Save As dialog box, right-click the file you want to delete.
2. Select Delete .
3 Click the Yes button.

How to Undelete a File (page 291)

1. Go to the Windows desktop.
2. Double-click the Recycle Bin icon.
3. Right-click the file you want to undelete.
4. Select Restore .
5. Click the Close button.

How to Rename a File (page 293)

1. In the Open or Save As dialog box, right-click the file you want to rename.
2. Select Rename .
3. Type a new name and press Enter. The file is renamed.

How to Copy a File to Another Folder (page 294)

1. In the Open or Save As dialog box, right-click the file you want to copy.
2. Select Copy .
3. Change to the folder where you want to place the file.
4. Right-click a blank area of the folder and file list.
5. Select Paste .

How to Copy a File to a Floppy Disk (page 294)

1. In the Open or Save As dialog box, right-click the file you want to copy.
2. Select Send To .
3. Select your floppy disk from the submenu.

How to Move a File (page 295)

1. In the Open or Save As dialog box, right-click the file you want to copy.
2. Select Cut .
3. Change to the folder where you want to move the file.
4. Right-click a blank area of the folder and file list.

5. Select ⌗Paste⌗.

CHAPTER 17

How to Hide or Display a Toolbar (page 302)

1. Select ⌗View⌗ → ⌗Toolbar⌗.

2. To hide a toolbar, uncheck it.

3. To display a toolbar, check it.

How to Display or Hide Other On-Screen Items (page 304)

1. Select ⌗Tools⌗ → ⌗Options⌗.

2. Select the View tab.

3. Check items you want to display. Uncheck items you want to hide.

4. Click the OK button.

How to Customize a Toolbar (page 306)

1. Display the toolbar you want to customize.

2. Select ⌗View⌗ → ⌗Toolbars⌗ → ⌗Customize⌗.

3. Click the Commands tab.

4. Do any of the following:

 ✳ To move a button on a toolbar, drag it to a new location on the toolbar.

 ✳ To delete a button on a toolbar, drag it off the toolbar.

 ✳ To add a button, select the category and then the command you want. Drag the command from the Customize dialog box to the toolbar on screen.

How to Create a New Toolbar (page 310)

1. Select ⌗View⌗ → ⌗Toolbars⌗ → ⌗Customize⌗.

2. Click the Toolbars tab.

3. Click the New button.

4. Type the toolbar name and click the OK button.

5. Click the <u>C</u>ommands tab.

6. Select the category.

7. Drag the command from the Customize dialog box to the new toolbar on screen.

8. When you are finished adding buttons, click the Close button.

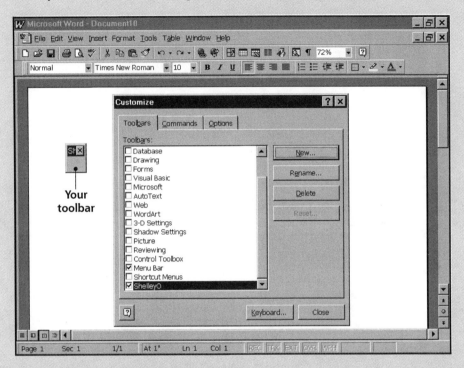

How to Record a Macro (page 316)

1. Select [<u>Tools</u>] → [<u>Macro</u>] → [<u>Record New Macro</u>].

2. Type a macro name.

3. Select the template through which you want to make the macro available.

4. Type or modify the description.

5. Click the OK button.

6. Perform the actions you want to record.

7. When you complete all the steps you want to record, click the Stop Recording button.

How to Play Back a Macro (page 318)

1. Select `Tools` → `Macro` → `Macros`.

2. Click the name of the macro you want to run.

3. Click the Run button.

VISUAL INDEX

Memo

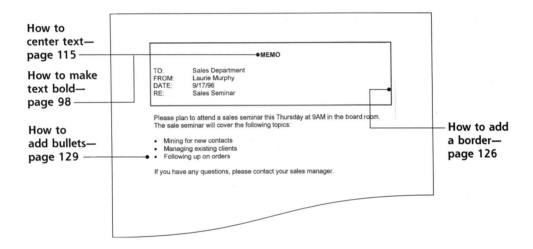

How to
center text—
page 115

How to make
text bold—
page 98

How to
add bullets—
page 129

How to add
a border—
page 126

●MEMO

TO: Sales Department
FROM: Laurie Murphy
DATE: 9/17/96
RE: Sales Seminar

Please plan to attend a sales seminar this Thursday at 9AM in the board room.
The sale seminar will cover the following topics:

- Mining for new contacts
- Managing existing clients
- Following up on orders

If you have any questions, please contact your sales manager.

Business Letter

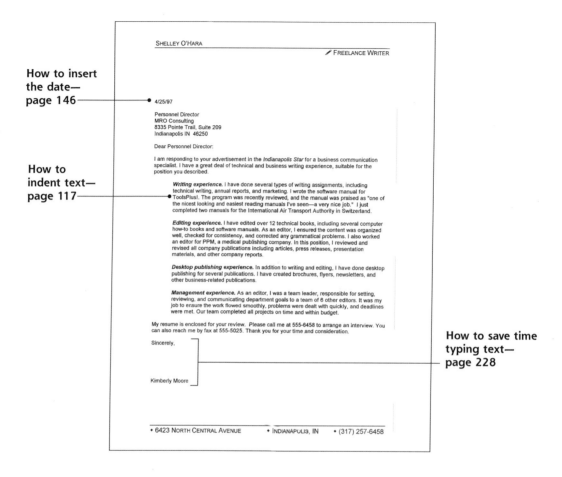

How to insert the date—page 146

How to indent text—page 117

How to save time typing text—page 228

SHELLEY O'HARA

✎ FREELANCE WRITER

4/25/97

Personnel Director
MRO Consulting
8335 Pointe Trail, Suite 209
Indianapolis IN 46250

Dear Personnel Director:

I am responding to your advertisement in the *Indianapolis Star* for a business communication specialist. I have a great deal of technical and business writing experience, suitable for the position you described.

Writing experience. I have done several types of writing assignments, including technical writing, annual reports, and marketing. I wrote the software manual for ToolsPlus!. The program was recently reviewed, and the manual was praised as "one of the nicest looking and easiest reading manuals I've seen—a very nice job." I just completed two manuals for the International Air Transport Authority in Switzerland.

Editing experience. I have edited over 12 technical books, including several computer how-to books and software manuals. As an editor, I ensured the content was organized well, checked for consistency, and corrected any grammatical problems. I also worked an editor for PPM, a medical publishing company. In this position, I reviewed and revised all company publications including articles, press releases, presentation materials, and other company reports.

Desktop publishing experience. In addition to writing and editing, I have done desktop publishing for several publications. I have created brochures, flyers, newsletters, and other business-related publications.

Management experience. As an editor, I was a team leader, responsible for setting, reviewing, and communicating department goals to a team of 6 other editors. It was my job to ensure the work flowed smoothly, problems were dealt with quickly, and deadlines were met. Our team completed all projects on time and within budget.

My resume is enclosed for your review. Please call me at 555-6458 to arrange an interview. You can also reach me by fax at 555-5025. Thank you for your time and consideration.

Sincerely,

Kimberly Moore

♦ 6423 NORTH CENTRAL AVENUE   ♦ INDIANAPOLIS, IN   ♦ (317) 257-6458

Personal Letter

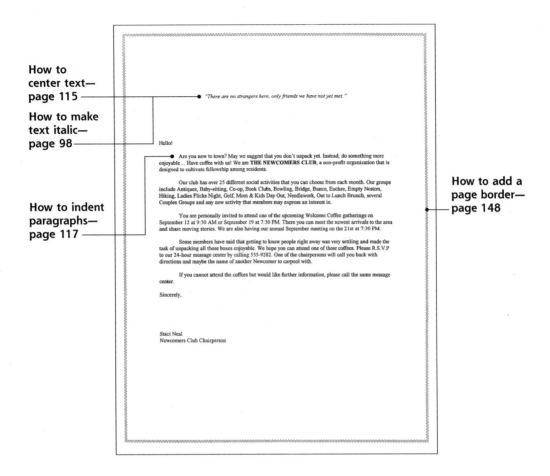

How to
center text—
page 115

How to make
text italic—
page 98

How to indent
paragraphs—
page 117

How to add a
page border—
page 148

"There are no strangers here, only friends we have not yet met."

Hello!

Are you new to town? May we suggest that you don't unpack yet. Instead, do something more enjoyable… Have coffee with us! We are **THE NEWCOMERS CLUB**, a non-profit organization that is designed to cultivate fellowship among residents.

Our club has over 25 different social activities that you can choose from each month. Our groups include Antiques, Baby-sitting, Co-op, Book Clubs, Bowling, Bridge, Bunco, Euchre, Empty Nesters, Hiking, Ladies Flicks Night, Golf, Mom & Kids Day Out, Needlework, Out to Lunch Brunch, several Couples Groups and any new activity that members may express an interest in.

You are personally invited to attend one of the upcoming Welcome Coffee gatherings on September 12 at 9:30 AM or September 19 at 7:30 PM. There you can meet the newest arrivals to the area and share moving stories. We are also having our annual September meeting on the 21st at 7:30 PM.

Some members have said that getting to know people right away was very settling and made the task of unpacking all those boxes enjoyable. We hope you can attend one of these coffees. Please R.S.V.P to our 24-hour message center by calling 555-9282. One of the chairpersons will call you back with directions and maybe the name of another Newcomer to carpool with.

If you cannot attend the coffees but would like further information, please call the same message center.

Sincerely,

Staci Neal
Newcomers Club Chairperson

Resume

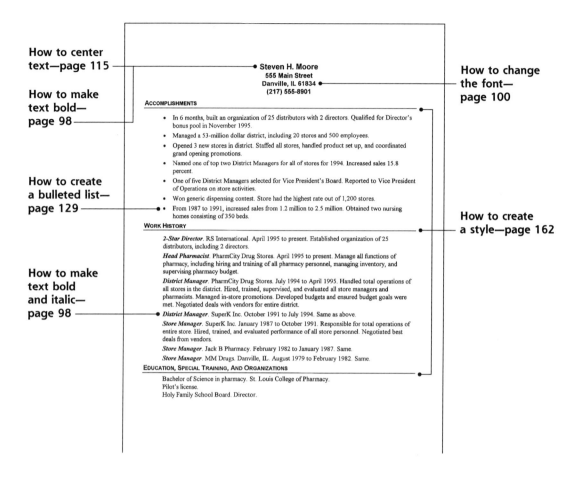

How to center text—page 115

How to make text bold— page 98

How to create a bulleted list— page 129

How to make text bold and italic— page 98

How to change the font— page 100

How to create a style—page 162

Steven H. Moore
555 Main Street
Danville, IL 61834
(217) 555-8901

ACCOMPLISHMENTS

- In 6 months, built an organization of 25 distributors with 2 directors. Qualified for Director's bonus pool in November 1995.
- Managed a 53-million dollar district, including 20 stores and 500 employees.
- Opened 3 new stores in district. Staffed all stores, handled product set up, and coordinated grand opening promotions.
- Named one of top two District Managers for all of stores for 1994. Increased sales 15.8 percent.
- One of five District Managers selected for Vice President's Board. Reported to Vice President of Operations on store activities.
- Won generic dispensing contest. Store had the highest rate out of 1,200 stores.
- From 1987 to 1991, increased sales from 1.2 million to 2.5 million. Obtained two nursing homes consisting of 350 beds.

WORK HISTORY

2-Star Director. RS International. April 1995 to present. Established organization of 25 distributors, including 2 directors.

Head Pharmacist. PharmCity Drug Stores. April 1995 to present. Manage all functions of pharmacy, including hiring and training of all pharmacy personnel, managing inventory, and supervising pharmacy budget.

District Manager. PharmCity Drug Stores. July 1994 to April 1995. Handled total operations of all stores in the district. Hired, trained, supervised, and evaluated all store managers and pharmacists. Managed in-store promotions. Developed budgets and ensured budget goals were met. Negotiated deals with vendors for entire district.

District Manager. SuperK Inc. October 1991 to July 1994. Same as above.

Store Manager. SuperK Inc. January 1987 to October 1991. Responsible for total operations of entire store. Hired, trained, and evaluated performance of all store personnel. Negotiated best deals from vendors.

Store Manager. Jack B Pharmacy. February 1982 to January 1987. Same.

Store Manager. MM Drugs. Danville, IL. August 1979 to February 1982. Same.

EDUCATION, SPECIAL TRAINING, AND ORGANIZATIONS

Bachelor of Science in pharmacy. St. Louis College of Pharmacy.
Pilot's license.
Holy Family School Board. Director.

Manuscript

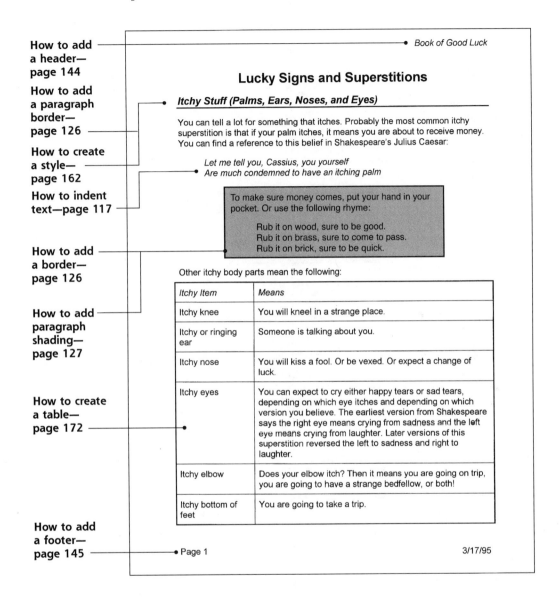

Book of Good Luck

Lucky Signs and Superstitions

Itchy Stuff (Palms, Ears, Noses, and Eyes)

You can tell a lot for something that itches. Probably the most common itchy superstition is that if your palm itches, it means you are about to receive money. You can find a reference to this belief in Shakespeare's Julius Caesar:

Let me tell you, Cassius, you yourself
Are much condemned to have an itching palm

To make sure money comes, put your hand in your pocket. Or use the following rhyme:

Rub it on wood, sure to be good.
Rub it on brass, sure to come to pass.
Rub it on brick, sure to be quick.

Other itchy body parts mean the following:

Itchy Item	Means
Itchy knee	You will kneel in a strange place.
Itchy or ringing ear	Someone is talking about you.
Itchy nose	You will kiss a fool. Or be vexed. Or expect a change of luck.
Itchy eyes	You can expect to cry either happy tears or sad tears, depending on which eye itches and depending on which version you believe. The earliest version from Shakespeare says the right eye means crying from sadness and the left eye means crying from laughter. Later versions of this superstition reversed the left to sadness and right to laughter.
Itchy elbow	Does your elbow itch? Then it means you are going on trip, you are going to have a strange bedfellow, or both!
Itchy bottom of feet	You are going to take a trip.

Page 1

3/17/95

Report

How to
center text—
page 115

How to make
text bold—
page 98

How to change
the font size—
page 103

How to create
a bulleted list—
page 129

How to insert
an Excel chart—
page 267

How to create
a header—
page 144

How to
insert an Excel
worksheet—
page 262

How to create
a footer—
page 145

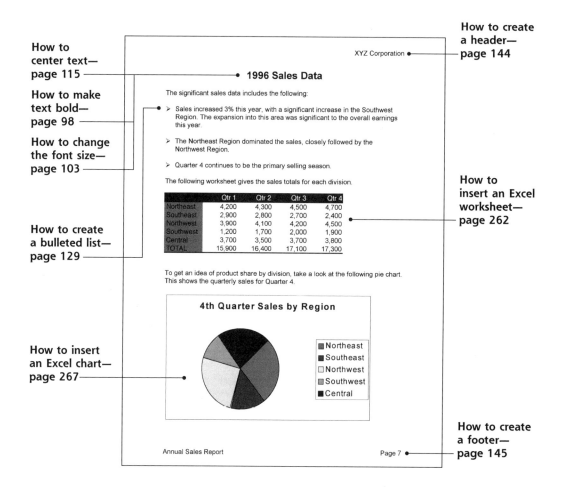

XYZ Corporation

1996 Sales Data

The significant sales data includes the following:

> Sales increased 3% this year, with a significant increase in the Southwest Region. The expansion into this area was significant to the overall earnings this year.

> The Northeast Region dominated the sales, closely followed by the Northwest Region.

> Quarter 4 continues to be the primary selling season.

The following worksheet gives the sales totals for each division.

	Qtr 1	Qtr 2	Qtr 3	Qtr 4
Northeast	4,200	4,300	4,500	4,700
Southeast	2,900	2,800	2,700	2,400
Northwest	3,900	4,100	4,200	4,500
Southwest	1,200	1,700	2,000	1,900
Central	3,700	3,500	3,700	3,800
TOTAL	15,900	16,400	17,100	17,300

To get an idea of product share by division, take a look at the following pie chart. This shows the quarterly sales for Quarter 4.

4th Quarter Sales by Region

- Northeast
- Southeast
- Northwest
- Southwest
- Central

Annual Sales Report   Page 7

Flyer

How to center text—page 115

How to make text bold—page 98

How to change the font size—page 103

How to create a bulleted list—page 129

How to insert a clip art image—page 192

How to set tabs—page 121

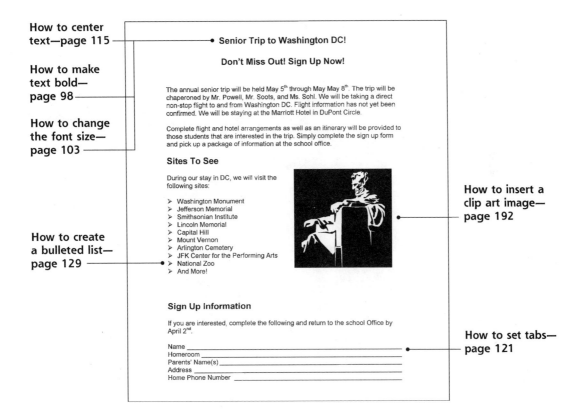

Senior Trip to Washington DC!

Don't Miss Out! Sign Up Now!

The annual senior trip will be held May 5th through May May 8th. The trip will be chaperoned by Mr. Powell, Mr. Soots, and Ms. Sohl. We will be taking a direct non-stop flight to and from Washington DC. Flight information has not yet been confirmed. We will be staying at the Marriott Hotel in DuPont Circle.

Complete flight and hotel arrangements as well as an itinerary will be provided to those students that are interested in the trip. Simply complete the sign up form and pick up a package of information at the school office.

Sites To See

During our stay in DC, we will visit the following sites:

➢ Washington Monument
➢ Jefferson Memorial
➢ Smithsonian Institute
➢ Lincoln Memorial
➢ Capital Hill
➢ Mount Vernon
➢ Arlington Cemetery
➢ JFK Center for the Performing Arts
➢ National Zoo
➢ And More!

Sign Up Information

If you are interested, complete the following and return to the school Office by April 2nd.

Name _____
Homeroom _____
Parents' Name(s) _____
Address _____
Home Phone Number _____

Booklet

How to change to landscape orientation—page 139

How to center text— page 115

How to change the font— page 100

How to set up columns— page 210

How to create a table— page 172

How to insert a column break— page 214

How to create a numbered list—page 130

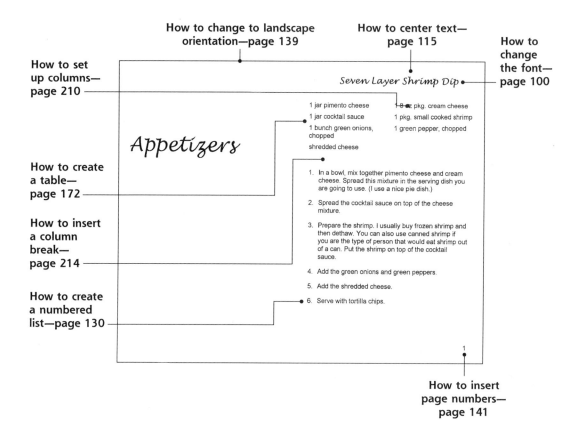

Seven Layer Shrimp Dip

Appetizers

1 jar pimento cheese
1 jar cocktail sauce
1 bunch green onions, chopped
shredded cheese

1 8-oz pkg. cream cheese
1 pkg. small cooked shrimp
1 green pepper, chopped

1. In a bowl, mix together pimento cheese and cream cheese. Spread this mixture in the serving dish you are going to use. (I use a nice pie dish.)

2. Spread the cocktail sauce on top of the cheese mixture.

3. Prepare the shrimp. I usually buy frozen shrimp and then dethaw. You can also use canned shrimp if you are the type of person that would eat shrimp out of a can. Put the shrimp on top of the cocktail sauce.

4. Add the green onions and green peppers.

5. Add the shredded cheese.

6. Serve with tortilla chips.

1

How to insert page numbers— page 141

Newsletter

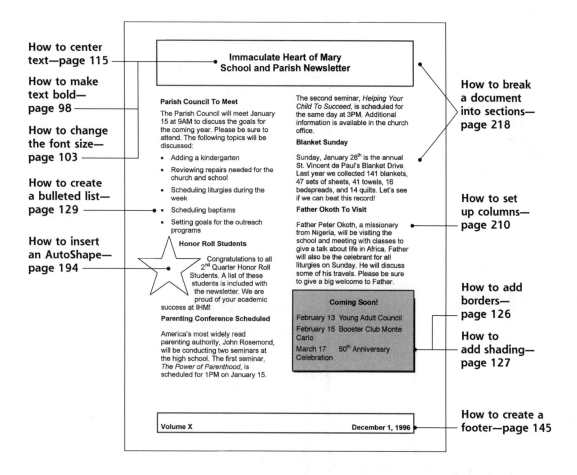

How to center text—page 115

How to make text bold—page 98

How to change the font size—page 103

How to create a bulleted list—page 129

How to insert an AutoShape—page 194

How to break a document into sections—page 218

How to set up columns—page 210

How to add borders—page 126

How to add shading—page 127

How to create a footer—page 145

Immaculate Heart of Mary School and Parish Newsletter

Parish Council To Meet

The Parish Council will meet January 15 at 9AM to discuss the goals for the coming year. Please be sure to attend. The following topics will be discussed:

- Adding a kindergarten
- Reviewing repairs needed for the church and school
- Scheduling liturgies during the week
- Scheduling baptisms
- Setting goals for the outreach programs

Honor Roll Students

Congratulations to all 2nd Quarter Honor Roll Students. A list of these students is included with the newsletter. We are proud of your academic success at IHM!

Parenting Conference Scheduled

America's most widely read parenting authority, John Rosemond, will be conducting two seminars at the high school. The first seminar, *The Power of Parenthood*, is scheduled for 1PM on January 15.

The second seminar, *Helping Your Child To Succeed*, is scheduled for the same day at 3PM. Additional information is available in the church office.

Blanket Sunday

Sunday, January 28th is the annual St. Vincent de Paul's Blanket Drive. Last year we collected 141 blankets, 47 sets of sheets, 41 towels, 16 bedspreads, and 14 quilts. Let's see if we can beat this record!

Father Okoth To Visit

Father Peter Okoth, a missionary from Nigeria, will be visiting the school and meeting with classes to give a talk about life in Africa. Father will also be the celebrant for all liturgies on Sunday. He will discuss some of his travels. Please be sure to give a big welcome to Father.

Coming Soon!

February 13 Young Adult Council

February 15 Booster Club Monte Carlo

March 17 50th Anniversary Celebration

Volume X

December 1, 1996

Two-Column Brochure

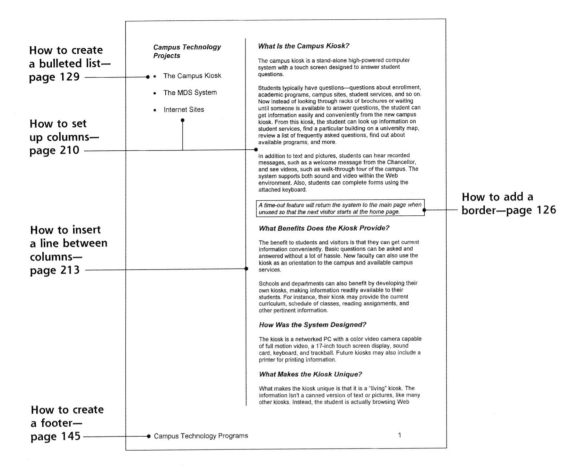

How to create a bulleted list—page 129

How to set up columns—page 210

How to insert a line between columns—page 213

How to create a footer—page 145

How to add a border—page 126

Campus Technology Projects

- The Campus Kiosk
- The MDS System
- Internet Sites

What Is the Campus Kiosk?

The campus kiosk is a stand-alone high-powered computer system with a touch screen designed to answer student questions.

Students typically have questions—questions about enrollment, academic programs, campus sites, student services, and so on. Now instead of looking through racks of brochures or waiting until someone is available to answer questions, the student can get information easily and conveniently from the new campus kiosk. From this kiosk, the student can look up information on student services, find a particular building on a university map, review a list of frequently asked questions, find out about available programs, and more.

In addition to text and pictures, students can hear recorded messages, such as a welcome message from the Chancellor, and see videos, such as walk-through tour of the campus. The system supports both sound and video within the Web environment. Also, students can complete forms using the attached keyboard.

A time-out feature will return the system to the main page when unused so that the next visitor starts at the home page.

What Benefits Does the Kiosk Provide?

The benefit to students and visitors is that they can get current information conveniently. Basic questions can be asked and answered without a lot of hassle. New faculty can also use the kiosk as an orientation to the campus and available campus services.

Schools and departments can also benefit by developing their own kiosks, making information readily available to their students. For instance, their kiosk may provide the current curriculum, schedule of classes, reading assignments, and other pertinent information.

How Was the System Designed?

The kiosk is a networked PC with a color video camera capable of full motion video, a 17-inch touch screen display, sound card, keyboard, and trackball. Future kiosks may also include a printer for printing information.

What Makes the Kiosk Unique?

What makes the kiosk unique is that it is a "living" kiosk. The information isn't a canned version of text or pictures, like many other kiosks. Instead, the student is actually browsing Web

Campus Technology Programs

1

Three-Column Brochure

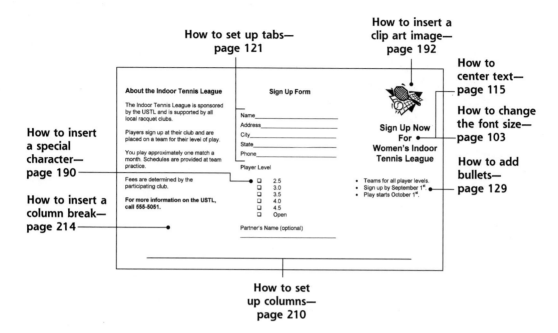

How to set up tabs—
page 121

How to insert a
clip art image—
page 192

How to
center text—
page 115

How to change
the font size—
page 103

How to insert
a special
character—
page 190

How to add
bullets—
page 129

How to insert a
column break—
page 214

How to set
up columns—
page 210

About the Indoor Tennis League

The Indoor Tennis League is sponsored by the USTL and is supported by all local racquet clubs.

Players sign up at their club and are placed on a team for their level of play.

You play approximately one match a month. Schedules are provided at team practice.

Fees are determined by the participating club.

For more information on the USTL, call 555-5051.

Sign Up Form

Name_____
Address_____
City_____
State_____
Phone_____

Player Level

☐   2.5
☐   3.0
☐   3.5
☐   4.0
☐   4.5
☐   Open

Partner's Name (optional)
_____

**Sign Up Now
For
Women's Indoor
Tennis League**

- Teams for all player levels.
- Sign up by September 1st.
- Play starts October 1st.

TROUBLESHOOTING GUIDE

I f you have a problem with Word 97, you can consult this troubleshooting guide, which covers common problems. Use the following list to review the covered problems and find where that problem is solved.

All the stuff on my screen disappeared.

If everything on the screen disappears, you may have selected the Full Screen
view, which hides the title bar, menu bar, toolbars, and status bar and just displays a big white area for typing text (see Figure A-1). If this happens, click the
Close Full Screen button to return to Normal view.

   If you see a gray background and the menu and toolbars (see Figure A-2), it
means you do not have a document open. You can choose to create a new document using File, New or open an existing document using File, Open.

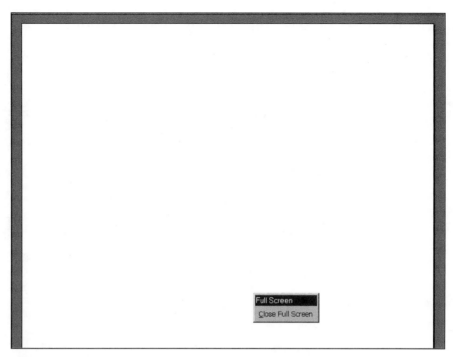

Figure A-1

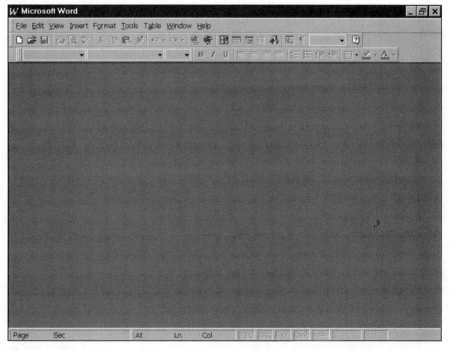

Figure A-2

My toolbars look different from the ones shown in the book.

You can customize the toolbars, adding other buttons, deleting buttons, or changing the order of the buttons. You can also move the toolbars around on-screen. (For information on customizing toolbars, see Chapter 17.) To reset a toolbar so that it contains the original buttons, follow these steps:

1. Open the **View** menu, select **Toolbars**, and then **Customize**. You see the Customize dialog box (see Figure A-3).

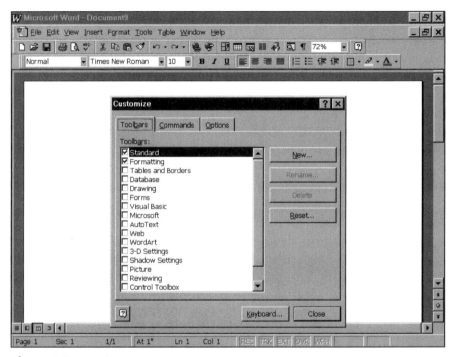

Figure A-3

2. Select the toolbar you want to reset.

3. Click the Reset button.

4. When prompted to confirm this change, click the OK button.

5. Click the Close button.

I can't move past a certain spot in the document.

The end of the document is marked by a short horizontal line. You cannot move past this spot. If you try to click beyond this spot, nothing happens.

I opened a menu by mistake.

If you open a menu or dialog box by mistake, press Esc to close the menu or dialog box without making a selection.

I don't see that Office Assistant all the time.

The Office Assistant is a tool you can use to get help (see Chapter 1). This feature is on by default, so you probably see the animated character in its little window when you start using the program. The Office Assistant may also appear when you perform certain tasks. To turn off the Office Assistant, click the Close button (the X) in the Assistant window. To turn on the Office Assistant, click the Help button on the toolbar.

I see dots between words, arrows, and some other weird mark at the end of each paragraph.

You can choose to display paragraph marks and space marks in your document (see Figure A-4). These elements do not print. To turn them on, click the Show/Hide ¶ button. To turn them off, click this button again.

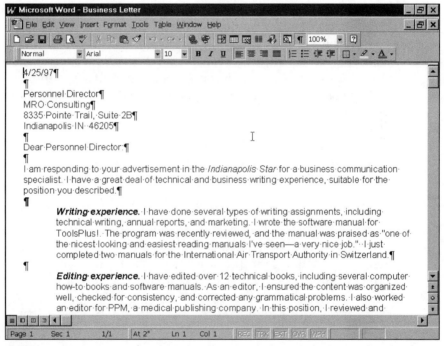

Figure A-4

I deleted text by mistake.

If you delete text by mistake, click the Undo button to undo the deletion. You can also undo formatting and other editing changes.

Text started disappearing when I started typing.

Word normally is in Insert mode; that is, new text is inserted when you type. You can also use Overtype mode. In this mode, text is overwritten as you type. You may have accidentally switched to Overtype mode by pressing the Insert key. If you see OVR in the status bar, press the Insert key on the keyboard to return to Insert mode.

The text I type is in all CAPS.

If you type text and it is in all CAPS, you most likely pressed the Caps Lock key by accident. Press this key again to turn off Caps Lock.

Text wasn't inserted in the right spot when I started typing.

Remember that the insertion point indicates where text will be added, and the mouse pointer indicates the location of the mouse pointer. They can be in two different spots. If you point to the spot where you want to add text, but don't click to move the insertion point, you don't move the insertion point. Be sure to point and click.

I thought I was selecting text, but somehow the text got moved.

If you select text, release the mouse button, and try to drag the text to extend the selection, Word thinks you want to move the selected text. This feature is called drag-and-drop editing. If you see a different mouse pointer (a box with an arrow), you know that you are moving text. You can undo the move by clicking the Undo button.

If you have this same problem a lot, you may want to turn off drag-and-drop editing. To do so, open the Tools menu and select the Options command. Click the Edit tab. Uncheck the Drag-and-drop text editing check box.

I want to paste text, but the paste command is grayed out.

Before you can paste text, you must first cut or copy something. If the Paste command is unavailable, it means you have not yet cut or copied something to the Clipboard.

I see red squiggly lines under some words.

Word automatically checks your spelling as you type. If a word is underlined with a red curvy line, it means Word thinks the word is misspelled. You can see alternative spellings for that word by right-clicking on it and then selecting the correct spelling. See Chapter 4 for more help on checking spelling.

I see green squiggly lines under some words and phrases.

Word also automatically checks the grammar in your document. Word uses a green curvy underline to point out what it thinks are grammatical errors. You can display suggested corrections by right-clicking on the highlighted word or phrase. For more information on checking grammar, see Chapter 4.

I can't move to the very top of the document.

In Normal view, you don't see the margins, so it looks as if the text is at the very top. In Page Layout view, you do see the margins, and the text looks like it is not at the top of the page. Even though there's white space, it doesn't mean you are not at the top of the document. You are just seeing the margin space. You cannot move to this space.

To change views, open the View menu and select the view you want.

I don't see my columns side by side.

Columns are displayed side-by-side only in Page Layout view. You are probably in Normal view. To change to Page Layout view, open the <u>V</u>iew menu and select the <u>P</u>age Layout command.

My text looks really small (or really big), but I haven't changed the font.

If you have not made a change to the font size but text looks really big or really small, you probably have zoomed the document. Open the <u>V</u>iew menu, select the <u>Z</u>oom command, and check the zoom percentage. The normal zoom is 100%.

I don't have some of the fonts mentioned in this book.

The fonts you have available depends on what you have installed on your computer system and what type of printer you have. Your printer comes with some built-in fonts, plus you can purchase font packages to add fonts to your system. Some programs come with additional fonts.

My paragraph formatting changed unexpectedly.

The formatting for a paragraph is stored with the paragraph mark. Each time you press Enter, the paragraph options for that paragraph are carried down to the next paragraph. And if you delete the paragraph mark, the paragraph takes on the formatting of the following paragraph.

If something bizarre happens, try undoing the change using <u>E</u>dit, <u>U</u>ndo. If you have trouble visualizing where the paragraph marks appear, you can display them by clicking the Show/Hide ¶ button.

I created a bulleted list, but now I can't get rid of the bullets.

When you press Enter within a bulleted list, Word adds another list item. To turn off bullets, click the Bullets button again.

I can't delete a number from the numbered list.

If you create a numbered list, Word adds the numbers automatically. You cannot delete them. To turn off the numbers, click the Numbering button.

Word starts making formatting changes without my selecting any command.

Word's AutoFormat feature makes some formatting corrections as you type. For example, if you type an asterisk and press Tab, Word creates a bulleted list. To review or change which formatting changes are made, follow these steps:

1. Open the **Tools** menu and select the **AutoCorrect** command.

2. Click the AutoFormat As You Type tab. You see the AutoFormat changes that are made automatically as you type (see Figure A-5).

3. To turn off an option, uncheck its check box. To turn on an option, check the check box.

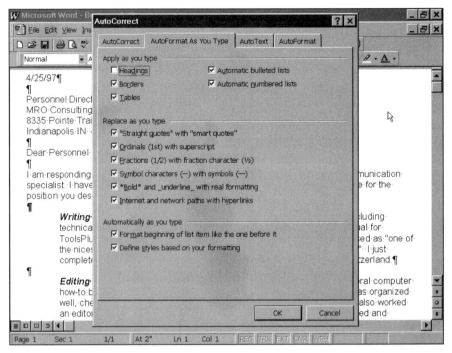

Figure A-5

4. Click the OK button.

I can't see the header (or footer) I created.

In Normal view, you won't see your headers or footers. To view these items, change to Page Layout view or Print Preview.

I don't want a page number or header or footer on the first page.

For some documents, you may not want to include a header or footer on the first page.

If so, you can turn it off by following these steps:

1. Open the **File** menu and select the **Page Setup** command.

2. Click the Layout tab. You see the Layout tab options (see Figure A-6).

3. Check the Different first page check box.

4. Click the OK button.

5. Go to the first page of the document and select the **View** → **Header and Footer** command. The header area should say First Page Header.

6. If you don't want to include a header or footer on the first page, simply leave it blank. If you've already added a header, delete the header or footer on this page.

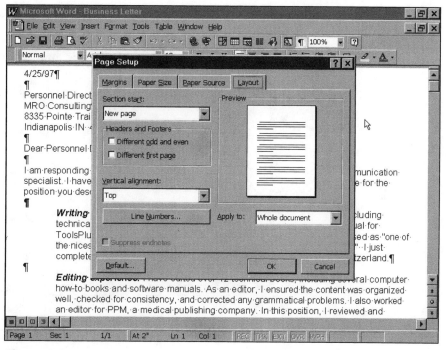

Figure A-6

7. Click the Close button.

I created a style, but now I don't like it and want to make a change.

You can modify a style by following these steps:

1. Open the Format menu and select the Style command. You see the Style dialog box.

2. Select the style you want to modify.

3. Click the Modify button. You see the Modify Style dialog box (see Figure A-7).

4. Click the Format button and select the type of formatting you want to change: Font, Paragraph, Tabs, Border, Language, Frame, Numbering. (Only some options are available for character styles.) Word displays the appropriate dialog box. For instance, if you select Font, you see the Font dialog box.

5. Make the selections you want and click the OK button.

6. Follow steps 4 and 5 for each change you want to make.

7. When you are finished making changes, click OK to return to the Style dialog box.

8. To apply the new style to the selected paragraph, click the Apply button. To close the dialog box without applying the style, click the Close button.

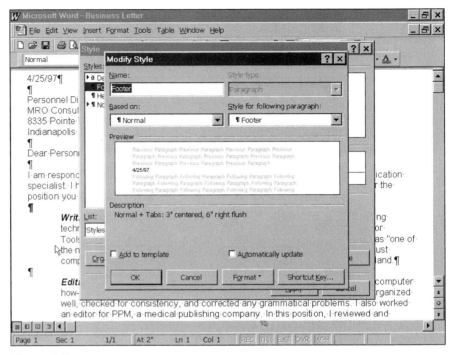

Figure A-7

I can't delete a table.

Deleting a table is tricky. You can't just drag across it and press the Delete key. Doing so deletes all the entries, but leaves the table grid.

To delete the table, follow these steps:

1. Select the table using the Table → Select Table command.

2. Open the Table menu and select the Delete Rows command.

My table columns aren't the right size.

When you create a table using the Insert Table button, Word bases the column width on the size of the page margins and the number of columns you have. Each column is the same size. You can adjust the column width if necessary.

Follow these steps:

1. Place the mouse pointer on the right border of the column you want to change. The pointer should look like two vertical lines with arrows on either side.

2. Drag the border to resize the column width. Drag to the left to make the column smaller. Drag to the right to make the column wider.

My table has borders, but I don't want them.

When you insert a table using the Insert Table button, Word adds a border around each cell. You may want to turn off this border.

To do so, follow these steps:

1. Select the table using the `Table` → `Select Table` command.

2. Click the down arrow next to the Border button in the toolbar.

3. Click the No Border button. If you can't see the rows and columns, you need to turn on gridlines by following the remaining steps.

4. Open the `Table` menu and select the `Show Gridlines` command. These gridlines are displayed on-screen but do not print.

Most of the table commands are unavailable.

To access the table commands, you must be within a table. Place the insertion point within the table and try again.

I inserted a picture, but I can't see my text.

Depending on the type of picture, Word handles the text and picture differently. Sometimes the picture appears right on top of the text. Sometimes the text flows around the picture — usually part above and part below, but nothing on the sides of the picture.

To control how the text flows around the picture, follow these steps:

1. Click the object you want to change.

2. Open the `Format` menu and select the `AutoShape` command for shapes you've drawn or the `Object` command for clipart images. You see the Format Object (or AutoShape) dialog box.

3. Select the Wrapping tab. You see the different options you can use for text wrapping (see Figure A-8).

4. Select the wrapping style you want. You can select Square, Tight, Through, None, or Top & Bottom. The pictures of each option are pretty self-explanatory.

5. For Square, Tight, and Through, select where you want to wrap to: Both sides, Left, Right, or Largest side. Again, the picture in the dialog box gives you a good idea of the effects of each option.

6. Click the OK button. Word wraps the text accordingly.

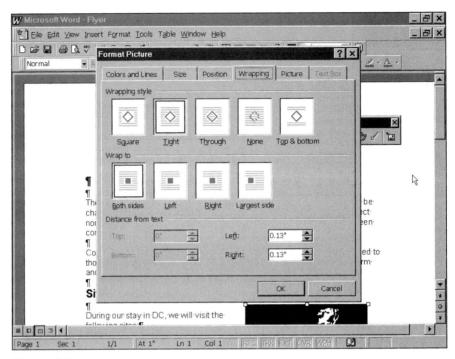

Figure A-8

My picture moves around.

By default, Word moves the picture with the text. (That is, the text where the insertion point was when you inserted the picture.) If you don't want the picture to move, you can change this option.

Follow these steps:

1. Click the object you want to change.

2. Open the ⌊ **Format** ⌋ menu and select the ⌊ **AutoShape** ⌋ command for shapes you've drawn or the ⌊ **Object** ⌋ command for clipart images. You see the Format Object (or AutoShape) dialog box.

3. Select the Position tab.

4. Uncheck the Move object with text check box.

5. Click the OK button.

I've set up columns, but how do I get to the next column?

You can move to the next column by filling the first column with text. If you want to force a column break, don't continually press Enter until you jump to the next column. Instead, insert a column break.

Follow these steps:

1. Open the [Insert] menu and select the [Break] command. You see the Break dialog box.

2. Click the Column break option button.

3. Click the OK button.

When I resize one column, the other columns change size.

Keep in mind that there's only so much room on the page. When you increase the size of one column, you leave less room for other columns. To get more room, you can make the left and right page margins smaller. You can also decrease the amount of space between the columns.

I created a template, but I forgot something or want to change something.

When you use the File, New command to use a template, you are creating a regular document based on the template. If you make a change, you don't alter the template. In some cases, you will want to update the template. In that case, you have to open the template file.

Follow these steps:

1. Open the [File] menu and select the [Open] command. You see the Open dialog box.

   Change to the folder for templates. If you used the default folders when you installed Word 97, this folder is named \Program Files\Microsoft Office\Templates. Use the Up One Level button to move to this folder.

2. Change to the template folder that contains your template. Remember that the templates folder has several subfolders for different document types (memos, reports, and so on). When you saved your template, you selected one of these folders. Select that same folder here.

3. Display the Files of type drop-down list and select Document Templates. You should see your template listed.

4. Click the template you want to edit.

5. Click the Open button. Word displays the template on-screen.

6. Make any editing or formatting changes to the template.

7. Save the template using the [File], [Save] command. Word saves the template in the same folder with the same name. The next time you use this template to create a document, it will include all the editing and formatting changes you made. Any previous documents based on the template remain unchanged.

My mail merge didn't work.

If a mail merge didn't work as expected, check the following:

* Be sure your main document includes the appropriate merge fields to insert the data. If not, edit the main document and insert the fields. See Chapter 14 for information on editing a main document.

* If you need to edit the data source, display the Mail Merge Helper dialog box and click the Edit button under the Data source. Select the file name and then make any changes, as described in Chapter 14.

* The main document and data source must be associated. If that association is lost, you can tell Word which data source to use. In the Mail Merge Helper dialog box, click the Get Data button and select Open Data Source. Select the data source file.

I can't find a document that I've saved.

When you save a document, you place it within a folder. If you can't remember which folder you used, you can search for the document. See Chapter 16 for help on managing documents.

Some features don't work as described here.

Word enables you to customize a lot of program options. For instance, you can turn on and off, a lot of the features. If something does not work as described, check the Options dialog box to see whether something has been changed. Chapter 17 covers customizing in more detail.

My macro didn't work.

If your macro did not work as expected, you can modify it by editing the various commands. If you are not familiar with the macro commands, the easiest way is to rerecord the macro and enter the same name. When prompted to replace the existing macro, select Yes.

GLOSSARY

AutoCorrect — A Word feature that automatically corrects certain misspellings and typographical errors.

AutoFormat — A Word feature that automatically makes formatting changes to your document.

AutoShape — A Word feature that enables you to draw simple shapes, such as circles, rectangles, boxes, stars, banners, and arrows in a document.

AutoText — A Word feature that makes it easy to insert commonly used text (words, phrases, sentences, paragraphs) into your document quickly and without typing the entire entry.

Bookmark — A spot in a document or selection of text that you name so you can easily refer or go to that spot.

Button — A small icon included in a toolbar. Each button is a shortcut to a commonly used command or feature.

Cell — The intersection of a row and a column in a table.

Character style — A set of formatting options applied to text. This type of style can include changes to the font, size, style, color, or any other text attribute.

Clip art — Artwork created by someone else that you are free to use in your document.

Clipboard — Windows feature that temporarily stores any text or object you cut or copy. You can then paste the item to a new location in the document, to another document, or to another application.

Customize — To make changes to the default options so that a feature works the way you want it to.

Data source — One of two documents needed for a mail merge. The data source includes the list of variable information (such as a list of names and addresses) that you want to merge with the main document to create personalized letters.

Default — The option that is selected and used unless you make a change.

Dialog box — A window that appears on-screen when you select some commands and prompts you for additional information about how to carry out that command.

E-mail — Stands for electronic mail. E-mail is a message sent via a network or modem to another user.

File — The contents of a document, named and stored in a particular folder on your hard disk or floppy disk.

Folder — A division of your hard disk. Each folder has a name, and folders can be stored inside of other folders. You can set up folders for the different types of documents you create.

Font size — The type size of a font. Fonts are measured in points, and there are 72 points to an inch.

Font style — An attribute, such as italic or bold, applied to a font.

Font — A set of characters in a particular typeface.

Footer — Text or graphics that are printed at the bottom of each page in a document.

Format — To change the appearance of text, paragraphs, pages, graphics, and so on.

Header — Text or graphics that are printed at the top of each page in a document.

HTML — The formatting language used to set up documents for the World Wide Web. HTML stands for HyperText Markup Language.

Hyperlink — A link that you can click to jump to a file, location in a file, a page on the World Wide Web, or a page on another network.

Insertion point — An on-screen indicator that looks like a flashing vertical line. This line indicates where new text will be inserted if you start typing.

Internet — A network of networks — commercial, educational, organizational, government, and personal networks. You can go to any sites on the networks if you have a modem and an Internet account.

Intranet — A network within a company or organization that is set up and uses the same method for displaying contents and navigating as the Internet.

Justified text — A text alignment. Instead of having an uneven right margin, space is added in between words to keep the left and right margins even.

Landscape orientation — A page layout where text is printed across the long side of the page.

Macro — A set of stored Word commands and instructions you can play back with one command.

Mail merge — A type of operation used to create personalized letters from two sources: a main document and a data source. Also known as form letters.

Main document — In a mail merge, the document that contains the text you want to include in each letter as well as the merge fields that insert the variable information.

Margin — The space left around each edge of the page.

Menu — A drop-down list of commands. The names of the menus appear under the title bar.

Merge field — A special type of code used in mail merge documents to tell Word when to insert variable information, such as a name or address, in a document.

Paragraph style — A set of formatting options applied to the paragraph. This type of style can include alignment changes, indents, borders, shading, and other paragraph formats.

Portrait orientation — A page layout where text is printed across the short side of the page.

Ruler — An on-screen formatting tool you can use to set indents or tabs.

Scroll bar — Strips along the right and bottom of the window that show you your relative position in the document. You can click the scroll arrow to scroll in that direction or drag the scroll box up or down to scroll through a document.

Section — A division of a document. Each section can have its own unique page formatting options.

Select — To drag across text or click on an object. Once selected, you can modify that item.

Selection bar — The white border along the left edge of the screen. You can use this area to select lines, paragraphs, or the entire document.

Status bar — The bar along the bottom of the screen that gives you information, such as the page number and insertion point position, about the current document.

Style — A set of formatting options applied to text. You can create both character and paragraph styles.

Symbol — A special character such as the copyright symbol ©.

Tab — A notch at the top of dialog boxes that contains more than one page of options. You can select the tab you want to view those options. This tab is different from the Tab key, which moves text to the next tab stop.

Template — A document that may include text, styles, formatting, AutoText entries, and macros set up for your use.

Thesaurus — A Word feature that enables you to look up synonyms for words in your document.

Title bar — The bar that appears along the top of the window and displays the program name and document name.

Toolbar — An on-screen row of buttons. Each button is a shortcut to a commonly used command or feature. By default, Word displays both the standard and formatting toolbars on-screen.

Visual Basic — The programming language included with Word. You can use this language to create simple macros to complex programs.

Wizard — An automated template that prompts you to make selections and enter text to create a document.

Word wrap — A Word feature that automatically wraps words when they reach the end of a line. You don't need to press Enter to end one line and start the next.

World Wide Web — Part of the Internet. Information on the World Wide Web is published as pages, and the pages can include text, graphics, sounds, animations, videos, and links to other pages. You move from page to page by clicking the links.

INDEX

(continued)

(continued)

(continued)

(continued)

(continued)

(continued)

IDG BOOKS WORLDWIDE REGISTRATION CARD

RETURN THIS REGISTRATION CARD FOR FREE CATALOG

Title of this book: **Discover Word 97**

My overall rating of this book: ❏ Very good [1] ❏ Good [2] ❏ Satisfactory [3] ❏ Fair [4] ❏ Poor [5]

How I first heard about this book:

❏ Found in bookstore; name: [6] _____ ❏ Book review: [7] _____

❏ Advertisement: [8] _____ ❏ Catalog: [9] _____

❏ Word of mouth; heard about book from friend, co-worker, etc.: [10] _____ ❏ Other: [11] _____

What I liked most about this book:

_____
_____

What I would change, add, delete, etc., in future editions of this book:

_____
_____

Other comments:

_____
_____

Number of computer books I purchase in a year: ❏ 1 [12] ❏ 2-5 [13] ❏ 6-10 [14] ❏ More than 10 [15]

I would characterize my computer skills as: ❏ Beginner [16] ❏ Intermediate [17] ❏ Advanced [18] ❏ Professional [19]

I use ❏ DOS [20] ❏ Windows [21] ❏ OS/2 [22] ❏ Unix [23] ❏ Macintosh [24] ❏ Other: [25] _____
(please specify)

I would be interested in new books on the following subjects:
(please check all that apply, and use the spaces provided to identify specific software)

❏ Word processing: [26] _____ ❏ Spreadsheets: [27] _____

❏ Data bases: [28] _____ ❏ Desktop publishing: [29] _____

❏ File Utilities: [30] _____ ❏ Money management: [31] _____

❏ Networking: [32] _____ ❏ Programming languages: [33] _____

❏ Other: [34] _____

I use a PC at (please check all that apply): ❏ home [35] ❏ work [36] ❏ school [37] ❏ other: [38] _____

The disks I prefer to use are ❏ 5.25 [39] ❏ 3.5 [40] ❏ other: [41] _____

I have a CD ROM: ❏ yes [42] ❏ no [43]

I plan to buy or upgrade computer hardware this year: ❏ yes [44] ❏ no [45]

I plan to buy or upgrade computer software this year: ❏ yes [46] ❏ no [47]

Name: _____ Business title: [48] _____ Type of Business: [49] _____

Address (❏ home [50] ❏ work [51]/Company name: _____)

Street/Suite# _____

City [52]/State [53]/Zipcode [54]: _____ Country [55] _____

❏ **I liked this book!** You may quote me by name in future
IDG Books Worldwide promotional materials.

My daytime phone number is _____

IDG BOOKS

THE WORLD OF
COMPUTER
KNOWLEDGE

❏ YES!

Please keep me informed about IDG's World of Computer Knowledge.
Send me the latest IDG Books catalog.